Do-It-Yourself
Contracting
To Build
Your Own Home

Do-It-Yourself Contracting To Build Your Own Home

A Managerial Approach / Second Edition

Richard J. Stillman

Chilton
Book
Company/
Radnor,
Pennsylvania

For Philip and Grace Joseph
Thank you for making it all possible

Contents

Acknowledgments

This book has been written thanks to the invaluable advice, information, and support provided by many cooperative people. My family has been especially kind. Not only have they put up with a difficult author, but my wife, Darlene, provided valuable administrative assistance; our son Thomas was the photographer; daughter Ellen was my in-house manuscript critic; and Richard, our older son, himself an author and teacher, offered much encouragement and advice on home repairs.

To Helen and Roy Fisher, my appreciation for many years of wise counsel in the financial-management aspects of housing. Becky Copley has been my indispensable secretary, typist, and copy editor for the last three years. Thanks, too, to the staff at Chilton Book Company for their expert advice and contributions to the book.

Many others have been generous with their time and advice. These include subcontractors, bookstore managers, lawyers, architects, insurance experts, bank and savings and loan officials, business executives, consumer organizations, colleagues, students, and friends. In particular, I want to mention Weston Strauch, B. F. Doss, the Honorable Joseph W. Sanders, Robert De Marco, Merlin Toups, Walter C. Balser, Dr. Martin Klein, John Petitbon, Luis Soto, Sidney J. Comer, and Joseph A. Martin.

Of course, for any errors or other weaknesses, the responsibility is entirely mine. Suggestions for improvements are welcome and will be incorporated in future editions.

Do-It-Yourself
Contracting
To Build
Your Own Home

Introduction
What This Book Can Do
for You

This book can help you obtain the home you could not otherwise afford. Inflation and increasing energy costs may have pushed even a modest "dream home" beyond the reach of your pocketbook, but you can save money—and have that dream home—through do-it-yourself contracting.

The main purpose of this new edition is to tell you how to save money and time in contracting to build your own home, as well as how to obtain a better-quality residence. *Do-It-Yourself Contracting to Build Your Own Home* will also be of considerable value if you hire a contractor or architect or buy a ready-made home. Whether you build or buy, you can be more certain of getting a fair deal because you will understand the process of home construction and be able to compute the costs involved. You can then compare the total cost of subcontracting with estimates from a contractor for building a comparable home or with the asking price of already built homes. The same analysis can be applied to building an entire home, adding a garage, extra room, swimming pool, or any other home improvement.

Small builders and subcontractors can also profit from the managerial approach presented in this book. Most contractors are small-scale entrepreneurs with little or no business background. *The Wall Street Journal* ("Out of the Mud," by Jeffrey A. Tannenbaum, June 27, 1972) reports that the building industry "traditionally has been split up among thousands of small firms, usually headed by former carpenters, bricklayers, or other construction workers who made the grade.'' My conversations with contractors have shown that many of them lack the understanding of management principles needed to build a home efficiently and may find this book a useful introduction to the subject.

Teachers of management, business, or public administration may find this book useful as a case study. Some colleges are using such books to illustrate management principles, and I find it an effective tool in my own classes.

The book is based on my experience in various parts of the United States, Europe, and the Far East. For the twenty-three years I was an Army officer, I rented homes in turn in San Francisco, Washington, D.C., Syracuse, San Antonio, Paris (France), and New Orleans. In each area I studied the housing market with the intention one day of subcontracting my own home. The move to my current job as a professor of management provided this opportunity. My homebuilding experience proved that using sound management principles can save up to 25 percent in costs and accomplish the job in one-third the time. It also results in a finer home because of the personal interest and attention paid. The managerial principles presented in the first edition are still valid today and will be in the years ahead. The impact of inflation and the energy shortage, however, have required changes in housing decisions. Chapter 2 is devoted to coping with inflation and the energy crisis, and information on these topics is included throughout the book.

The appendixes contain much useful information. If you are unfamiliar with mortgages, read the sample one in Appendix C. In Appendix D you can refer to inflation and interest tables to see what will happen to your dollars in the years ahead; this can be an important factor in deciding when to build. Appendixes E and F spell out the cost of mortgage money and the variation in monthly payments, based on several rates of interest. The Glossary contains definitions of various financial, housing, and management terms so you can familiarize yourself with the language used in these fields.

Successfully managing the building of your own home is a challenge. It requires a conscientious effort—a lot of hard and productive work. Still, the rewards can be great. Besides the satisfaction of actually participating in the building of your dream home, there are also the savings in time, money, and materials. However, *a word to the wise:* Do not undertake such a project if you are devoid of managerial aptitude or unfamiliar with local building codes. For those who accept the challenge, though, please let me know the results.

Chapter One
A Managerial Approach
to Building Your Home

The managerial approach to building your home presented in this book will enable you to obtain a home you could not otherwise afford, especially in times of inflation and increasing costs of labor and energy. Many people have found the management approach to homebuilding has saved them money, cut construction time, and given them a better-quality house. Building your own home requires considerable hard work, personal attention, and managerial aptitude. So examine your own limitations before starting such a venture. After reading this book, you will be better able to decide if you should subcontract your home or hire a contractor to build it for you. In either case, you will have a much better idea of costs and what is involved in building a home. This background should permit you to make wiser decisions regarding the home of your choice.

This chapter presents an overview of some management principles and how you can apply them to subcontract your home. These management principles have universal application; they can be used at work, in social organizations, and in managing your money. In subsequent chapters we will use these principles to manage the building of your home to save both money and time.

WHY A MANAGERIAL APPROACH TO HOMEBUILDING?

A home is usually the largest single investment a person makes in his lifetime. It is very important, therefore, to examine every aspect thoroughly. This need for a careful study is supported by comments obtained in a large metropolitan area where homes varied in cost from $100,000 to $375,000. In most cases, the owners stated that major pitfalls could have been avoided if greater care had been taken before purchase. Here are the remarks of two dissatisfied homeowners that typify the magnitude of problems people face when they fail to use sound management concepts.

> We bought our house the way we would buy a pair of shoes. Looked at the house one afternoon and within an hour signed an agreement. It's been a financial nightmare. Our monthly payments, closing costs, utilities, and maintenance expenditures have exceeded by 40 percent what the salesman estimated. My wife had to get a job and we are still going further in debt. We can't sell at anywhere near the price we paid. How stupid of us not to have taken our time and studied up on what we were getting into.

The following remarks were based on an interview with an owner of a $225,000 home in an exclusive neighborhood.

> A friend suggested I contact his cousin to build my home. The guy seemed pleasant and had built a few houses in the city. But it's been a damn nightmare. From the start, he alienated everybody. He made the neighbors mad by trampling their shrubbery with his trucks, using their water without permission, and throwing cement and other debris on their lawn. He fought every suggested change I made and then charged us twice the going price. He had no idea what communication or management was all about. For example, we asked for a fine quality redwood fence. Instead, I received a tan color of cheaper grade. His excuse: "I told the subcontractor what to do but he screwed up." I ended up painting it red. As you can imagine, it looks terrible.
>
> The house was to be finished in six months and it took ten. Many things didn't work when I moved in. He promised to fix everything, but I ended up paying to have someone else do it. My wife and I spent an excessive amount of time supervising work that our builder was supposed to do. But he hardly ever showed up. To make matters worse, the plumber and others wouldn't take instructions from us so we wasted more time trying to contact him. It was a mess. The house has nearly

caused my wife a nervous breakdown. She is still taking tranquilizers.

Want to avoid similar problems? Read on.

A MANAGEMENT MODEL

What is management? It means achieving an objective by utilizing personnel, money, and material; it means performing the functions of planning, organizing, and controlling; it means working within a framework of line, staff, and service responsibilities; and it means being involved in making decisions.

Look at a management model (Figure 1–1) to help you clarify this definition. An example is provided that will enable you to relate the management model to your homebuilding project. The model presents

Figure 1–1   An overview of the five major components of management.

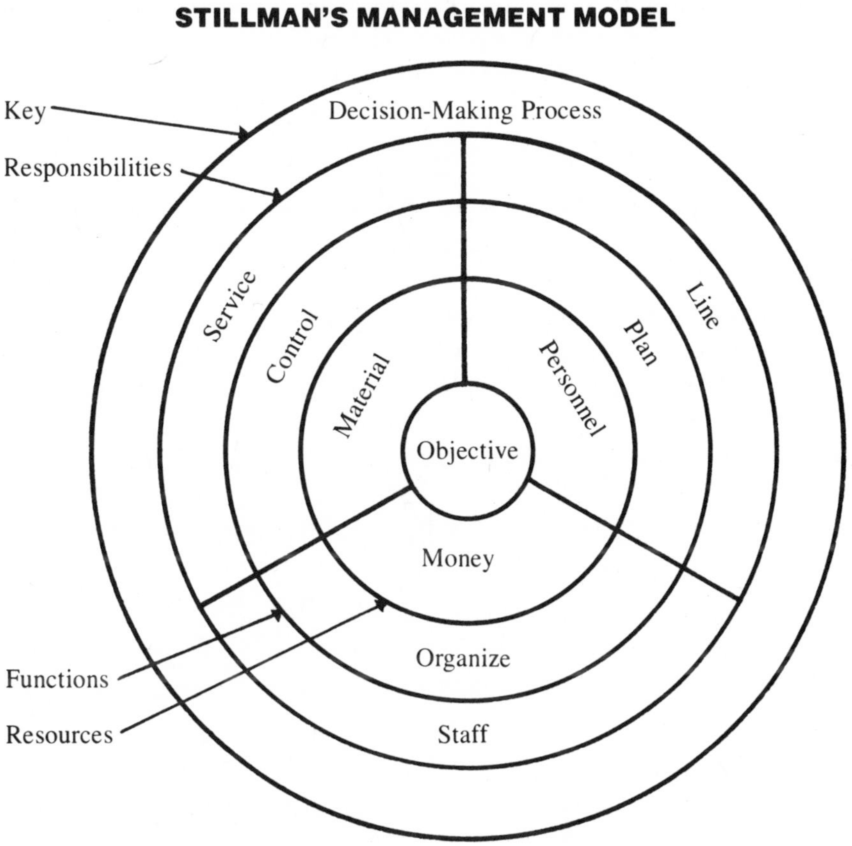

STILLMAN'S MANAGEMENT MODEL

a graphic overview of the five major management components: objective, resources, functions, responsibilities, and decision-making process.

OBJECTIVE

Management must establish a primary goal for its organization. A homebuilder may decide his objective is to build a residence in a designated area, utilizing subcontractors and completing the project within four months at a 25-percent savings in total cost. Whatever your objective, it must be realistic and feasible. It should be adopted only after you have given appropriate thought to available resources (personnel, money, material) and the other components of the management model.

The objective should provide answers to the questions of what, when, where, how, and why. Figure 1–2 presents these answers as they pertain to a homebuilder.

Establishing a primary objective also means you'll need to develop subobjectives or subgoals. The more complex the homebuilding project, the more involved these subgoals become. They may also include short-, medium-, and long-term objectives. The objective is at the heart of management, and all management efforts should be focused on accomplishing that objective.

RESOURCES

Once your management objective is established, you must determine which resources are required to accomplish your objective most efficiently. Any organization, to operate effectively, requires adequate manpower, financial resources, and equipment.

Manpower requires one full-time individual (you, for example) who has overall responsibility. This individual may draw upon forty-

Figure 1–2 The five questions the management objective should answer.

WHAT	Build a residence
WHEN	Within four months
WHERE	In a designated area
HOW	Subcontracting
WHY	Save 25 percent

nine different subcontractors from time to time, as well as advice from a lawyer and several qualified technicians in the homebuilding industry. Money is needed to pay the subcontractors and all other expenses. Materials include lumber, roofing, concrete, sheetrock, and many other supplies. In essence, the three resources of personnel, money, and material result in one outcome: a completed home. It is your responsibility as manager to use these three resources efficiently in order to obtain the quality of home you desire at a reasonable price.

FUNCTIONS

The third circle in the management model refers to the three basic management functions: planning, organizing, and controlling. For you as a manager to accomplish your objective effectively, you must be capable of performing these three functions:

1. Plan what you are going to do.
2. Do what you plan.
3. Check what you have done.

Later chapters will emphasize the importance of using a budget to serve as a *planning* document and as a means of *control* to determine how the actual expenditures compare with the planned estimate. The actual building of the house encompasses the *organizational* or "doing" aspect. These three management functions apply in every type of homebuilding, from the smallest cottage to the largest mansion.

RESPONSIBILITIES OF MODERN MANAGEMENT

Now that we have established our objective, determined our resources, and recognized our functions, let us look at the areas of responsibility that may be utilized to accomplish our objective. The homebuilder must decide what *line, staff,* and *service* areas are most appropriate.

Line activities include such production-area subcontractors as carpenters, plumbers, electricians, and roofers. These people are the doers and comprise the operational aspect of management.

In addition to the line requirement, there is need for staff responsibilities. These are the activities that help the line people or operators accomplish their various assignments. The homebuilder will perform the vast majority of the staff work himself: keep the financial records, serve as his own personnel manager, and provide his own research. He will hire a lawyer for legal work and rely on another member of the family or helper for clerical and administrative tasks.

The third area of responsibility may be categorized as service activities. These include custodial, maintenance, and storage duties. This service function, performed by the owner or a family member, includes sweeping the premises, running errands for the subcontractors, carrying refuse to the dump, and performing a multitude of other menial but vital tasks.

DECISION-MAKING PROCESS

The final ring in Figure 1–1 is the decision-making process. The decision-making process may draw upon all other components of the management model in order to arrive at a sound solution. In making management decisions, these questions should be kept in mind:

1. What is your objective?
2. Do you have the necessary facts to make a sound decision?
3. What are your alternatives?
4. Have you chosen the most profitable alternative?

ORGANIZATION

One approach to organizing your homebuilding project effectively is to consider yourself the business manager with overall responsibility (see Figure 1–3).

If you undertake this project as a single person, there isn't any question who is boss, but marriage presents a different story. Accordingly, you may wish to have co-presidents rather than the arrangement in this chart.

Assume you designate yourself as president and your spouse agrees to be executive vice-president—with authority to act in your behalf if you should be absent. This organizational system should be developed during the initial planning stage. Be specific in delineating responsibilities, but make your organization flexible so changes can be made if necessary. You should have a workable filing system and a person to

Figure 1–3 A hypothetical organization to manage construction of a home.

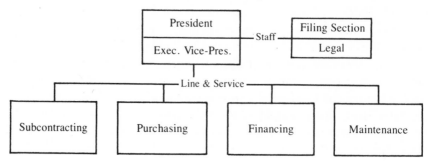

handle all correspondence and the purchasing of material. Use a lawyer for legal matters. In addition to assuming overall responsibility, someone should make the financial arrangements and be in charge of each subcontractor—plumber, electrician, carpenter, roofer, bricklayer, and so on. Name one person to take charge of the maintenance chore, but everyone can pitch in when necessary.

GUIDELINES

During the planning and building phases, you may wish to consider the following guidelines, which are highlighted throughout the book.

1. Don't let the magnitude of this homebuilding project frighten you. Look at the various tasks and break down each to its smallest component. From such a perspective, each job becomes relatively easy.

2. Time is a valuable commodity; employ it to your advantage. A management approach to homebuilding minimizes the time required to complete the project.

3. Be flexible and imaginative. A home should be attuned to the times, present and future. This includes consideration of the fact that one day you may wish to sell your house.

4. Make your homebuilding project a family affair by encouraging active participation of all members.

5. Go first class. Better materials and quality workmanship cost less in the long run and give greater satisfaction. Shop carefully. Obtain at least three competitive quotes when possible.

6. Maximize your down payment, contract for the shortest-term mortgage you can afford, and pay off the balance as rapidly as possible—if you have found the locality where you expect to settle for at least three years.

7. Minimize your costs by eliminating the middleman wherever possible.

8. Deal only with reputable people who have a good record of achievement and stand behind their work. Inspect their work and ask for references.

9. Pay all bills by check, but keep an adequate amount of money in your checking account to allow you to secure the best prices from "hungry" subcontractors or suppliers who prefer cash "on the barrel head" rather than waiting thirty days for their money. The remainder should either be drawing interest or borrowed only at the time required.

10. Your home should be a major growth investment. The lot, house, and maintenance should be viewed in this perspective.

11. During the planning and construction, capitalize on any mem-

ber of your family's experience in these areas of homebuilding. If someone paints well, for example, use this skill.

12. Timing is important. This applies to availability of materials, personnel, and money, as well as weather conditions.

13. Make every effort to get along with people, including suppliers, subcontractors, other builders, inspectors, bank officials, and neighbors.

14. It pays to be in good physical and mental condition, since you may be working ten to twelve hours each day and will find the task physically and mentally challenging.

15. Before making any major decision, determine the impact of inflation and the energy shortage. This determination should include such factors as size of home; insulation; location; personnel, money, and equipment cost projections; labor-saving devices; and new developments like alternative heating and cooling systems.

16. Smaller is better. Smaller homes, like smaller cars, cost less to build and maintain. Build only the size home to meet your needs and make it energy efficient. The size and cost should also relate to nearby homes for ease in selling.

17. Earnings (salary and other income) should keep pace with rising home costs. Prepare your budget with care to include estimated income and expenses for the next five years. It is not desirable to exceed 25 percent for housing costs unless you can make definite cuts in other areas like food, clothing, vacations, or recreation.

18. Energy will become scarcer in the years ahead and costs will rise. It is essential therefore to plan wisely in building your home.

SUMMARY

Management principles can help you save both money and time. The management model presents a graphic overview, consisting of five components that will facilitate sound decisions. Similarly, the organization chart can help delineate responsibilities.

Familiarize yourself with the managerial guidelines that include flexibility, imagination, quality, involving family members, maximizing the down payment, and paying off the mortgage in the shortest practical period. Eliminate the middleman where possible, deal with reputable people, pay bills by check, and remember that time is money.

Chapter Two
Your Home, Inflation, and the Energy Shortage

Inflation and the energy crisis have had a major impact on housing decisions in recent years. Although the rise in home values has exceeded inflation as measured by the Consumer Price Index (CPI), mortgage rates are currently near record levels and fuel costs (heating oil, for example) have nearly doubled in some areas during the past year.

Thus the energy crisis requires a fresh approach to subcontracting your home. Sound management calls for planning energy-saving measures carefully before you build that dream home. Before subcontracting a home, it is essential to estimate if your savings and income will permit you not only to build the house but also meet all monthly payments for the next five years. The average budget allows about 25 percent for housing costs; if you wish to skimp in other areas, like recreation and vacations, you can increase this percent, but be sure to stick with your budget. You must also decide if it is wise to wait for a decline in mortgage rates or housing costs (labor and material). (The amortization tables provided in the Appendix can help you reach a decision.)

In considering housing and energy costs, ''smaller is better'' should be the watchword for most homebuilders. A location near schools, churches, hospitals, public transportation, work, and shopping facilities looms ever more important. And so much the better if you can walk, jog, or bicycle to work and shopping facilities. The cost of installation and maintenance of heating and cooling units, as well as choice insulation, storm windows, and other measures are ever more important.

This chapter provides information that will help the potential home-builder cope with inflationary housing costs and the energy crisis. Suggestions will be made to enable a homebuilder to save money and take appropriate energy-saving measures both before and after construction.

RISING HOME COSTS

Housing costs take about a fourth of the average family budget in the United States. Individuals who purchased homes in recent years have, in general, done well. Figure 2–1 shows the rapid dollar rise in new homes since 1972. Note that between 1967 and 1972, prices rose at a much slower rate and actually declined between 1969 and 1970; between 1972 and 1979, however, prices of new homes more than doubled in value. The average yearly sale prices of new houses between 1967 and 1980 are listed in Table 2–1.

Two essential questions a potential homebuilder should answer are: What will a house I subcontract now be worth in the years ahead? Will

Figure 2–1 Average yearly sale price for new one-family homes in the U.S. Source: *Construction Reports,* "New One-Family Houses Sold and For Sale." Dept. of Commerce, Bureau of Census, and Dept. of Housing and Urban Development.

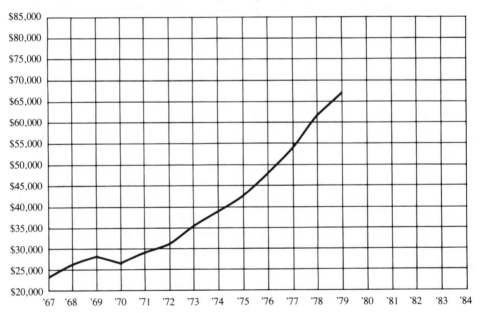

Table 2–1   Average Market Price of Homes

Year	Average Yearly Sale Price
1967	$24,000
1968	$24,600
1969	$27,900
1970	$26,600
1971	$28,300
1972	$30,500
1973	$35,500
1974	$38,900
1975	$42,600
1976	$48,000
1977	$54,200
1978	$63,500
1979	$72,500
1980	$78,000 (est.)

my investment keep pace with or exceed inflation? Figure 2–2 indicates that homes in recent years have done better than inflation. (Between 1967 and 1972, however, the CPI gained at a faster pace than new one-family home prices.) Keep in mind also that mortgage rates are very high today. Will they continue at this pace or come down? You must decide if it is wiser to delay subcontracting in order to take advantage of possible lower interest rates.

You may wish to see if you can obtain a variable mortgage. The variable concept works this way: if interest rates go down, mortgage payments decline; if interest rates go up, payments increase. You also may wish to check on the availability of increasing mortgage payments that rise over the years—hopefully in accordance with increases in your salary.

A successful money manager must plan wisely before making a major investment in a home. Keeping Figures 2–1 and 2–2 current can help you in making appropriate housing decisions. Although interest costs are high today, remember that by subcontracting you can save up to 25 percent, making the higher mortgage cost less than if you bought a new or used home. Furthermore, any savings gained by delaying building until interest rates drop further may be offset by rising construction costs. Delaying construction also means you will spend less time living in your dream house.

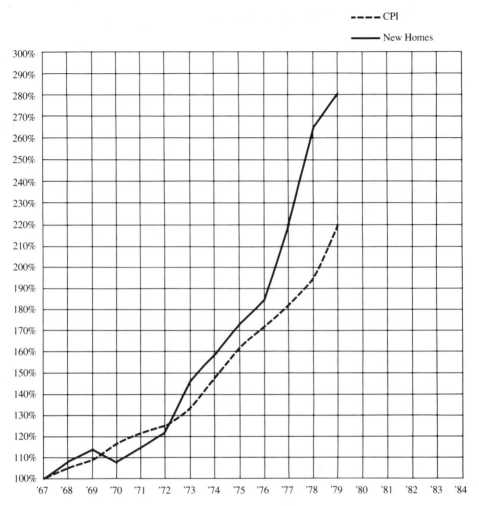

Figure 2–2 Comparative rises in Consumer Price Index (CPI) and average sales prices of new one-family homes.

RISING FUEL COSTS

In 1979 home costs in general increased by 18 percent, in contrast to 13 percent for the CPI. (The Consumer Price Index is a measure of change in the prices of goods and services in major expenditure groups such as food, housing, clothing, transportation, health, and recreation.) In some areas of the United States, however, fuel prices increased at a much faster rate—as high as 100 percent. In other localities the rate of increase was lower than the CPI because of the type of fuel used.

As shown in Table 2–2, families in one southern community that used natural gas experienced a sizable increase in heating and cooling

Table 2–2   Sample Gas Heating and Cooling Costs for One-Family Dwellings

1970	$549
1971	564
1972	640
1973	784
1974	877
1975	975
1976	1033
1977	1112
1978	1298
1979	1331

costs over a ten-year period. These homes averaged between 2200 and 2400 square feet (excluding garage). A similar sampling of water rates found an increase of 150 percent from $121 in 1970 to $281 in 1979. (These rates include water, sewer, quality control, and city sanitation.)

These costs, shown in Figure 2–3, point up the fact that prices for home heating gas increased steadily over the ten-year period, with a total increase of 226 percent. Although heating oil costs in one New England community doubled (a 100-percent increase) from 1978 to 1979, coal costs, in contrast, only rose 4 percent for a West Virginia family for the same year.

Important information can be acquired by studying different fuel costs. First, you can determine which type of heating and cooling sys-

Figure 2–3   Sample gas heating and cooling costs for one-family homes.

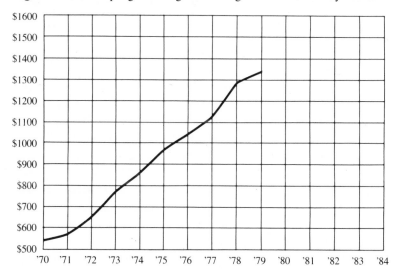

tem, or combination thereof, will be most suitable for your subcontracted home. Second, you can estimate both the price of the unit (including installation and upkeep) and the annual fuel costs over a five-year period.

RISING MAINTENANCE COSTS

It is very important to determine not only the initial building costs to subcontract your home but also the annual expenses. It is sad indeed to build your dream home and then find you are forced to move because you are unable to meet mortgage payments and other yearly housing costs.

In estimating yearly costs for maintenance and repairs, you should consider the age of your home and what items will need repairs due to normal wear and tear. If you have children and pets, this figure normally will be higher than for an older couple with no children or pets. The size of your home is also a factor in determining costs. Some people are more particular than others in replacing such items as leaky washers, peeling paint, and damaged doors. Your best gauge will be based on several years of good record keeping. On newer homes of average size, this amount varies from $175 to $900. Equipment replacements and miscellaneous costs also vary, based on factors discussed above for maintenance and repairs. Be sure to allow adequate amounts for inflation. Also recognize that emergencies occur (miscellaneous); allow $100 to $1000 for this purpose. The experience of one of my neighbors is a good example: "We have two teenagers who are just learning to drive. I've had $765 in unexpected repairs this year because of damage to our garage and gate. Unfortunately, I had made no provision in my budget and had to borrow money—at 21 percent."

Estimate with care your housing expenses over a five-year period using a format like that in Figure 2–4.

Because housing costs take about 25 percent of a family's income each year, you should determine if your income will keep pace with your estimated costs to maintain your home in the next five years. This should include staying roughly within the 25 percent guideline. Keep in mind that in recent years housing costs have been increasing at a faster rate than inflation as a whole. Most families should allow for a 20 percent annual rise in costs to maintain their homes. This increase in housing bills may require cutting expenses in other areas, such as recreation or travel, in order not to exceed your income and be able to meet mortgage payments and other annual home costs. Last year I received the following sad note from a colleague in New England:

ESTIMATED YEARLY COST TO MAINTAIN MY HOME: 19__ to 19__					
Costs	*1st year*	*2d year*	*3d year*	*4th year*	*5th year*
1. Mortgage					
2. Taxes and Assessments					
3. Insurance					
4. Heating and Cooling					
5. Utilities— (other than heating & cooling) Water, gas, electricity					
6. Phone					
7. Maintenance and repairs					
8. Equipment					
9. Miscellaneous					
TOTAL					

Figure 2–4 Suggested form for estimating housing expenses.

We had saved our money for twenty one years in order to have a beautiful home of our own. Frequent moves over the years caused us to rent in order to depart for new assignments quickly. We finally scraped enough money together to secure a home we really wanted. My teaching job was secure with a tenured position and pay raises kept pace with inflation. My wife taught in grade school and our incomes, $39,240, I thought sufficient. But we paid 12¾ percent for our mortgage plus 6 points and our heating costs doubled in one year. In addition, the roof required a major repair ($2,948) and other unexpected repairs and maintenance required $4,653. Then one of our parents became ill and we had to pay nursing home costs. We could not meet all the expenses and were forced to sell the home that meant so much to us—and at a $10,000 loss.

ENERGY CONSERVATION

Every potential homebuilder should give serious consideration to the future energy situation in the United States. It is apparent that this problem will increase in the years ahead. How does the energy crisis affect the homeowner of tomorrow?

Check with care the size and energy efficiency of your home before you build it. Consider such questions as: Do you have adequate insulation? Are windows and other glass areas insulated or double glazed? Are the exterior doors adequately insulated? Are heating and cooling units the most efficient and economical? How far is home from work? Do you plan to use all the floor space? What are current and projected utility rates in your community? These and other questions on energy conservation should be answered to your satisfaction before subcontracting your home.

There are other energy conservation measures to consider before building. Because energy will become more expensive with each passing year, your goal should be to buy the most efficient equipment to meet your needs.

STORM WINDOWS

Plan to use storm windows regardless of the area in which you plan to build. Even in places like Florida, storm windows keep warm air inside in cold weather and hot air out in summer. Such protection will reduce your home energy bill for both heating and cooling.

Some people who subcontracted their homes cut costs by making their own storm windows. This requires some carpentry skill, tools, and mechanical ability. Making storm windows requires accurate measuring to determine material needs. First, purchase lumber (or metal) accessories to prepare the frame, including screen mouldings. Next, buy vinyl or Mylar plastic sheeting to place in the frames. Storm windows should be installed with screws, not nails. Use metal screws for metal window frames and wood screws for wood frames. If possible, buy material that does not have to be painted. Caution: If done well, this do-it-yourself approach can save you up to 50 percent; if not, it can far exceed the cost of buying ready-made storm windows.

Although storm windows may be taken down and stored in the attic, garage, or basement in the summer, some families use the windows year round. If your house is air conditioned, storm windows can cut fuel costs in summer as well.

INSULATION

Adequate insulation in a home retards the flow of heat from one substance to another. (This retardation occurs when two materials of unequal temperature are placed side by side.) When your home is heated in the winter, heat leaves the warmer inside wall material and is absorbed by the colder outside material until the temperature of each is equalized. In the summer, the warmer outside air flows to the inside of the house. This process (called "heat exchange") can be retarded, or slowed up, by insulation. The wall itself is of some help, but the essential ingredient is adequate insulation.

It is important to provide adequate insulation in the ceiling, walls, and, where appropriate, under raised floors in the home you subcontract. (See Figure 2–5, which points out where to insulate your home.) Adequate insulation will keep your house at the desired temperature in all seasons at a lower cost. You will enjoy not only savings from lower heating and cooling bills (regardless of the source of energy used—coal, oil, electricity, gas, or solar) but also savings in the initial purchase of equipment, for the size of the heating and cooling units can be smaller if you have provided adequate insulation.

Another advantage to good insulation is the increased value of your home when you sell it. A look at your utility bills as well as at some of your insulation will point up to potential buyers the desirability of owning your home.

The Department of Energy has prepared excellent information on the amount of insulation required in various sections of the country. Instead of inches of insulation required the government uses the term R-value, which indicates how well the insulation resists the flow of heat. In this standard measurement, the higher the R-value number, the greater is the capability of the insulation. Higher R-values are required in colder climates. The Department of Energy suggests R-values shown in Figure 2–6 for various heating zones.

Another helpful chart prepared by the Department of Energy shows the relationship between R-value and inches of insulation (Table 2–3).

Although the Department of Energy material is an excellent guide, you must determine your own needs in terms of cost. Obtain recommendations from local companies specializing in insulation, as well as from utility companies. Keep in mind that after a certain point, the costs of material and labor may begin to outweigh any energy savings to be gained from installing more insulation.

Where to Insulate

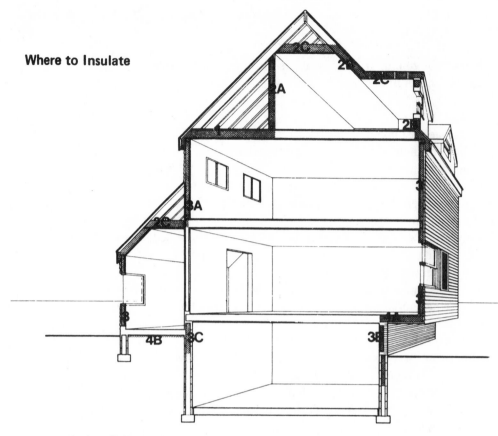

1. In unfinished attic spaces insulate between the floor joists to seal off living spaces below. [1]

2. In finished attic rooms with or without dormers, insulate . . .
   - **2A** between the studs of "knee" walls;
   - **2B** between the studs and rafters of exterior walls;
   - **2C** ceilings with cold spaces above.

3. All exterior walls, including . . .
   - **3A** walls between living spaces and unheated garages or storage areas;
   - **3B** foundation walls above ground level;
   - **3C** foundation walls in heated basements. These need only be insulated to 2 feet below ground level. (In certain extremely cold climates of northern Maine, Minnesota, and Alaska, specialists should be consulted for foundation wall insulation.)

4. Floors above cold spaces, such as vented crawl spaces and unheated garages. Also insulate . . .
   - **4A** any portion of the floor in a room that is cantilevered beyond the exterior wall below;
   - **4B** slab floors built directly on the ground. [2]

---

1 Well-insulated attics, crawl spaces, storage areas, and other closed cavities should be well-ventilated to prevent excessive moisture build-up.

2 Slabs on grade are almost always insulated, in accordance with building codes, when the house is constructed.

Figure 2–5 Where to insulate. Source: *Insulation*, Dept. of Energy, May 1979.

U.S. Heating Zones

Recommended R-Values

Heating Zone	Attic Floors	Exterior Walls	Ceilings Over Unheated Crawl Space or Basement
1	R-26	R-Value of full wall insulation, which is 3½″ thick, will depend on material used. Range is R-11 to R-13.	R-11
2	R-26		R-13
3	R-30		R-19
4	R-33		R-22
5	R-38		R-22

Figure 2–6 Department of Energy recommended R-values. Source: *Insulation,* Dept. of Energy, May 1979.

A word of caution about insulation. As the Department of Energy states:

> A major problem that can be associated with installing insulation is moisture control. If the water vapor in the warm, moist air inside your house permeates the insulation, it can cause the insulation to lose its effectiveness; if the moisture becomes depos-

Table 2–3   Department of Energy R-Values Related to Inches of Insulation

	Batts or Blankets		Loose and Blown Fill*				
R-Value	Glass Fiber	Rock Wool	Glass Fiber	Rock Wool	Cellulose Fiber	Vermiculite	Perlite
R-11	3½ in.	3 in.	5 in.	4 in.	3 in.	5 in.	4 in.
R-13	4	3½	6	4½	3½	6	5
R-19	6	5	8½	6½	5	9	7
R-22	7	6	10	7½	6	10½	8
R-26	8	7	12	9	7	12½	9½
R-30	9½	8	13½	10	8	14	11
R-33	10½	9	15	11	9	15½	12
R-38	12	10½	17	13	10	18	14

*The R-Value for urea-formaldehyde foam is 4.2 per inch of thickness. However, a recent bulletin (Use of Materials Bulletin No. 74, Sept. 15, 1977) from the Department of Housing and Urban Development (HUD) indicates that the effective R-Value of this type of fill is only 3.3 per inch when installed, due to a 6 percent average linear shrinkage. Therefore, urea-formaldehyde foam in a 3½ inch wall cavity would have an R-Value of 10.5.

Source: *Insulation,* Department of Energy, May, 1979.

ited in the building structure, it could eventually cause mold growth, paint peeling, or structural rotting. To guard against moisture problems, use vapor barriers with insulation and adequately ventilate the house.[1]

FREE HEAT

The location of your house is important not only in regard to its distance from schools, churches, shopping centers, hospitals, and work but also in its position on the lot you have selected. This includes careful attention to the placement of windows and doors. Take full advantage of the free heat provided by the sun. Windows should face in the direction that affords the most warmth from the sun. Avoid putting windows on the colder (north) side. Plant trees and shrubs to provide maximum shade for the house, thus reducing energy costs in the summer.

CEILING FANS

You may wish to consider installing ceiling fans in your home. Each fan circulates the air throughout a particular room, keeping you comfortable and fuel bills down. Ceiling fans normally pay for themselves within a few years. However, it is essential to buy first quality fans that

[1] Department of Energy, *Insulation,* May 1979, p. 4.

are quiet and durable. The blade should be long enough to circulate the air thoroughly (usually 52 inches). Ceilings should be nine feet or higher for the fans to be most effective, although the fans can be adapted to fit in smaller rooms. Install the fans in the rooms where they will receive the most use—the kitchen, den, study, and bedroom.

From an energy conservation standpoint, ceiling fans can be real money savers. One family I know kept meticulous records on utility costs before and after installation of Hunter ceiling fans. They report: "In 1978, prior to the installation of our six ceiling fans at a cost of $1,200, our utility bills ranged from a high of $300 to a low of $150 and totaled $2,640 for the year. After installation, our utility costs varied from $260 to $125, with a one year purchase and installation expense of $2,280. This is a savings of 360, or nearly 14 percent. Keep in mind that our utility bills were raised about 20 percent in 1979, so the real savings was even greater. The fans permit us to be just as comfortable in the summer (with a four degree lower thermostat setting). The fans will pay for themselves in three to four years. And besides the energy conservation factor, we think the fans are quite attractive."

HEAT PUMP

A heat pump, a central unit that can both cool and heat your home, is one alternative to oil. Its energy source is electricity, and it requires no water or other fuel. The heat pump is one of the most efficient cooling and heating systems on the market. Check out your area to be sure electricity costs will be within your budget over a five-year period (see Figure 2–7). Because additional heating may be required in very cold weather, contact people in your area who have heat pumps to see if they are doing the job satisfactorily, and find out their costs.

Heat pumps work like refrigerators, which transfer heat out of the refrigerator and into the kitchen. In hot weather, heat pumps transfer heat (not air) from the inside of a home to the outside. On cold days, a heat pump reverses itself and transfers heat (not air) from the outside to the inside of a home. With the appropriate automatic thermostat installed, a heat pump can provide the desired temperature regardless of season.

The initial cost of a heat pump, plus annual upkeep, should be checked carefully before purchase. It does save energy and costs less to operate than other types of electric heating, delivering two units of heat for each unit of electricity it uses. It is essential, however, to have the required insulation (exterior walls, ceilings, and raised floors) for the

ESTIMATED HEATING AND COOLING COSTS						
System	Initial Cost	Annual Maintenance (Five-Year Period)				
		1st	2nd	3rd	4th	5th
Oil						
Gas						
Electricity						
Coal						
Solar Energy						
Wood						
Combination of systems						

Figure 2–7 Estimating your heating and cooling costs.

heat pump to be effective. And keep in mind that systems other than electric may prove to be more economical for your home.

In addition to the conventional heating and cooling systems using oil, gas, electricity, coal, or wood, there is also solar energy, which offers great potential in some localities in the United States. Before subcontracting your home, it is important to determine the initial costs of various heating and cooling systems, as well as the yearly maintenance charges for a five-year period. (The form shown in Figure 2–7 permits you to itemize your estimates.) This material should be reviewed with care before you make any decisions.

SOLAR ENERGY

Consider the possibility of using a solar energy system for part or all of your heating requirements if you live in certain areas of the country. Several private firms now offer solar energy units. Before you buy one, check carefully to see that such a system will meet your needs better than the available alternatives.

The advantages of a solar energy system include possible long-term savings, higher resale value, energy conservation, environmental safety, and clean operation. Disadvantages include higher initial costs, special designs required for your home, and the need for an auxiliary system. Another point to consider is that not much is known about the reliability of solar systems over a long period of time.

Heat for solar energy is stored in either a large tank of water (1000–2000 gallons), in spare heating systems, or in a bin of small rocks (for systems that use air as a heat-transfer medium). If a bin is used, the hot air flows through the space between the rocks and heats them. Such a bin is about 2½ times larger than the tank used in a water storage system. Radiation is absorbed by a collector, placed in storage with or without the assistance of a transfer medium, and then distributed to the living area of your home. The performance of each operation is maintained and monitored by either automatic or manual controls. An auxiliary heater provides backup when the solar system is not working.

ACTIVE AND PASSIVE SYSTEMS

There are two basic types of solar heating systems—active and passive. Active systems are divided into liquid and air. They use pumps and pipes (or fans and ducts) to carry heat from the collectors to and from storage to the living area. Passive systems use the structure of the house as both the collector and storage medium. In the passive system, movable wall panels, or flaps, can be used to direct the heat throughout the living area. (See Figure 2–8.)

An active system can be used in either a new or an existing home. When designing your new home, consider a passive system when the main concern is space heating. The design of a passive solar home requires great care regarding siting, north-south orientation, protective landscaping, and high-quality construction (see Figure 2–9)—all factors you can control by subcontracting your home.

SOLAR HEATING REQUIREMENTS FOR NIGHTS AND COLD, CLOUDY DAYS

On sunny days the heat generated in the collectors is transferred to the storage system. A second set of pipes (for liquid) or ducts (for air) is used to circulate heat from storage to the rooms in your home. There should be sufficient heat in your storage medium to last a few days, but if you have several cloudy or very cold days in a row and the heat in storage is exhausted, an auxiliary heater takes over. It would be too costly for your solar system to keep your home warm much longer than

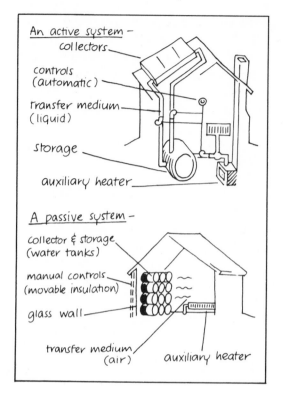

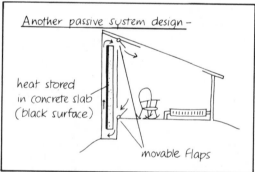

Figure 2–8 Active and passive solar heating systems. Source: *Solar Energy and Your Home,* Dept. of Housing and Urban Development.

a few days; most systems are designed therefore to provide only 50 to 75 percent of your total heating needs.

An auxiliary system can be any one of the standard heating systems that use oil, electricity, gas, or coal. It is a good idea to have a full-sized backup system, because it will be used when the weather is at its worst or when maintenance on the solar energy system is necessary.

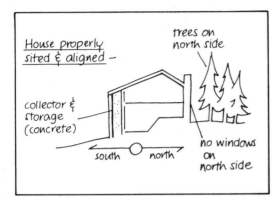

Figure 2–9 Siting, landscaping, and alignment for a solar energy system. Source: *Solar Energy and Your Home*, Dept. of Housing and Urban Development.

SOLAR ENERGY SYSTEMS AND AIR-CONDITIONING CAPABILITY

The heat from a solar energy system can be used to drive an air-conditioning compressor, but solar air-conditioning systems are currently very expensive when compared to conventional systems. In view of the extensive research and development in this area, however, discoveries may be made that will reduce costs. Passive air-cooling systems, currently available, are inexpensive and efficient, but they only work well in areas with low humidity and cool nights.

I suggest you also contact the following associations for names and addresses of local members who can provide helpful information. (See the list of Recommended Reading at the back of this book for further reference material.)

American Institute of Architects
1735 New York Avenue, N.W.
Washington, D.C. 20006

The American Society of Heating,
Refrigerating and Air Conditioning
Engineers
345 East 47th Street
New York, N.Y. 10017

National Association of Home Builders
15th and M Streets, N.W.
Washington, D.C. 20005

Solar Energy Industries Association
1001 Connecticut Avenue, N.W.
Washington, D.C. 20036

ENERGY CONSERVATION CHECKLIST BEFORE BUILDING

	Yes	No
1. Is insulation adequate in walls, ceiling, and, if appropriate, raised floors?	____	____
2. Are windows double-pane or storm windows?	____	____
3. Do drapes, with insulation, fit snugly?	____	____
4. Are doors, thresholds, door sweeps, all cracks, windows caulked and/or weather-stripped?	____	____
5. Were all forms and combinations of heating and cooling considered prior to making a decision—oil, gas, wood, coal, electricity, solar?	____	____
6. Are there storm doors? (Like storm windows, they provide a dead air space, which is an excellent insulator.)	____	____
7. Were energy alternatives considered prior to selecting kitchen equipment?	____	____
8. Is a fireplace desirable from an energy-saving standpoint?	____	____
9. Can a fireplace be used on those fall and spring days to provide adequate heat instead of using the furnace? (Don't forget to include the initial installation expense, in addition to upkeep and wood-burning materials.)	____	____
10. Will using the fireplace (to heat one or several rooms) in cold weather be more costly than using the central heating system because more heat from a fireplace rises through the chimney than enters the room?	____	____
11. If a chimney is used, will the damper fit snugly to prevent fireplace drafts?	____	____
12. Is a wood stove more appropriate than a chimney with brick fireplace, from an energy conservation viewpoint? (If so, has the cost of wood been considered?)	____	____

PLANNING FOR ENERGY SAVINGS

It is in the planning stage that you can do the best job to make your home energy efficient. The accompanying "Energy Conservation Checklist" provides measures you may wish to consider *before* building your home. Space is provided for you to come up with other ways to keep your home energy expenses to a minimum.

DAY-TO-DAY ENERGY CONSERVATION

Once your home is completed, it is essential to implement sound energy conservation measures to stay within your budget. Review your planned

	Yes	*No*
13. Are house windows located to take full advantage of the sun?	_____	_____
14. Is thermostat placed in a hall or location away from exterior doors, windows, and drafts? (Otherwise, the heating and cooling system will go on and off when the remainder of the house will be at the desired temperature.)	_____	_____
15. Is it necessary to heat the garage?	_____	_____
16. Can portable heaters (or window cooling units) be used more economically in certain localities of the home instead of central heating and cooling?	_____	_____
17. Are doors provided for rooms that may not be used? (Rooms not used shouldn't be heated or cooled; it is cheaper to close the doors if they are properly sealed.)	_____	_____
18. Are trees and shrubs planted wisely to reduce the wind force and provide shade? (Check with your local county agent for free information.)	_____	_____
19. Are the appliances planned the most energy-efficient units—air conditioner, refrigerator, water heater, freezer, dryer, dishwasher, clothes dryer, oven, and range? (Where appropriate, check the energy-efficient rating labels required for air conditioners by the federal government.)	_____	_____
20. Are fluorescent lights used wherever feasible because of lower utility costs (kitchen, bathrooms, etc.)?	_____	_____
21. Are electrical outlets placed on interior walls to reduce loss of air (hot or cold) inside of the house?	_____	_____
22. Will ceiling fans be appropriate for certain rooms?	_____	_____
23. Other (itemize)	_____	_____

energy conservation program yearly to determine if you are taking a sufficient number of actions to save money. The accompanying checklist itemizes energy-saving measures you may wish to consider. You are limited only by your imagination and creativity in devising ways to cut your energy costs. One family has a yearly brainstorming session where they all get together and exchange ideas on how to be more economical at home. The meetings have paid off handsomely in cutting money budgeted for housing. Last year this permitted them to enjoy a longer vacation.

DAY-TO-DAY ENERGY CONSERVATION CHECKLIST

———————————, 19———
(Date last checked)

	Yes	No
1. Thermostat set at 65° F in winter.	———	———
2. Thermostat set at 78° F in summer.	———	———
3. Lights turned off when not used.	———	———
4. Range used for cooking, not heating.	———	———
5. During long vacations: air-conditioning units turned off (or at least turned to a higher thermostat setting); only pilot light left on in water heater; perishable food in the freezer and refrigerator used up so that controls can be set to highest temperature; home has lived-in look or neighbor checks daily to pick up papers, mail, etc.	———	———
6. All water faucets checked for leaks and repaired promptly. Worn washers replaced without calling plumber.	———	———
7. Local utility company called to see if they will make a free inspection of home to suggest latest energy conservation measures.	———	———
8. Hot water heater at medium or low range (110° F or less).	———	———
9. Pilot light turned off in heating unit (furnace in the summer).	———	———
10. Heating and cooling units are serviced in accordance with warranty instructions. Filters kept clean.	———	———
11. Other (itemize)	———	———

SUMMARY

In deciding whether or not to subcontract your home, it is essential to consider the costs of inflation and the energy crisis. With mortgage rates at record levels and fuel costs doubling, you must estimate if your savings and income will permit you to meet all monthly payments for the next five years. It may be wise to wait for a possible decline in rates and costs. Research the purchase and fuel costs for heating and cooling units with care. Select a lot close to work, schools, and shopping districts, and design your home to maximize the conservation of energy. Once in your dream house, check that conservation measures are taken.

Chapter Three
Planning Your Dream
House

The first management function is adequate planning. To be a successful homebuilder, you must spend sufficient time during the planning phase. Adequate planning means determining if this is the correct time to build: read relevant available literature;[1] speak with building experts; and observe quality, residential construction firsthand. Give serious consideration to location, design, expenditures, time available for the project, and selection of subcontractors and desired materials. If this planning goes well, all other requirements should fall into place. Some people have told me they spend between eight months and two years planning to build their dream house.

TIMING—SHOULD I BUILD NOW?
During this period of inflation, energy shortage, and high interest rates, I am frequently asked, "Is it wise to build now?" My answer is,

[1] The federal government has good documents available. Pointers can be obtained from two HUD publications, *Minimum Property Standards (One- and Two-Family Dwellings)*, HUD No. 4900.1, 1973 ed. with amendments; and *Manual of Acceptable Practices*, No. 4930.1, 1973 ed. Helpful information can also be acquired from the Department of Agriculture publication, *Wood-Frame House Construction*, Agriculture Handbook No. 73 (Washington, D.C.: Government Printing Office, April 1975 rev.).

"Yes." If you intend to live in a community for at least three years, you should do well by making such an investment. Prices of housing materials and labor are going up each year and there is no indication that inflationary pressures will not continue in the future, although the rate should be somewhat slower than the 1979–80 rise. It will hit hardest at the pocketbooks of fixed-income people; even if the rates are lowered, they will be reduced in a lesser proportion than building costs will rise.

Another aspect you should consider is the availability of subcontractors and suppliers. If there is a major building boom in your area, it could delay your completion by months. The large contractors usually tie up the best subs, and some materials may not be in local stock. Recently I talked with a small builder who was most unhappy:

> I have waited 12 weeks for my plumber to return and install the bath fixtures—excuses, excuses, excuses. Last year he would have come begging, but now he has so much work he claims to be working 14 hours a day including Sunday. This delay already has cost me $6,000. I am paying 16 percent on the $150,000 I borrowed for these four duplexes. Vandalism and theft have been terrible. As you can see, holes have been punched in my celotex, my pipes have been broken, paneled doors kicked in, sliding glass partitions jammed, and a small fire destroyed part of one house. Stupidly, I didn't have insurance to cover the fire loss. To make matters worse, some of my good lumber was carted away and 500 of my bricks disappeared. I will be lucky to break even on this job.

Figure 3-1 PERT chart used during the planning phase of building a house.

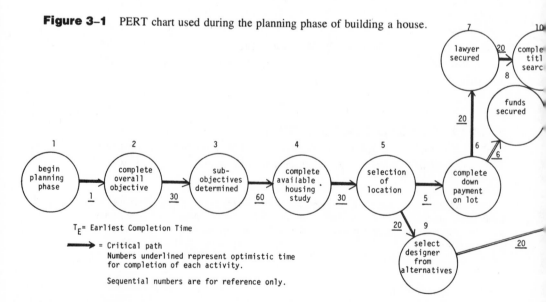

Timing is also important because of seasonal weather conditions. In some areas, floods, typhoons, heavy snows, drenching rains, excess heat, hard freezes, or hurricanes can play havoc with house construction. Determine when it is most convenient for you to supervise the project. In most areas, it is helpful to get the actual building under way in late spring; longer days are advantageous to a homebuilder. Your subs work their people on an hourly wage and are delighted to put in long hours to finish their work and get paid. This helps you in your objective to complete the house on schedule.

PERT AND TIMETABLE

PERT (Program Evaluation and Review Technique) is a managerial technique that helps you plan each step involved in completing a project. It is a valuable tool that can assist you in identifying and analyzing possible problem areas. An analysis of these potential difficulties can result in modifications that may reduce or eliminate the problems altogether.

One approach a successful builder employed was to use PERT for both the planning and building phases (see Figure 3–1). He developed a planning schedule that seemed feasible: a nine-month optimistic schedule and an alternative twelve-month schedule, which allowed for unplanned incidents. The detailed schedule, much like a budget, provides both a plan and a control technique. You may wish to use a format similar to Figure 3–1 in the planning phase of subcontracting your home, but be sure to design it to meet *your* requirements.

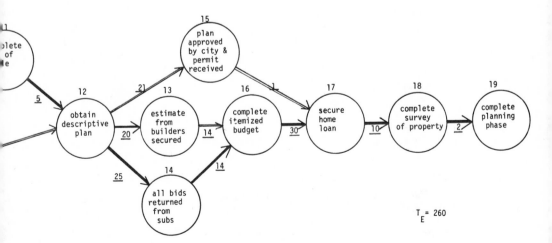

A timetable listing events in chronological order can also be of valuable assistance in checking on your progress. Such a timetable should list all major steps in planning your home. A model timetable is shown here. You will want to tailor the timetable to your own specific goals.

LOCATION

Location is of prime importance. The following features should be considered: distance to work, transportation facilities, taxes, people currently living in the residential area, availability of police and fire departments, proximity of good schools if you have or plan to have children, suitability of land to provide relative safety (e.g., high ground will provide relative safety during a flood), and area where property values are rising.

With the ever-increasing cost of gasoline, it may be wise to limit your search to within a five- to ten-mile radius of your place of employment. Make certain to determine the travel time between home and office. Also determine the quality of public transportation available, for you and your family may have to depend on it.

Figure 3–2 Sample form for rating lots under consideration.

LOT RATING WORKSHEET

	Lot A	Lot B	Lot C	Lot D	Lot E	Lot F
Proximity to work						
Convenience to school						
Convenience to church						
Play area nearby						
Quality of police and fire protection						
Adequacy of zoning restrictions						
Convenience to shopping facilities						
Location in relation to factories						
Size of lot in relation to price						
Appearance of neighborhood						
Amount of quiet and privacy						
Trees and shrubs						
Drainage						
Total points						

SCALE

Outstanding	*4 points*	*Fair*	*2 points*
Good	*3 points*	*Poor*	*1 point*

Today, more people are searching for a house within walking, jogging, or biking distance of work and stores. This saves time and money, improves your health, and helps alleviate ecology and energy problems.

Real estate taxes, present and planned, must be considered in determining where to live. Take the time to look at alternative lots. Speak to neighbors in the immediate area and consider privacy, if it's important to you. Give consideration to the homes adjacent to your lot. Will neighbors be looking in your backyard even with a six-foot fence?

The area you select should have a strong neighborhood association that checks to make sure homes meet minimum specifications. Pride in neighborhood appearance should be encouraged. One family developed

---

PLANNING TIMETABLE

1. Begin planning phase. Discuss techniques to meet needs—PERT, management model, planning steps.
2. Overall objective—a home within one year to meet family requirements and within financial resources.
3. Subobjectives:
   a. Location
      1. Walking distance to work
      2. Professional residential area
      3. Near good schools
      4. High ground to provide relative safety in the event of hurricane
      5. Area where property values are rising
   b. Cost
   c. Type
4. Complete study of available housing:
   a. Read articles
   b. Obtain ideas from authorities
   c. Visit sites
5. Select from alternatives the desired location.
6. Complete down payment on lot.
7. Secure lawyer.
8. Secure funds for lot.
9. Select designer from alternatives.
10. Complete title search.
11. Complete act of sale.
12. Obtain description of materials and necessary plans.
13. Secure estimate for comparison from builders.
14. All bids returned from subs.
15. Plan approved by city and permit received.
16. Complete itemized budget.
17. Secure home loan.
18. Complete survey of property.
19. Complete planning phase—review.

a rating scale for comparing each lot under consideration (see Figure 3–2).

BUILDING RESTRICTIONS

Building restrictions established by the city and the subdivision should be studied very carefully. Be sure to obtain the most current copy and

Figure 3–3 Sample building restrictions established for one area.

BUILDING RESTRICTIONS FOR
LAKE OAKS SUBDIVISION
A – Single Family Dwelling Sites

These restrictions apply to Squares No. 3, 4, 5, 6, 7, 8, 9, 10, 11, 5087, 5088, 5089 and 5090 in "Lake Oaks Subdivision", which is in Zone Four of the Lakefront Development of The Board of Levee Commissioners of the Orleans Levee District, in the City of New Orleans, Louisiana. Said subdivision is bounded by Lake Pontchartrain on the north, property of American Radiator & Standard Sanitary Corp. and St. Roch Ave. on the east, various properties on the south and Elysian Fields Ave. on the west.

SECTION I
DEFINITIONS
MAP

Where reference is made to the Map of "Lake Oaks", it refers to the Map entitled, "LAKE OAKS ON LAKE PONTCHARTRAIN, NEW ORLEANS, LOUISIANA, BOARD OF LEVEE COMMISSIONERS OF THE ORLEANS LEVEE DISTRICT," dated December 1, 1960, File No. L. D. 3106, signed by A. L. Willoz, C. E. Registration No. 73.

ORLEANS LEVEE BOARD

Where the name "Orleans Levee Board" appears it shall mean "The Board of Levee Commissioners of the Orleans Levee District."

MAIN BUILDING

The building that will be inhabited, containing rooms such as Living Room, Kitchen, Dining Room, Parlor, Bedroom, Library, etc.

ACCESSORY BUILDING

A subordinate building, attached to or detached from the main building, the use of which is incidental to that of the main building and not used as a place of habitation, such as a Living Room, Kitchen, Dining Room, Parlor, Bedroom, Library, Bathroom, etc.

HEIGHT OF BUILDING

The height of a building is the perpendicular distance measured in a straight line from the top of the highest point of the roof beams in the case of flat roofs, and from the average height of the gable in case of a roof having a pitch of more than twenty degrees with a horizontal plane, downward to the established grade in the center of the front of the building.

SECTION II
APPROVAL OF BUILDING PLANS

Prior to beginning the construction of a residence, garage, swimming pool, fence, or other structure, the owner shall submit reproduced copies of detailed plans and specifications of the proposed building or structure to the Orleans Levee Board. With plans the owner shall have to furnish an affidavit, certifying that the value of the house shall be equal or above the minimum in Section XVI. No work shall be done on the building until such written approval is received and building permit obtained from the City of New Orleans.

The approval of all structures by the Orleans Levee Board will be based on the requirements of these restrictions and on appearance.

Owners are cautioned that all structures erected on any parcel of ground in Lake Oaks must comply to Zoning Ordinances of the City of New Orleans. There may be cases where the City Ordinances are more restrictive than these title restrictions, in which case the former will govern.

SECTION III
GENERAL

All lots in Squares No. 3, 4, 5, 6, 7, 8, 9, 10, 11, 5087, 5088, 5089, and 5090, of Lake Oaks Subdivision shall be devoted to single family dwellings. On these lots all the usual uses normally allowed to private homes such as by professional men who operate Dentists' and Doctors' Offices, Nurseries, Clinics, etc., therein will not be permitted.

SECTION IV
FRONTAGE

No residence shall be built on less than one lot as shown on Map of "Lake Oaks". When any purchaser wishes to buy more than one site in order to erect a larger permitted residential building, this may be done provided that said lots or fractional lots shall aggregate a width of at least as wide as adjacent lots and shall be treated as one lot. The restrictions applying to a single lot should apply to such larger site. No resubdivision of lots shall be done which would leave remaining on the square a lot of an area or width below the average standard for said square, as indicated on the Map of "Lake Oaks". No lot shall be shifted as to frontage. No lot shall be renumbered or lose its identity even when subdivided. No lot shall be resubdivided for private sale or otherwise unless first approved by the Orleans Levee Board.

HEIGHT

Residences shall not exceed thirty-five (35) feet in height.

SECTION V
MINIMUM FRONT, SIDE AND REAR YARDS

(a) No part of any building of a residence shall be built closer than twenty (20) feet minimum distance from the front property line of the lot, nor closer to either side property line of the lot than six (6) feet minimum distance, however, the combined width of both side yards shall be a minimum of twenty-five per cent (25%) of the width of the lot, but need not exceed twenty-one (21) feet. Corner Lot 21, Sq. 4, Lots 1 and 20, Sq. 5 and Lot 19, Sq. 5087 shall have twenty (20) feet set backs on front and side streets. All other corner lots shall have twenty (20) feet set back on front street and twelve and five tenths feet (12.5) on side street. No detached garage shall be constructed closer than sixty (60) feet from the front property line and when outside the required rear yard area shall not project into the side yards.

An attached or detached carport may be constructed in the side yard area, provided its columns or wall are not closer than six (6) feet from the side property line, however, the roof may project two (2) feet into six (6) feet area. An attached or detached carport shall be considered a building for storing automobiles and having no more than one side enclosed. The other three sides must be completely open. Storage areas, utility rooms, tool rooms, etc., in such carports will not be permitted within the side yard area. Cooling towers and condensers must be erected in the rear of the main building and not project into side yard areas. No cooling towers or condensers shall be erected on roof of any building. When an accessory building is outside the required rear yard area it shall not project into the side yards. Clothes lines shall be in the rear of main building and shall not project beyond the side building lines.

(b) Bay or bow oriel, dormer and other projecting windows, stairways, landings or other structural parts shall not project beyond the front and side building lines.

(c) Cornices, roof overhangs, gutters, spouting, chimneys, brackets, pilasters, grill work, trellises, and other similar projections and any projections for purely ornamental purposes may project beyond the front and side building lines, however, not exceeding two (2) feet.

(d) Unenclosed, uncovered or covered porches, balconies and steps, shall not project beyond the front or side building lines.

(e) The rear yard measured from the farthest back projection of the principal building to the rear property line shall be not less check with the local association to see if there are plans to modify any of the present restrictions.

The rules regarding home construction may include height of the house; advance approval of the plans; garbage receptacle standards; minimum front, side, and rear yards; instructions for services such as gas, telephone, and electric power; grading of site; restrictions on hedges and shrubbery; fences; and swimming pool standards. Figure 3–3 shows the building restrictions established for one area.

than twenty per cent (20%) of the depth of the lot, except that in deep lots said yard need not exceed at any point, a maximum of twenty-five (25) feet and on shallow lots no rear yard shall be less, at any one point than a minimum of fifteen (15) feet.

(f) The front of a corner lot shall be its narrower dimension.

SECTION VI
VEHICLES

No trucks, trailers, automobiles or other commercial vehicles bearing advertisements are to be stored or parked on residential property or on streets, except when making deliveries. Passenger vehicles, owned by a resident, shall be stored on the resident's ground and not on the street.

SECTION VII
GARBAGE RECEPTACLES

Each residence of Lake Oaks Subdivision shall be required to install a garbage receptacle between the front sidewalk and curbing, by the owner of said residence. This receptacle shall be of sufficient capacity to take care of the garbage cans used by said residence and shall be of an approved design. The receptacle shall be installed underground and shall have a neat cover flush with the sidewalk surface. Details of garbage receptacle shall be made part of the plans and specifications of the residence to be submitted to The Board of Levee Commissioners of the Orleans Levee District for approval. No garbage cans are to be exposed on the street or sidewalk in front of a residence.

SECTION VIII
SERVICES

All services, such as gas, telephone, electric power, sewers, drains and water pipes shall be placed underground from the property line to the building.

Relative to electric service, the owner shall lay, or have laid, a cable underground from his meter to a New Orleans Public Service Inc's., transformer vault in the rear of the lot.

Relative to telephone service, the owner shall provide, at his own risk and expense, an open trench not less than fifteen (15) inches in depth from his house to a telephone terminal box in rear of his property. Location of this trench is to be designated by the telephone company. The Southern Bell Telephone and Telegraph Company will then lay the necessary cable in this trench and the owner, after the cable is laid, will then backfill this trench at his own expense.

SECTION IX
TRANSFORMER VAULTS AND EASEMENTS

To serve the sites in the Lake Oaks Subdivision with an electric underground system, transformer vaults will be erected in the rear of lots adjoining an easement owned by the Orleans Levee Board within which the primary cables serving the transformers will be located. These vaults will be constructed of brick or concrete and will be located as indicated on Map of Lake Oaks Subdivision, File No. L. D. 3106.

Public easements to permit walking through from street to street are provided in Squares 7, 8, 9, 10 and 11, and also between Squares 5 and 6. These easements are indicated on Map of Lake Oaks Subdivision File No. L. D. 3106.

On the lots listed below there are indicated on the plan of Lake Oaks four (4) foot easements, which are reserved for underground electric conduits and cables to be installed and maintained by the New Orleans Public Service Inc., as part of the Electrical Distribution Systems serving the residences of Lake Oaks Subdivision. The conduits will be encased in concrete and will be at least three (3) feet below ground surface which will permit landscape plantings and erection of permissible structures under Section V.

Sq. 3	Lot 2
Sq. 4	Lot 5
Sq. 4	Lot 24

Although the probability is remote, repairs to the conduits may become necessary, and in such event, the New Orleans Public Service Inc., has the right to enter these easements to make the necessary repairs.

When such repairs have been completed, the New Orleans Public Service Inc., will be responsible to restore the surfaces of the easements to their. original condition upon completion of said work.

SECTION X
SWIMMING POOLS

Swiming pools, if and when erected are to be of approved, substantial and neat construction, and will only be permitted provided they are entirely surrounded by a fence not less than thirty-six (36) inches in height and shall conform to all fence requirements recited in Section XII. The vertical inside faces of a pool shall be built no closer than six (6) feet to either side property line nor closer than thirty (30) feet to the front property line, not closer than six (6) feet to the rear property line. The finished top-side or surface deck shall not be constructed higher in elevation than one foot above the established site grade of the residence. Equipment such as diving boards, etc., shall not be higher than five (5) feet above site grade of the residence. The pool shall be so designed as to prevent splashings from the pool from draining into adjacent properties.

SECTION XI
PARKS

Lake Oaks Park is a public park, owned by the Orleans Levee Board, and is for use of the General Public of the City of New Orleans. This park will be maintained by the Orleans Levee Board.

Interior Parks are reserved for the common use of the property owners of Lake Oaks and nothing shall be placed thereon, or no use shall be made thereof, to the detriment, inconvenience or annoyance of the resident, or owner of any part or portion of ground adjacent thereto. These parks are owned and are to be maintained by the Orleans Levee Board.

SECTION XII
FENCES

Fences will be permitted as noted below:

Front yard fences, if and when erected, shall not exceed eighteen (18) inches in height and shall be of neat and substantial construction.

Side fences, when erected between the front building line and front property line, shall not exceed eighteen (18) inches in height.

Side and rear yard fences, if and when erected between front building line and rear property line, shall not exceed five (5) feet in height and shall be of neat and substantial construction.

On corner lots, fences shall not be erected closer than the required setback from any street or park property line.

Plans showing location and details of fences must be submitted for approval to the Orleans Levee Board before they are erected.

SECTION XIII
GRADE OF SITE

The established grade of lots is not to be raised by any individual owner so as to adversly affect an adjacent property owner or owners in the same square.

SECTION XIV
PLANTING

Hedges and shrubbery may be grown along property lines, but shall be restricted to a height of two (2) feet along the front yard property line, and shall be restricted to a height of seven (7) feet on side and rear property lines.

Trees planted in the required side yards of one lot may not project into the required side yards of adjacent owners, except upon agreement between the affected owners that said projection is not objectionable.

All trees, shrubbery, flowers, lawns or other vegetation on private residential lots shall be kept in good order by the owners and/or their tenants.

SECTION XV
GRASS CUTTING ON VACANT SITES

For the purpose of keeping the Subdivision in an orderly condition, the Orleans Levee Board reserves the right and assumes the responsibility to cut the grass on vacant building sites for the period of time commencing after the improvements are completed to December 31, 1962. In cutting the grass on vacant property the Orleans Levee Board is to be held harmless for any damage by the owners of such vacant property. Upon termination of this period it will be the responsibility of the owners of each lot to maintain the grass in a presentable condition.

SECTION XVI
MINIMUM COST OF RESIDENCES

The total construction cost of any residence shall be at least equal to or in excess of one and one-half (1½) times the market value of the lot, on which constructed, at the time construction begins.

PURCHASE ARRANGEMENTS

The next step is to make arrangements to purchase the desired lot. The best arrangement is buying directly from the owner. If you can't, you should work through an able real estate agent who is a member of the local real estate board. This will permit you to arrive at a fair price in comparison to similar lots recently sold. (The sale prices of all lots appear weekly in some local papers.) Before hiring a lawyer, secure his itemized charges. (See Figure 3–4 for sample charges.)

TITLE SEARCH AND INSURANCE

Have a title search and title insurance. The purpose of a title search is to determine if the lot is clear of prior claims. Your lawyer will usually check the records back fifty to seventy-five years for this purpose. You can expect to be charged 1 percent of the property price for this service.

Figure 3–4   Itemized legal charges involved in purchasing a lot.

	Buyer	Seller
PAYABLE AS COURT COSTS:		
Mortgage certificate		10.00
Paving certificate		4.00
Conveyance certificate		7.00
Tax certificate		8.00
Registration of act in conveyance office	4.50	
Registration certificate	1.50	
Cancelling mortgage Registration in archives, New Orleans		4.50
PAYABLE AS LEGAL FEES:		
Passing act of sale	120.00	
Preparing, ordering, and obtaining certificates		50.00
Conducting title examination	50.00	
Executing release of mortgage		50.00
Less: deposit on costs	−60.00	
PAYABLE AS OTHER COSTS:		
Pro Rata Tax Adjustment:		
City taxes (to buyer)	237.24	
State taxes (to seller)		20.60
Purchase Price:		
Close out balance on loan with savings and Loan Association (to S & L)	11,385.29	
Seller's portion (to seller)	4,814.71	
TOTAL DISBURSEMENTS	$16,553.24	$154.10

Thus, on a $20,000 lot, it will cost you $200. Make certain you get what you pay for. That is, be sure the attorney spells out in a letter the length of time the title search covered.

In order to avoid or reduce this cost, you may wish to check the records yourself or obtain the services of a title searcher who specializes in this work. His fee should be no more than half the lawyer's charge. In fact, some lawyers use the services of these title searchers and then charge the client the full price. See Figure 3–5 for a sample letter spelling out the details of a title search that you should request from your lawyer.

Title insurance provides you protection in the event it is later discovered that you don't really own the property. The charge is normally 1 percent of the value of the home. If this amounts to $100,000, your title insurance may cost $1,000. Title companies specialize in this type of business. It pays to shop around for the best price, but consider the reputation of the company first.

Figure 3–5 Sample lawyer's title examination.

Dear _____:

I have examined the title to the above described property, and based upon the records and documents available for inspection, the title is approved subject to the certificates obtained and copies of survey. Certificates have been received clear of any discrepancies in prior transfers dating back through two preceding transferors.

Mortgage certificates indicate that there is presently an outstanding mortgage and vendor's lien in the amount of $_____ in favor of _____ Savings and Loan Association, such mortgage being evidenced by a note executed by _____ in favor of the above mentioned mortgagee on December 20, 1975.

This open vendor's lien in favor of _____ Savings and Loan Association, recorded in M.O.B. _____ folio __, of _____, will be cancelled subject to payment of the outstanding balance of $_____ to the vendor, _____ Savings and Loan Association.

The last survey of this property was conducted more than two years ago, and it is suggested that an up-to-date survey be secured prior to construction.

Regular city and state tax certificates and special paving, sewerage, and water certificates have been secured and indicate that payment of all taxes has been accomplished. City and State property taxes, it is understood, will be prorated among the vendor and vendee as indicated in the Act of Sale.

Yours truly,

Title insurance protects the lender only and not the purchaser. The purchaser can protect himself by paying an additional sum of money. Be sure to check this out before making a decision. If you let your lawyer take care of title insurance, he may charge an extra amount or receive a kickback from the company selected.

If the records indicate you have clear title to your lot, the next step is to sign the "agreement to purchase" (see Figure 3–6).

PLANS AND MATERIALS

Keep your costs for plans at a minimum. If you can find someone—not necessarily licensed but competent—who has worked for an architect and has just started his own business, he will be delighted to prepare your plans for a reasonable fee. Be sure the person is well qualified. You may find your wisest choice is a recognized architect.

You may wish to develop sketches of your house, as well as detailed specifications. You can find excellent ideas in books that deal with plans for homes. Also visit newly constructed homes and houses for sale that appeal to you. One person wrote me:

> I looked for homes that were similar to what we wanted to sub-contract. On Sundays my wife and I would dress well and ask owners if we could see the inside of their homes. Most people were pleased to comply. In two instances we obtained copies of plans that made it easy to sketch out what we wanted. The sketching was easy for us because we took a basic drafting course at a local university. We also learned the importance of checking all dimensions for errors prior to construction.

An architect or a draftsman can use the sketches to make up the necessary (often ten or more) sets of drawings (five plans per set: foundation, floor plans, interior and exterior wall elevations, plot plan, and typical interior and exterior wall sections). It is important to work closely with this person to make certain your desires are conveyed clearly to him and that your proposals are feasible. You can keep your architect or draftsman happy and keep your costs down by not making changes after his drawings have been finalized. (See Appendix A for a complete set of drawings.)

I am amazed at the number of people who buy a home and never ask to see the drawings. They provide valuable information that could be an important factor in arriving at your decision to buy or not to buy.

The draftsman or architect should also provide you with necessary copies of "description of materials." It is important to be specific about materials for every item in your home—foundation, exterior walls, floor

AGREEMENT TO PURCHASE OR SELL

For exclusive use of "Realtors"

FORM ATP-OS NO. 3
Revised and approved January, 1971
Standard Form Real Estate Board of New Orleans, Inc.

Member Real Estate Board of New Orleans, Inc.

_____ Agent _____ , La., _____ 19 ___

1. _____ offer and agree to purchase _____ seli

2. _____

3. _____

4. On grounds measuring about _____ or as per title.

5. Property sold and purchased subject to all title and zoning restrictions on record, or by laws or ordinances for the sum of _____

6. _____ ($ _____) Dollars,

7. on the terms of_____ cash _____

8. _____

9. _____

10. This sale is conditioned upon the ability of purchaser to borrow upon this property as security the sum of $_____ by a mortgage loan or

11. loans at a rate of interest not to exceed _____ % per annum, interest and principal payable on or before _____ years

12. in equal monthly installments.

13. Should purchaser, seller or agent be unable to obtain the loan stipulated above within _____ days from acceptance hereof, this contract shall then be
14. null and void and the agent is hereby authorized to return the purchaser's deposit in full. Commitment by lender to make loan, subject to approval of title, shall constitute ob-
15. taining of loan.
16. Property sold subject to the following lease or leases:

17. Tenant _____ Rental _____ Expiration _____ Options _____

18. _____

19. Possession and occupancy by purchaser at passing of act of sale or on _____

20. All recorded sewerage, utilities and street surfacing charges bearing against the property as of this date to be paid by_____
21. Real Estate Taxes and rentals (if any) to be prorated to date of act of sale.

22. All costs and fees for necessary certificates and vendor's closing fee to be paid by seller. Cost of survey by_____

23. Act of sale at expense of purchaser to be passed before _____ Notary, at any time after

24. _____ 19 _____ , and prior to _____ 19 _____ . In the event bona fide curative work in connection with title
25. is required, the parties herewith agree to and do extend the time for passing of act of sale by thirty days.
26. Upon acceptance of this offer, vendor and purchaser shall be bound by all its terms and conditions and purchaser becomes obligated to deposit with seller's agent immediately

27. _____ % of the purchase price amounting to $_____ , and failure to do so shall not void this agreement but shall be considered as a breach
28. thereof and seller shall have the right, at his option, to demand liquidated damages equal to the amount of the deposit or specific performance, and purchaser shall, in either
29. event, be liable for agent's commission, attorney's fees and costs.
30. This deposit is to be non-interest bearing and shall be placed in any bank in Metropolitan New Orleans, without responsibility on the part of the agent in case of failure or
31. suspension of such bank.
32. The seller shall deliver to purchaser a merchantable title, and his inability to deliver such title within the time stipulated herein shall render this contract null and void,
33. reserving unto purchaser the right to demand the return of the deposit from the holder thereof, and reserving unto agent the right to recover commission.
34. In the event the seller fails to comply with this agreement for any other reason, within the time specified, the purchaser shall have the right either to demand the return of
35. his deposit in full plus an equal amount to be paid as penalty by the seller; or the purchaser may demand specific performance, at his option.
36. In the event the purchaser fails to comply with this agreement within the time specified, the seller shall have the right to declare the deposit, ipso-facto, forfeited, without
37. formality beyond tender of title to purchaser; or the seller may demand specific performance.
38. In the event the deposit is forfeited, the commission shall be paid out of this deposit, reserving to the seller the right to proceed against the purchaser for the recovery of
39. the amount of the commission.
40. If this offer is accepted, seller agrees to pay the agent's commission of _____ which commission is
41. earned by agent when this agreement is signed by both parties and when the mortgage loan, if any, has been secured.
42. Either party hereto who fails, for any reason whatsoever, to comply with the terms of this offer, if accepted, is obligated and agrees to pay the agent's commission and all
43. reasonable attorney's fees and costs incurred by the other party, and/or agent in enforcing their respective rights.

44. _____

45. This offer remains binding and irrevocable through_____

46. Submitted to _____ (Signed)_____
Listing Agent or Owner

47.
48. By _____ Address
Selling Agent I/We accept the above in all its terms and conditions.

_____ , La. _____ (Signed) _____

_____ 19 _____

Address

Figure 3-6 Sample "Agreement to Purchase or Sell." Courtesy of Real Estate Board of New Orleans, Inc.

framing, roofing, windows, interior doors and trim, cabinets, heating, plumbing, and so on. For example, for roofing specify "asbestos shingles, Johns-Manville, American colonial." Don't simply ask for "asbestos shingles" because there is a great difference in quality and price of roofing materials. It is your responsibility to provide the architect or draftsman with the specific details on material. If undecided, indicate a well-known item and add "or equivalent." Being as precise as possible will permit more accurate estimates by builders and subcontractors. (See Appendix B for a sample description of materials.)

Experience indicates that it pays to buy the best materials. Careful shopping, however, may reveal large price differences in similar first-quality materials. Don't hesitate to ask for discounts. In the long run, the cost difference is recovered in durability, reduced heating and cooling bills, and appearance.

Preparing a description of materials may sound like a big undertaking, but this is not so. Your designer will probably have many sets from previous work, and good builders also have copies. In addition, the owner of a home you admire may provide you with his plans. Once you have several descriptions of material in hand, you need only make appropriate modifications to suit your needs.

ARCHITECT

If you desire a custom-designed home with architectual detailing, you should engage the services of an architect. You will probably have greater peace of mind by having a professional do your plans and specifications. If you decide to use an architect, it is important to select a firm with a good reputation. The architect should be a member of the American Institute of Architects (AIA). Make sure that the written contract specifies precisely what work the architect will perform for his fee.

The normal fee for designing, drawing, supervising, and inspecting is 6 to 7 percent of the cost of constructing the home. This would amount to $6,000 or $7,000 on a $100,000 dwelling. Consult with several firms before making a decision (and be prepared to pay a consultation fee). If you only wish an architect to design and draw up plans and specifications, the fee for these services may be 2 to 3 percent of the construction cost of the home. A nonlicensed architect's fees may be lower than 2 to 3 percent, but his drawings would need to be stamped by a licensed professional in order to obtain a permit to build.

You may also obtain services of architects on an hourly basis at fees ranging from $10 to $50 per hour. The lowest price for obtaining plans and specifications is usually obtained from a draftsman. The price may range anywhere from $250 to over $1,000. Where an architect creates, designs, and draws up the plans, a draftsman typically only copies a set of drawings that have been created by someone else. These drawings must also be stamped by a licensed professional before you can obtain a permit to build.

BUILDERS AND ESTIMATES

After the plans and description of materials are completed, you can let out three sets to reputable builders in the community, who will give you their prices to construct this exact house. You will then have a comparison of their costs versus your costs. Keep in mind that any additions after signing with a builder will cost you extra.

I checked with fourteen individuals who had contracted to have their homes built and found that the original estimate had been increased by 8 to 26 percent because of additional charges the builders had made. One of my neighbors had a patio overhang extended four feet—it cost him an extra $1200.

BUDGET

Keep in mind other costs, such as landscaping, fencing, drapes, and moving expenses. Itemize every cost in your budget; it is a significant planning tool. See the format shown in Figure 3–7; you may be able to

Figure 3–7   A budget format.

BUDGET OF_____

Item	First Estimate	Revised Estimate	Actual	Contracted With: (Name, address, phone, principal to contract)
Preliminary Costs				
[Includes such items as lot, taxes, insurance, lawyer's fee, building permit, and survey.]				
Foundation:				
Piling (#9)	$ 950.00	$ 912.00	$ 912.00	Smith Pile Drivers, Inc.
•				121 Richton Ave.
•				711-3000
•				Mr. John Smith
Materials				
Lumber	6,579.79	6,641.50	6,766.14	Doc Lumber Company
•				5164 Collins Avenue
•				401-6111
•				Mr. J. J. Doe
Total*	xxx	xxx	xxx	

*In arriving at your total, you may wish to pay yourself a fair return and include this figure in the overall price. This economic opportunity cost means that if you hadn't spent time on this job you could have done other productive work. However, if you had contracted a builder there would also be time expended. A query of four persons indicated they averaged three hours per day over an eight-month construction period. Buying a new or used home also involves use of time—loan negotiations, etc.

obtain a form for this purpose from a lending agency. Don't forget to allow up to 10 percent in your budget for unforeseeable items.

BIDS

Once you have listed all the items necessary to build your home, it is time to contact subcontractors and supply houses for prices. Leads on the most reliable firms can be obtained from successful builders, observation of quality homes in progress and talks with the subcontractors concerned, and friends who did their own subcontracting. All three sources should prove valuable.

If possible, get bids from three suppliers and subcontractors before you make your final decision. Do not always take the lowest bid or accept the first price. In order to secure bids on lumber, electrical requirements, plumbing, and so on, it is necessary to provide these firms with your plans and description of materials; this is the primary reason for having ample sets made. Be sure to have copies returned. (The city and local jurisdictional board may also require copies for their files.) Be careful not to accept inferior substitute material for what you specify in the description of materials.

Once you have selected the best deal, it is only a matter of tabulating the prices to determine the overall cost of building your home. This total can be compared with what the three builders estimated. You may find a 25 percent difference with even the lowest bid. If the spread is close or the project appears insurmountable, you may wish to go the builder route—or buy a home. But don't be discouraged at this point!

ELECTRICITY EFFICIENCY RATING

The importance of having an energy-efficient home cannot be overemphasized. The years ahead will bring an increasing scarcity of energy and rising energy costs. Accordingly, it is highly desirable to buy the most efficient products and materials for your home. This determination can be made best during the planning phase, when you prepare your description of materials and develop the specific costs.

How do you go about buying the most efficient units? Many appliances have energy ratings. Suppose you decide to have a workshop in your garage and desire a window air-conditioning unit. (Air conditioning is often the largest user of electrical energy in a home.) Factors to consider in selecting the appropriate unit include the location of the room (northern or southern exposure takes a smaller size), the number of people using the room (the more people, the larger the unit), the amount of insulation (a better-insulated room will require a smaller unit), and the dimensions of the area (a larger room will require a larger unit).

After you have accumulated the above information, visit reputable dealers to determine the appropriate size air conditioner for your workshop. To find the most energy-efficient unit, select the air conditioner that has the least wattage for the cooling capacity you desire. Let us assume you select a room air conditioner unit rated at 20,000 British Thermal Units (BTU).[2] It is then to your advantage to buy a quality unit with the lowest wattage. Reason: the higher the wattage (for a similar BTU) the greater the dollar cost.

The operating efficiency of a unit can be determined by using the following formula:

$$\frac{\text{British thermal units (BTU)}}{\text{watts}} = \text{Electrical Efficiency Rating (EER)}$$

If you found three units of comparable quality rated at 20,000 BTU that had wattages of 2,000 (unit 1), 2,200 (Unit 2), and 2,500 (Unit 3), the formula would provide the EERs as follows:

Unit 1: $\dfrac{20,000}{2,000} = 10.00$

Unit 2: $\dfrac{20,000}{2,200} = 9.09$

Unit 3: $\dfrac{20,000}{2,500} = 8.00$

It is apparent from the EER results that Unit 1 is the best buy. It provides 10 BTU per watt in contrast to Unit 2, which furnishes 9.09, and Unit 3, which furnishes only 8 BTU per watt.

The above method should be employed in selecting appliances to be used in subcontracting your home. Look at refrigerators, dishwashers, washing machines, dryers, ovens, ranges, compactors, electric garage-door openers, and garbage disposals. After deciding which appliances are suitable for your home, determine the EER for each appliance. It should be an important factor in your decision as to what appliance is correct for your home.

---

[2] A British thermal unit is the quantity of heat necessary to raise one pound of water one degree Fahrenheit at or near 39.2 degrees.

ENERGY GUIDE

There is another piece of information on large appliances that can be helpful to you in making wise, energy-efficient selections. The Federal Trade Commission requires Energy Guide labels to appear on water heaters, washing machines, refrigerators, freezers, room air conditioners, and dishwashers. The labels list the costs per year for operating different models. Data provided on the Energy Guide vary based on the type of appliance. A refrigerator, for example, has an Energy Guide indicating the capacity of the refrigerator—freezer, manufacturer, model number, type of defrost, estimated annual energy costs for the highest and lowest comparable models, and the cost of this model. The FTC Energy Guide states: "Your cost will vary, depending on your local energy rate and how you use the product." The dollar cost is based on the national average electric rate per kilowatt hour.

SUMMARY

Adequate planning is essential to build your home economically and efficiently. A detailed timetable that includes many opportunities for review of completed steps will make your job much easier. The timetable will also serve as a checklist, so that no job is undertaken out of order, and no job is overlooked. Detailed plans prevent cost overruns and construction delays; they are the map to the house of your dreams.

Chapter Four
Money—The Essential
Ingredient

Now that you have done a good job of planning and have all your facts in hand, you are in a position to visit lending agencies. Officials at banks, mortgage firms, insurance companies, and savings and loan associations should be impressed with your knowledge and the thoroughness of your work. Check your budget once more to be sure that all estimated expenses are listed and that your computations are correct. Go over your description of materials to see that each item is specified.

Your objective now is to obtain the money under the best possible terms. The loan you seek to build your home is called a mortgage. Title or ownership of the home will rest with the lending agency until you have paid your debt. Familiarize yourself with the terms of your mortgage *before you sign it*. Reading the sample mortgage in Appendix C will help acquaint you with the terminology.

INTEREST COSTS

One of the most important considerations will be the interest you must pay and the number of years you will be making payments. Even ½ percent represents a significant amount of money. Table 4–1 shows the cost of a $40,000 mortgage based on different interest rates of varying duration.

Table 4–1   Cost of a $40,000 Mortgage by Interest Rate and Duration

Interest Rate	Years							
	5	10	15	20	25	30	35	40
9	$ 9,840	$20,840	$33,080	$46,400	$ 60,800	$ 75,920	$ 91,740	$108,160
9½	10,420	22,120	35,240	49,520	64,900	81,200	98,040	115,680
10	11,000	23,440	37,400	52,720	69,100	86,480	104,480	123,040
10½	11,600	24,800	39,620	55,920	73,400	91,760	110,920	130,720
11	12,200	26,160	41,840	59,120	77,700	97,160	117,500	138,240
11½	12,800	27,520	44,120	62,400	82,000	102,680	124,080	145,920
12	13,400	28,880	46,460	65,760	86,400	108,200	130,660	153,760
12½	14,000	30,280	48,800	69,120	90,900	113,720	137,380	161,440
13	14,620	31,680	51,140	72,480	95,400	119,360	144,100	169,280
13½	15,240	33,120	53,480	75,920	99,900	125,000	150,820	177,120
14	15,860	34,560	55,940	79,440	104,500	130,640	157,540	184,960
14½	16,800	36,000	58,340	84,720	109,100	136,400	164,400	192,800
15	17,100	37,480	60,800	86,480	113,700	142,160	171,260	200,640
15½	17,800	38,800	63,200	90,400	118,000	147,920	178,400	208,000
16	18,400	40,400	65,600	93,600	123,000	153,200	184,980	216,480

If you are able to pay off your mortgage rapidly, it cuts your charges markedly. The interest on a five-year loan at 12 percent amounts to $13,400, in contrast to $108,200 at the same rate for 30 years—a difference of $94,800. A 20-year loan at 11 percent costs $38,040 less than the same loan for 30 years.

Interest rates in the 1979–80 period varied from 10 to 17 percent. There will always be variations in this highly competitive area of home loans. It is therefore wise to shop around and check the different types of institutions—banks, savings and loan associations, mortgage companies, and insurance firms.

You will have a stronger bargaining position if you can make a larger down payment. Lending institutions are concerned about risks and a larger down payment (other things being equal) reduces their risk. It is true that the mortgagor (person borrowing the money) can be taken to court by the mortgagee (lender) for failure to meet payments, but legal proceedings are costly and time-consuming. All lenders wish to avoid this action.

A 20 percent down payment is recommended—more if feasible. (If you build a house knowing you will leave the area within three years, you can support a case for making the minimum down payment and extending the loan over the longest term; this is because more people will be able to take over the loan.) In Table 4–2, note the difference in cost when two people bought similar houses for $100,000.

Table 4-2   Effect of Down Payment on Total Cost

1	2	3	4	5	6	7
Percent Down	Amount of Down Payment	Principal Amount of Loan	Duration of Loan (years)	Interest Rate	Total Interest	Total Cost (2 + 3 + 6)
20	$20,000	$80,000	30	12	216,242	316,242
5	$ 5,000	$95,000	30	12	256,787	356,787

Lenders are eager to provide funds to "blue chip" borrowers—individuals who make a healthy down payment and have an excellent credit rating. They can be expected to meet all their loan obligations and so receive the best terms. Borrowers should strive for this category because they will be eligible for the lowest interest charges and thus will place themselves in the strongest bargaining position. Although a good credit risk may wish to make the maximum down payment and pay off his loan as rapidly as possible, the loan officer may try to have him take the mortgage for a longer time. The lender's reasoning is apparent from the statistics, which show that home costs increase in direct relation to the duration of the mortgage. He may try to convince the borrower that the actual interest charged does not tell the whole story.

The loan official may mention the income tax write-off as a great advantage. If someone is in the 30 percent tax bracket (on the average) for the life of the loan and it costs 10 percent to borrow money, it means the tax deduction may reduce it as low as 7 percent. This is still a sizable charge, and a person would be fortunate to do as well (after taxes) on his own investment portfolio. It is better to forget the tax advantage and proceed to use the money saved on interest to build your own sound money management program.[1]

IMPACT OF INFLATION AND TAXES ON BORROWING

Because inflation can reduce your borrowing costs, it should be taken into consideration. The annual erosion in the purchasing power of the dollar is expected to continue. There are, however, two unknowns: the annual percentage increase and the specific items that will rise. Assume

[1] For a detailed discussion of this topic, see the author's *Guide to Personal Finance: A Lifetime Program of Money Management,* 3d ed. (Englewood Cliffs, N.J.: Prentice-Hall, 1979); or *More For Your Money! Personal Finance Techniques to Cope with Inflation and the Energy Shortage,* (Englewood Cliffs, N.J.: Prentice-Hall, 1980).

that a home that could be subcontracted for $100,000 rises to $105,000 twelve months later. In this case, your dollar power has been reduced by nearly 5 percent ($105,000 − $100,000) ÷ 105,000. If you had borrowed the $100,000 last year to build the home, you could pay the money back with cheaper dollars.

Now assume your $100,000 loan could be obtained at 12 percent, with the entire interest and principal to be paid at the end of the twelfth month. In such a case the impact of inflation would in theory result in your paying nearly 7 percent interest ($112,000 − $105,000) ÷ $105,000.

Your actual interest savings will depend on the amount of inflation affecting your particular purchase.

UNDERSTANDING AMORTIZED HOUSING LOANS

It is important for the homebuilder to understand the difference between term loans, available from banks for interim financing, and amortized housing loans obtained from savings and loan associations, mortgage companies, and insurance firms.

A term loan requires regular interest payments made at established times. When the final interest payment is due, the total amount of the principal also must be repaid. For example, a person who borrows $100,000 at 12 percent for 10 years on a term basis will have to pay $1,000 per month interest for nine years and eleven months. The final payment will be $101,000 ($1,000 interest plus $100,000 principal).

In contrast to a term loan, an amortized loan requires equal monthly payments that include both interest and principal during the life of the loan. The amortized loan costs less in interest payments than term because interest costs are computed at the end of each month based on the outstanding balance. Because the principal is reduced each month, the monthly interest is reduced and more goes for paying off the principal. A person who borrows $100,000 at 12 percent for ten years will have interest costs totaling $120,000 for a term loan, in contrast to approximately $98,000 for an amortized loan.

Study amortization tables carefully before obtaining a loan to purchase your home. Such tables are available in real estate offices, savings and loan associations, and other lending agencies. The tables are necessary because computing amortized loan payments is very difficult. It is important to determine the difference in costs based upon interest rates offered at the time you intend to buy. A 1 percent lower rate can amount to $25,000 savings on a $100,000 mortgage over a 30-year pe-

MONTHLY PAYMENTS ON A $_____ LOAN AT ___% INTEREST OVER A ___ -YEAR PERIOD Monthly Payment per $1,000 = _____				
I Number of monthly payments	*II* Interest paid monthly	*III* Principal paid monthly	*IV* Total monthly payment (*II & III*)	*V* Total principal due (*balance*)
1				
2				
3				
4				
5				
6				
7				
8				
9				
10				
11				
12				
1st year total				
13				
14				
15				
16				
17				
18				
19				
20				
21				
22				
23				
24*				
2nd year total				
*To 240 monthly payments for a 20-year loan, 360 monthly payments for a 30-year loan, etc.				

Figure 4–1 Sample form for analyzing monthly payments on a loan.

riod. Even ¼ percent can save over $6,000. I suggest you break out your amortized loan information as shown in Figure 4–1. (See also Appendix E.)

TYPES OF MORTGAGE LOANS

Three types of mortgage loans are available—VA (GI), FHA, and conventional.

GI LOAN

Since the end of World War II, more than 10 million people have purchased homes with the assistance of GI loans under the guaranteed home-loan program of the Veterans Administration (VA). A GI loan is a loan made by a private lending institution to a veteran for any "eligible purpose," pursuant to Title 38, United States Code. (See *Loans For Veterans,* VA Pamphlet 26–4, rev. 1980, p. 2.)

The rate of interest on a GI loan fluctuates with the changes in the cost of borrowing money. The VA will guarantee no more than 60 percent of a loan, the top portion of the loan, in an amount not to exceed $25,000. Eligible individuals first apply to a lending agency. The major firms doing this type of business are mortgage brokers.

The GI loan provides the following advantages:

1. The interest rate is normally lower than the going rate at the time.

2. You have the right to repay your loan at any time without penalty.

3. No down payment is required.

4. The loan may be made for up to 30 years.

5. The veteran has the right to sell his home to whomever he pleases and whenever he desires.

The disadvantages you may encounter are:

1. There undoubtedly will be red tape when dealing with the government.

2. Add-on points are often charged, which may absorb much of the savings gained from the lower interest rate. A point is 1 percent of the amount of the mortgage loan. If a loan is for $50,000, one point is $500. Points are a one-time charge by the lender which enables him to raise the yield on his loan. Although the VA does not permit point payments legally, there are ways to do this "under the table" by asking a higher price for the home than if a conventional loan were used or by making no record of such point money being exchanged.

FHA

The Federal Housing Administration (FHA) also provides an opportunity to obtain a loan at less than the going rate. The FHA, like the VA, guarantees a loan for the lending agency, which approves the loan first. Anyone who has good credit, steady work, and the necessary cash down payment is eligible for an FHA loan. At the present time, the maximum mortgage that the FHA will guarantee for a single-family dwelling is $60,000.

The FHA calculates the maximum insurable loan by taking:

97 percent of the first $25,000 (the appraisal value)

95 percent of the excess

The advantages of the FHA loan are as follows:

1. There is a smaller down payment than with a regular loan. If a person purchases a $60,000 home, his down payment is only $2500. (The buyer may have to pay closing costs similar to those in a conventional loan.)
2. The interest rate is normally more reasonable.
3. The period of payment may be longer, with a 30-year maximum.

The prime disadvantage is the amount of time consumed in bureaucratic delay.

CONVENTIONAL

The key advantage to the conventional loan is that it eliminates government red tape. It is often more costly, however. Also, in periods of high interest rates, lending agencies are more selective and these loans may be difficult to obtain.

In the 1979–80 capital market, it was generally not possible to secure the best deal on a conventional loan. Two examples will serve to illustrate the picture. The branch manager of one large savings and loan firm was making no GI or FHA loans—money was too scarce and there were better opportunities in the regular home loan. He was making conventional loans up to 80 percent of appraised value. On a $100,000 home, this meant an $80,000 maximum loan, with interest charge of 12¾ percent and monthly payments to be completed in 20 years. So a buyer had to have $20,000 of his own money available or secure a second mortgage from some other source—at a higher rate of interest.

In the second case, a prominent lending institution on the West Coast required a 25-percent down payment on a $200,000 house. Although the bank would loan $150,000 at 12 percent, they stipulated that if the prime interest rate was raised before the contract was closed, the borrower had to pay the higher price. In addition, they would not grant the loan for a period in excess of 20 years. Consequently, monthly payments, including interest, taxes, insurance, and so on, approximated $1,800. Other costs of closing the deal amounted to an added $2,000 (tax reserve, title company fee, recording fee, and so on). In this situation, the buyer had to muster at least $52,000 to obtain the $200,000 house.

What are the current conditions of these three categories of loans? Because of the red tape, some savings and loan associations will not use FHA. One savings and loan official, when asked why he took VA, commented:

> There is governmental interaction, but it isn't as bad as the FHA. Mortgage companies handle FHA. Although you have to put down only 5 percent with FHA, mortgage companies have other means of making money. Some ask a commitment fee. This means that if you indicate your intentions in taking out a mortgage, you are charged for the paperwork involved even if you don't go through with the deal. There are also discount points, which may run from 6 to 8 percent the first year. Thus, if your house and lot are valued at $100,000, you would actually spend $6,000 to $8,000 more for the initial purchase by paying 6 to 8 discount points. It is very important for you as a home-builder to know exactly what all costs are in making a loan.

COMPUTING ALL COSTS

All types of lending agencies try to maximize their costs. It behooves each borrower to be sure he has calculated all charges correctly. With interest rates high, it pays to make the maximum down payment. Why let the bank charge you 12 to 20 percent when your money only earns 5 to 14 percent? The question of points should also be given a hard look. The number of points charged in my area ranged from two to eight. On $100,000, this one-time charge would amount to $8,000 at the highest rate. Another "hidden" cost is supervision; that varied from between 0 and 1 percent. (I observed the amount of supervision given my neighbor's home—about 30 minutes of casual observation during the entire construction period. I can think of better ways to spend $1,-000.) A performance bond or placement in escrow also involves a one percent charge.

What about insurance and taxes? Lending agencies love to take care of these items for you. A doctor friend told me his bank representative advised him that the bank could get a better tax assessment, "so let us handle it." He commented:

> My family has lived in this area for four generations; we know all the tax angles and can get the best deal. What the institution wanted was for me to pay my taxes up to a year in advance. They would invest my money until payment was due—a great deal for the bank, but I was getting taken. On insurance, I found their rates higher than the company we use for my medical affairs, so I told them impolitely to go to hell.

It makes better sense to cut your borrowing costs to the minimum by paying your own taxes and insurance. Shop around for insurance and obtain the policy best suited to your needs. During construction, obtain a policy protecting you from risks such as injury to workmen and others, theft, destruction of materials, and damage to neighbors' property. This builder's coverage is essential and can be obtained locally.

Subcontractors often carry this insurance; it is wise to obtain a copy of the policy before they begin work. The "certificate of insurance" should be from a reliable company. It itemizes type of insurance (employer's liability, workmen's compensation, comprehensive general), policy number, expiration date, and limits of liability. Adequate insurance protection is a must for both you and your sub.

CONVINCING YOUR LENDING AGENCY

Have your records available when you sit down with the lending agency, particularly when you subcontract your house. Your job will be to convince the loan officer that you can build a satisfactory home. He may point out that you lack experience to do the job properly and have inadequate buying power to obtain the best prices from subcontractors and supply houses. He may also indicate that interim interest between the time you start building and the time you move in could be considerable. For example, if it takes one year to build a home and you borrowed $100,000 (average amount) at 12 percent, it will cost $12,000.

The loan officer's points are valid in some cases. Emphasize your research and knowledge in the homebuilding field, as well as the fact that your subcontractors will be highly qualified. It is also helpful to indicate your close (daily) supervision.

The loan officer will know if you have done your homework. You may have found a first-class carpenter who will give you a "turn-key" job; that is, he will be present from the initial survey until you move in.

Another approach is to have a relative or friend who is in the contracting business available to help you. Some people who build their own homes have engineering backgrounds or are successful managers. One loan officer put it this way: "I want to be sure that when we lend our money, the man will be capable of meeting his payments. If he doesn't come up with an adequate home, or interim interest eats him up, I could be in trouble."

A normal agreement between you and a savings and loan association stipulates that the institution will hold in escrow the entire money needed for the house. If the house costs $100,000 to build, this amount will be set aside and payments will be made as subcontractors submit their invoices. You pay interest only on the amount used at the standard going rate. (Make certain you have a written agreement with the lender that you will be charged interest only on the amount actually used; there have been cases where borrowers paid interest on the entire amount from the day it was placed in escrow.) It is desirable to talk with at least three reputable lending institutions in order to get the best deal. A Dun and Bradstreet report can be obtained through your bank, and respected leaders in the community can also give you good advice. Friends and relatives who have used these lending agencies over the years when buying a home can provide valuable information.

Be sure to obtain every cost involved, and find out whether the rate charged will fluctuate over the years, based on the changing interest rates. Ideally, you should try to secure a loan where the institution will reduce interest in a declining period and not increase it again when the rate rises. In these times of high interest, it is very important for you to have an escape clause. Keep in mind that sometime during the duration of long-term loans (twenty to thirty years) interest rates will decline. You must have the opportunity to refinance at the lower rate or pay off the loan—with no penalty charge for early payment. *Be sure to read all the fine print.* If you don't understand something, ask the loan officer to explain. If still in doubt, check with an authority—preferably a lawyer qualified in this field.

What about buying your lot before building your home? Although savings and loan associations will lend you dollars on a lot if you intend to build in a couple of years, they will not make such loans for speculation purposes, and their rate is higher than for a regular mortgage loan. For this reason it is better to buy your lot just before you build. You obtain a lower interest rate on your lot in a package deal, and you don't tie up your money in idle land for a long period of time. Besides, you may change your mind about building in that particular location and have a difficult time selling it quickly at a fair price.

LOW-COST RESIDENTIAL MORTGAGES

Since 1977, many communities throughout the country have provided low-interest residential mortgages. This concept, first employed in Chicago, was based on a technique used by large corporations, in which in certain situations federal law permitted them to sell tax-free issues instead of taxable bonds. This resulted in a savings of millions of dollars to the companies in interest payments over the life of the bonds. The government, however, lost millions because the bonds were not subject to federal income tax.

The city of Chicago established a trust, and tax-free bonds were sold by brokerage firms to interested buyers. The funds derived from these bonds were then made available by the trust to a lending institution, which in turn made the money available to people who wished to purchase homes in the Chicago area.

The Chicago concept spread rapidly to other communities throughout the country. In Louisiana, for example, the Jefferson Parish Home Mortgage Authority announced that, effective September 5, 1979, 7.625 percent residential mortgages would be made available to the general public on a first-come, first-served basis. The response to these low-interest mortgage bonds was overwhelming. Unfortunately, few could take advantage of the low interest.

Table 4–3 Sample General Terms of Loans

	Single	Owner-Occupied Duplex
Maximum mortgage	$75,000.00	$75,000.00
Mortgage note rate (annual percentage rate 8.250%)	7.625%	7.625%
Repayment (monthly)	30 years	30 years
Participation fee	1¼%	1¼%
Origination fee	1%	1%
Down payment (minimum)		
1. Conventional	5%	10%
2. F.H.A.	Varies by regulation	Varies by regulation
3. V.A.	Varies by regulation	Varies by regulation
Restrictions		
1. Renovations	Functionally rehabilitate	Functionally rehabilitate
2. Occupancy	Owner	Owner
3. Residence—location	Jefferson Parish	Jefferson Parish
4. Assumption	Restrictive	Restrictive
Income requirements (maximum)	$30,000.00	$30,000.00
Refinance (renovations only)	Functionally rehabilitate	Functionally rehabilitate

The general terms of the Jefferson Parish (county) Home Mortgage Authority for a single-family dwelling and owner-occupied duplex are shown in Table 4–3.

The annual percentage rate (APR) was 8.25 percent at that time (September 1979), in contrast to more than an 11 percent APR being charged for conventional mortgage money in the New Orleans area. People stood in line for five days through rain and high temperatures, and with good reason! The savings over a thirty-year period were nearly $50,000 on a $55,000 loan.

Jefferson Parish stated that only those applicants whose annual adjusted gross income did not exceed $30,000 in the prior taxable year (including the adjusted gross income of all persons who intended to reside with the applicant in the same family residence) were eligible. In each case, these low-interest loans were provided for low- and middle-income groups. In addition, the parish made available workers to assist women, minorities, first-time homebuyers and citizens of low and moderate income of Jefferson Parish in qualifying for low-interest loans. Documents required at the time of appointment with lending institutions if individuals wanted to subcontract or purchase a home are shown in Table 4–4.

If the opportunity to obtain a low-cost residential mortgage becomes available in your community and you are eligible, take advantage of it. Or go one step farther: Muster political support in your city or county to establish some type of home mortgage authority to provide these low-rate loans for all income levels.

BANKS FOR INTERIM FINANCING

A commercial bank for financial assistance usually will provide only interim financing (construction loans). It may, however, work with a savings and loan association, which will take over the mortgage. As a result, you may need to utilize only one title search, lawyer, and so on. One businessman who used this dual method to subcontract his house commented:

> I can't overemphasize the importance of having an officer at the bank who knows you and believes in you. What happens is that this "friend in court" participates in the daily meetings that review all loan requests. Here the decisions are made to lend or not to lend. This man can be very influential if he supports your position, pointing out that you are a good risk and capable of doing the subcontracting. But to gain his support initially, I had to prepare a detailed budget and other data, as well as secure a qualified carpenter who would help supervise the job.

Table 4-4 Documents Required of Loan Applicants in Jefferson Parish

Document	Required For			
	Existing Home	New Home	Proposed Home	Renovations
1. Plans and specifications			X	X
2. Purchase agreement dated on or after August 30, 1979	X	X	X	
3. Building contract dated on or after August 30, 1979			X	X
4. 1978 tax return (Form 1040 and W-2 or other sufficient evidence of income)	X	X	X	X

This friendly relationship warrants a word of caution, particularly if you plan to use this friend in the future. Recently, a bank got burned by lending a good friend $100,000 to subcontract his house. He proceeded to spend money as if it were going out of style. He kept no valid records, and he had no written agreements with his subcontractors. When the money ran out, he came back to the bank for an additional $50,000. This time his good friend said "No." An investigation discovered that he had overspent his original estimate by $70,000 and the value of his property totaled only $35,000. The bank foreclosed on him.

INSURANCE COMPANY LOAN

It may be to your advantage to contact local representatives of reputable life insurance companies. If you go this route, they will require you to take out a life policy for the amount of the loan. This makes a nice profit for them annually on both the policy and the mortgage interest. You may find, however, that their interest costs are lower. If this is true and you need life insurance, this could be your best deal. Younger homebuilders in particular may be interested, in view of the lower premiums for their age bracket. Another advantage of obtaining a mortgage from some insurance companies is that the annual dividends can be applied to the loan and thus can reduce the length of time or the monthly payments required to pay off the mortgage.

A SECOND MORTGAGE

You may have your heart set on building your own home immediately. This decision may be made with full knowledge of the risks involved, including high interest rates. Assuming your first mortgage does not cover all your financial needs, the agency from which you obtain the first mortgage will hold your home and land as collateral. You estimate your building costs at $100,000; you have $10,000 in cash and a savings and loan association agrees to lend you $75,000. You are now short $15,000. One way to secure this money is to obtain a second mortgage.

The company willing to lend the money on a second mortgage will demand a higher rate of interest. If you fail to meet your payments, you may be forced to sell your property. If the sale brings only $70,000, it all may go to the first mortgage holder.

The second mortgage holder only obtains his money after the first mortgage is paid off completely. To protect himself he not only will charge a higher interest rate, but he also will lend you the money for a shorter period—usually no longer than ten years.

If you decide to take out a second mortgage, it is important to go to a reliable firm and find out all costs involved. The interest charge on the $15,000, for example, may be within the legal limit of your state, but there also may be hidden charges. And there may be no consumer protection against these expenses. Such costs may even include a placement fee for the company that leads you to the second mortgage broker. Read the second mortgage agreement carefully. Better yet, *avoid taking out a second mortgage*. If necessary, borrow from a friend, relative, your insurance policy, or take out a personal loan. It is best if you can subcontract your home without having to borrow a penny. This prevents any delay caused by obtaining the loan and securing clearance on the payment of invoices. It also eliminates brokers' snooping into your personal financial affairs. Lending agencies can be difficult just when you need their financial support the most.

Saving enough to buy a smaller home may be preferable to borrowing for an expensive one. The initial subcontracting gives you invaluable experience that can result in a more successful job the next time.

SUMMARY

Adequate financing is an essential ingredient for successfully subcontracting your home. Consider banks, savings and loan associations, insurance companies, and mortgage firms for the best deal. Be familiar with the pros and cons of using VA, FHA, or conventional loans. I recommend a 20 percent down payment as a minimum, and also advise paying off your mortgage as rapidly as possible.

It is important to consider all money costs in home ownership. Initially, you must obtain enough money to buy your lot and meet all payments to your lending agency, subcontractors, and suppliers. Once settled in your new home, there are mortgage payments, taxes, insurance, heat and utilities, maintenance, and major expenditures for large appliances and furniture. If there are second mortgage payments to be met, there is the added risk of foreclosure and of losing the home you have worked so hard to build.

If an opportunity to obtain a low cost residential mortgage becomes available in your community, and you are eligible, take advantage of it. Or go a step further: muster political support in your city or county to establish a mortgage authority that provides low rate loans for all income levels.

Most importantly, have all the facts of your plans and arrangements available prior to conferring with your loan officer. The more thorough your financial data, the better the chance of obtaining a loan and meeting your future payments.

Chapter Five
Building Your Home

The money is available, your planning is complete, and you are now ready to carry out your building plans. It is helpful to recheck your survey. Be certain you are building on land you own. Also review local requirements to be sure you build in accordance with city and subdivision restrictions.

At this point, you are ready to contact that first-rate carpenter you have selected. There is no substitute for the experience of a competent carpenter; he can help you immensely. As stated previously, you pay more if he gives you a "turn-key job," meaning that he is available from the time he lays out the forms for the foundation until the house is completed and the key is turned over to you. Mentioning this experienced carpenter to your lending agency, I am confident, helps in obtaining the loan.

YOUR JOB RESPONSIBILITIES

You can avoid possible confusion and conflict by having only one subcontractor on the job at a time. Time however is money. Besides, more losses occur (theft and pilferage), and prices rise in the interim. It seems as if delay builds on delay. Your big responsibility therefore is to be on the job. This could require working ten to twelve hours a day, including time on the site, taking care of financial records, doing the buying, and coordinating the day-to-day activities. Many people cannot spare this block of time but do utilize vacations, weekends, and evenings.

For the best results, it is essential for you, or a reliable substitute, to be on the job throughout the actual construction. You can also cut costs by participating in the building wherever possible. This may include assisting in the installation of heating and air conditioning, hauling and sorting bricks, and providing service to meet emergency needs.

Prompt decisions are required daily; if you are not present, the subcontractor may walk off the job. After all, he is paying his people by the hour. If you don't have the necessary materials or if you don't tell him what's expected, why shouldn't he leave? And it may be a long time before he returns—another job now may take priority.

Your presence on the job also prevents mistakes. For example, if you are paying the carpenter for paneling and the insulation has not been completed when he does this, you may never find out why it costs you so much to heat or cool the house.

There usually are no workmen on the job on weekends. This will permit you to shop for materials, clean the area, and bring records up to date. Whenever possible, conduct business on weekends at your housing site. It saves time to have representatives visit you with samples and catalogs of rugs, drapes, lighting fixtures, and so on. Most important, subcontractors usually charge time and a half (sometimes double time) for Saturday and Sunday work. However, you may find moonlighters who will work for reasonable rates during their free weekends, holidays, and evenings.

BUILDING TIMETABLE

Prepare a step-by-step building timetable, showing the sequence of events, comparable to the one shown here, but reflecting your specific requirements. A PERT chart can also be very useful during this construction phase (see Figure 5–1). If you do prepare a PERT chart and timetable, *they must be made to suit your requirements*.

What are some of the key points to look for while you are building your home? The PERT chart, for example, helped one family complete their home in two months, in contrast to their neighbors, who averaged six months for comparable homes. Examine the items listed in the "Building Timetable," and be sure to include all necessary steps required for your home. It may be helpful to refer to Appendix A, showing the blueprints of one home. But remember, use *your* blueprints to assist in preparing *your* timetable and PERT chart.

BUILDING TIMETABLE

1. Building phase begun. Discuss techniques to meet needs—
   PERT, management model, organizational, and control steps.
2. Stakes for piling laid.
3. Piling driven.
4. Temporary electrical hookup completed.
5. First city inspection completed.
6. Lumber delivered.
7. Exterior forms laid out.
8. Foundation plumbing completed.
9. First plumbing inspection completed.
10. Grading and preparation completed.
11. Lumber and other supplies delivered.
12. Termite inspection completed.
13. Concrete poured for foundation.
14. Garage secured.
15. Frames completed by carpenter.
16. Sheathing for exterior completed.
17. Roof covered with waterproof material.
18. Roof completed.
19. Windows and glass doors installed.
20. Inside plumbing completed.
21. Air conditioning and heating completed.
22. Bricks for home delivered.
23. Electric turbine vent completed.

Figure 5–1 PERT chart format used during the building phase. Your chart will reflect your own specific needs.

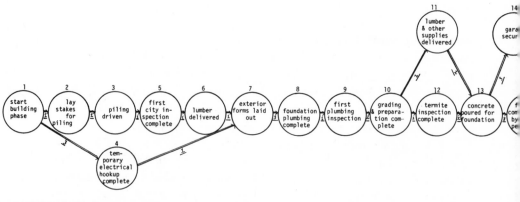

T_E= Earliest completion time

➤ = Critical path

Numbers underlined represent optimistic time for completion of each activity.

Sequential numbers for reference only.

24. Electrical and phone wiring completed.
25. Iron set above windows.
26. Insulation for walls and attic completed.
27. Bricking completed.
28. Sheetrock completed.
29. Slate porch completed.
30. Gutters installed.
31. Terrazzo floor completed.
32. Concrete for drive and walks completed.
33. Kitchen cabinets and plumbing fixtures installed.
34. Tile completed.
35. Outside air conditioning completed.
36. Inside door installed.
37. Ground cleaned and prepared for landscaping.
38. Painting completed.
39. Fence completed.
40. Rugs installed.
41. Flower and plant landscaping completed.
42. Plans filed.
43. Final inspection by city.
44. Light fixtures completed.
45. Wallpaper completed.
46. Drapes installed.
47. Insurance converted from construction to home.
48. Job completed. Move in.

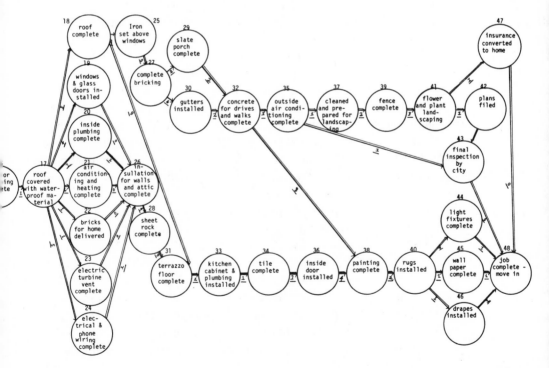

START OF BUILDING PHASE

At this time, you should prepare your PERT chart and timetable. The same format you developed at the beginning of the planning phase can be applied. You must realize that these are guidelines only and should be modified as you proceed with construction. Figure 5–1 shows a PERT chart representing the optimistic time for completion of the project. You may wish to develop as many as three PERT charts—optimistic, average, and pessimistic. Make several copies; keep one at home and have at least two others for you and your spouse to carry with you.

FOUNDATION

A good foundation is essential in the building of your home. Be present during the excavation, and check to see that the materials used meet your specifications. Many homes are constructed with basements. The objective here is to have a basement that will be free of water, which eventually can penetrate the floor and walls. Make certain that there is good outside grading that will carry any water away from the house.

A basement can't be built in every location. Sometimes, to prevent a house from sinking, pilings are necessary. If you use pilings, be sure that your carpenter or surveyor places the stakes in accordance with the architectural drawings. It is desirable to have the pilings driven in the ground shortly after the markings have been placed (some youngsters delight in rearranging these stakes). It also pays to watch the pile-driving crew to make certain they put the pilings precisely where the stakes are placed. Be sure to check the dimensions of the pilings to determine if they match the specifications.

You may wish to be present when all materials are delivered. If pilings are used, you can see that they are not dumped in the street or on the neighbors' property; you can also make sure they measure up to the quality ordered. You will be charged for the number used, so when the job is done, make your own count. The fewer blows it takes to drive them in the ground, the quicker the job can be done. If your neighbors have valuable china or other breakables, have the courtesy to notify them when this work will take place.

On occasion an operator has been noted to do a sloppy job. In one case a contractor had specified 35-foot pilings of adequate diameter but poor workmanship resulted in several breaking off at 20 to 25 feet. If the ground is hard, however, the pilings can be driven only to "refusal," which may result in their penetrating the ground less than the specified distance. In another situation the contract called for 35-foot pilings and only 20-foot lengths were used. The error was reported, but poor communication kept it from reaching the contractor until after the slab was poured. Result? The concrete flooring had to be broken and removed.

New pilings were then driven. Extra cost—$21,300. Delay—39 days. Yes, it does pay for a home builder to be on the job during construction!

The basement is the part of a home that is completely or partly below ground level. A good basement area can be used for recreational purposes, laundry facilities, heating units, extra bedrooms, and storage. The foundation should be built securely and sealed properly so that moisture will not penetrate the walls. A damp basement, a common complaint, can be prevented during construction by using the appropriate sealant for the wall and floor materials selected. Be present during digging of the hole to make certain it will be deep enough to accommodate the ceiling height you desire. The hole also should be reinforced to hold the weight of the rest of the home.

ELECTRICAL HOOKUP

Call the electric company to install a temporary hookup while the piles are being driven or before the start of any carpentry work. Your carpenter will need this power to cut the lumber for the exterior forms. (A gas-powered saw is expensive and not as efficient.) As a temporary expedient, ask a neighbor for permission to hook into one of his outlets. If this is necessary, offer to pay him and thereafter maintain his friendship. Your subcontractors might also use his water and park in front of his premises. You will be living beside him soon and it helps to start off on friendly terms.

FIRST CITY INSPECTION

If pilings are being used, it may be time for the city inspector to determine if they are satisfactory. The pile-driving company or contractor must inform the city at least twenty-four hours before work is to begin. You and the lending-agency representative should be present when the inspector arrives. Be nice to city inspectors; they can offer helpful advice. The following remarks of one city inspector are representative:

> I consider the piling check the most important one. If you don't have a solid foundation, the house is doomed from the start. People don't realize that these city inspections and the checks of the lending agency are in the homeowner's best interest. If they weren't made, some builders would take complete advantage of buyers. After all, most of what a contractor puts into a house is hidden. Only after a dwelling is occupied for a reasonable period will some of the failings come to light. I make four to five visits to a building site—during the foundation phase, framing, enclosing, and completion.

Don't pay your bill until after the city inspector has given his approval. If the invoice provides a discount within ten days and net at thirty, it makes sense to pay it within the discount period. Otherwise, be sure to make payment within the time allowed. Check with local city authorities to make sure that each required city inspection is accomplished at the appropriate time.

LUMBER

Lumber is a major cost in the construction of your home—a cost that is increasing every year. In one six-month period, according to the National Association of Home Builders, price increases on wood products added $1,200 to the construction cost of the typical new one-family house. The primary reason for the price surge is heavy demand for wood products from both homebuilders and foreign markets.

With lumber so expensive, it is essential that you as a homebuilder take appropriate precautions to use it wisely and protect it well. Work closely with your carpenter to meet his needs. If possible, order only the amount required for several days' work; let the lumber company, not your building site, be your storage facility. It is surprising the quantity that can disappear if left unguarded. Other reasons for keeping minimum amounts on your property include the greater risks from damage by vandals, deterioration by prolonged exposure to the elements, and injury to workers and the curious, ever-present youngsters who delight in playing in such surroundings.

Be present to check the amount of lumber actually delivered. Your carpenter also should be with you to confirm that the quality and size are what you ordered. If there are any damaged pieces or other irregularities in the material, be sure they are returned at once and replacements delivered promptly. Don't sign the delivery slip for any merchandise received at the site until you have checked it carefully.

Each day make a point to talk with your carpenter to be sure he has all the supplies required. If he doesn't have nails, for example, or if they are the wrong size, he may have to stop working until they arrive. Emergencies will occur, and by being present you can solve them quickly and perform mercy missions, such as going to the store for ice and soft drinks. When there are errands to run, you must understand exactly what materials are needed. It is disappointing to run five miles for nails and have the carpenter say, "That's not what I wanted; I asked for ten-penny galvanized nails."

EXTERIOR FORMS

Once the initial lumber is delivered, the carpenter is prepared to lay out the exterior forms so that the slab, if required, can be poured. It also permits the plumbers to come in to do their initial work.

FOUNDATION PLUMBING

Now that your exterior forms have been laid out, you can proceed to work with your plumber. He will prepare the foundation plumbing. You may find that the head plumber is the only member of a small firm that has achieved the master plumber level. He has the most knowledge and skill, so it is important that he be present during this phase of the project. If trouble is discovered later, it is terribly expensive to break through concrete that has set.

You will require both galvanized iron pipe and copper tubing. Copper, like lumber, is expensive. Be sure that the copper used is the size you specify: don't accept ⅜ inch if you want ⅝ inch. The amount of pressure and quantity of water for your toilet facilities are dependent upon the diameter of the tubing. You usually subcontract with the plumber for the entire job, including the foundation plumbing and all the inside facilities—tubs, toilets, sinks, and hot water heater. Unless you specify your copper size, he will try to keep his costs down by using smaller piping. And even if the specifications call for ⅝ inch, he may substitute a smaller size, which could go unnoticed until you wonder why the toilets flush so poorly. Specify the gauge of copper desired and the pounds per square inch (psi) to be delivered.

Check the location of your clean-out holes, so that if your toilets later become stopped up they can be flushed out readily. You should note the location of the outside water valve, so that if a leak develops you can turn off the water supply fast. Be sure that the inside water valves for the toilets, sink, etc., are in a convenient location and can be turned off easily in the event of an emergency. If you plan on any future additions, this is the time to stub in plumbing needs.

Once the plumber has completed his work, there should be an initial plumbing inspection. Hopefully your plumber has a friendly relationship with the inspector so that it will be done promptly. (I have been informed that to help expedite this procedure, money changes hands at times.)

GRADING, PREPARATION OF FOUNDATION, AND OTHER CONCRETE WORK

Your next subcontractor will prepare and pour your foundation, if such work is required. This is hard manual labor. Be present when the steel meshing, reinforcing rods, shell material, and other supplies arrive to be sure you have the quantity needed and that they meet your specifications. The contractor himself usually arranges to purchase these items and also orders the concrete. If a pumper is needed, be sure that you or the subcontractor has ordered one.

Call the day before to confirm that the concrete will be delivered and that the men arrive on time to lay the slab. This work begins early in the morning and is usually completed that afternoon. Check your weather reports; you cannot pour satisfactorily if it rains. A heavy downpour an hour or two after the slab has set, however, will help cure it.

These workers move fast and furious. In hot weather, it may be helpful for you to have ice and soft drinks. You may also find it a timesaver to have a portable john on the job site. Some workers prefer to take a short break periodically. If gas stations or other facilities are nearby, it may not be necessary to rent one, although some local building codes require a portable toilet on the site during construction. A city inspection may be required to examine the concrete work upon completion.

TERMITE PROTECTiON AND INSPECTION

Take out a contract for both the initial termite protection and the annual follow-up service. Be sure that the charges for the annual inspection are no higher than what you would pay a firm on a one-time basis. Your presence on the site at the time the service is rendered will permit you to observe where the openings are located and to see that each outlet is undamaged so the opening can be properly capped. Capping the openings simplifies the exterminator's annual visit to spray your home. The exterminator can also show you signs indicating the presence of termites.

GARAGE SECURED

It is helpful to enclose your garage as soon as possible; this will give you a place to store items and keep them safe overnight. This includes lumber, nails, tools, and other materials. A garage separated from the house means less noise inside the home.

Climate has a lot to do with whether a free-standing garage is desirable. A home builder in Florida saved $5,180 by not having an enclosed garage. Trees on his property provided ample shade for his car.

An attached garage needs adequate insulation, or appropriate wall board material to block out noise when the car is driven in and out. Local building codes may require a fire wall.

FRAMING

While the carpenter and his workers are completing the framing, you can meet with other subcontractors and suppliers on the job site. It is advantageous to build when housing starts are less frequent than normal or during slow periods, when lumber salesmen will make frequent trips to your home and work with carpenters to avoid lumber shortages and obtain millwork requirements. (Millwork refers to the doors, trim, shelving, window sills, and other finishing work.) It is helpful to use a lumber house that has both the framing lumber and millwork. A personal visit to the lumberyard beforehand will enable you to see the quality of their material. Your carpenter should be able to do the framing and install the millwork.

EXTERIOR SHEATHING AND COVERING FOR THE ROOF

You should proceed rapidly to enclose your house to protect it from the elements and provide a measure of security. Sheathing is an initial covering of waterproof material that is used on the exterior wall of a frame structure. Your description of materials should specify the type required, such as USG gypsum $\frac{1}{2} \times 2 \times 8$ v edge.

Some builders place sheets of plywood at the entrances to keep out intruders and stray animals. Once under cover, you can proceed at a rapid pace by utilizing several subcontractors inside while others are busy outside (see Figure 5–1).

ROOF

The roof, like the foundation, should be a long-lasting investment. It pays to use fine materials and employ a roofer who takes great care in his work.

A higher roof permits faster run-off of rain water and less accumulation of snow. Such a roof provides for greater storage space and results in greater warmth in the winter and a cooler interior in the summer. It is also convenient to have a high attic where workers can install and maintain your equipment more easily.

WINDOWS AND GLASS DOORS

The less maintenance work you have in the future, the better off you will be. Aluminum windows can be a substantial work saver.

Ample windows will give you a bright and sunny house. A large sliding glass door facing the backyard is also a worthwhile investment. Be sure that the glass door has adequate locks. It is possible to purchase glass that can even withstand bricks thrown at it.

Don't install your screens until the painting and other outside work is finished. Otherwise, your screens may be a mess; their replacement may be less costly than trying to clean them. If your supplier can't store them for you until needed, your garage may be a satisfactory haven. Cover your windows with paper after installation so that cleaning will be easier before you move in. If you ever have had to use razor blades to scrape paint and plaster from windows, you can appreciate the time and effort saved.

AIR CONDITIONING AND HEATING

Take care to select the appropriate size unit for both heating and cooling your home. In a number of speculation homes, I have found the air conditioning unit to be undersized and ineffective on very warm days. You may find it desirable to install two separate units; the second unit goes on automatically as needed. An electronic filter system does a good job of removing dust, smoke, and other particles in the air.

It pays to buy a fine quality heating and cooling unit from a reliable dealer. Check to see that appropriate insulation is used to wrap the air ducts and that they are of adequate size. A local or city inspector usually will check to see if the insulation complies with the local code. The outside air-conditioning unit should be located unobtrusively and close enough to the house so as not to reduce its efficiency.

ELECTRIC TURBINE

An electric turbine will go on and off automatically at preset temperatures to reduce the heat in your attic. It pays to buy one that will give reliable service over a long period of time. More reasonably priced turbines are wind driven, but they are not as efficient. A turbine usually is placed at the rear of the roof so it won't detract from the appearance of your home.

ELECTRICAL WIRING

If possible, have your electric utility company visit you to estimate the appropriate lighting needs for your home, including the number of outlets. Naturally, they are interested in maximizing electrical usage because it will give them more business. Nevertheless, it gives you a good basis for talking with your electrician. With the continuing increase in new electrical products, it's safer to have more rather than fewer outlets. Your local building code will specify the minimum number of outlets required for your home.

Be present while the wiring is being installed. Although your electrical inspector should pick up such points as wiring size and sufficiency of outlets, this doesn't always happen. Be specific about the number of circuits and types of breakers, including ground-fault interrupters.

TELEPHONE

The telephone company will be happy to work with you in determining the type of equipment best suited to meet your requirements. Be liberal in your estimate of future needs. Frequently, extra phone jacks can be provided at no extra charge.

INSULATION

The best time to make certain that you have adequate insulation is during the building phase. Be sure that the material received meets the specifications contracted for with your supplier and that the workers place it in the areas difficult to reach. It is important to stay with the workers because often that ensures that they fill areas that might otherwise be overlooked. The following comments by a local utility company may be helpful:

> In homes with little or no insulation, much of the heating generated by the heating system is quickly lost, thereby increasing heating costs. Adequate insulation, however, properly installed (especially in ceilings, as warm air rises), helps keep the heat in and the cold out, to let you enjoy maximum comfort, operating efficiency, and economy from your system. Insulation should be the equivalent of six inches of rock wool or fiberglass in ceilings, four inches in exposed walls, and two inches in floors of homes without slab foundations. Also, be sure to seal cracks around doors and windows with weatherstripping or caulking compound to prevent heated air from escaping.[1]

THE STILLMAN HOME

A brief description of our home will bring out some points that may be of interest to you in planning your own. You also may wish to refer to the blueprints of this house that appear in Appendix A. Please keep in mind that the design of our house reflects one family's views and desires. You will build and furnish a home to suit your own taste and temperament. This rare occasion to express yourself is one reason why prefabricated homes can never be adequate substitutes for custom-built dwellings. In America, we have seen craftsmanship give way to mass production in almost every field of endeavor. The last great exception is in the homebuilding industry. This privilege should not be sacrificed for the sake of cost and conformity. Furthermore, by subcontracting and utilizing sound management concepts, costs can be held to within the competitive range of prefabricated homes of a comparable size and design.

---

[1] "Insulation More Important Now Than Ever," *Homemaking,* New Orleans Public Service, Middle South Utility System.

Figure 5–2   A home that was subcontracted at a 25-percent savings.

EXTERIOR

To give the home a distinctive appearance, we selected an attractive, high-quality hard tan brick for the exterior. The brick is used across the entire width of the house and extends in short walls on either side up to the drive and side gates.

You may wish to use old bricks, which are available in most communities; wrecking crews are frequently tearing down buildings and enterprising businessmen purchase the bricks for resale after they have been cleaned and sorted. Some people buy cheaper bricks and then go to the expense of painting them. You may prefer wood to a brick exterior, but keep in mind that exposed brick is virtually maintenance free and painting wood can become quite expensive over the years. There is also a lower risk of fire with brick than with wood.

A wide overhang (24 inches) on the roof will provide shade and help shield your home in inclement weather. When you plan the exterior, it is a good idea to put drains in the ground so there will be rapid drain-off of water. Also, a front sidewalk that extends to the street is helpful for anyone getting out of a vehicle at the curb.

DRIVEWAY AND GARAGE

To add character, we used washed gravel to pave the drive. Our drive can accommodate two compact cars. Any drive should be wide enough to permit a van or repair vehicle to move in and out with ease. And with teenagers driving the family car, it pays to have ample width.

Thomas S. Stillman, T & D Photo Co.

Figure 5–3   Driveway and garage.

In Figure 5–3 you will see the garage door is in line with the driveway. Time and again we have seen homes that do not have a direct entry to the garage because they did not locate it on the property line. Several of our neighbors failed to do this; as a result, they cannot safely get a second car in and out of their garage. Those that try find they have frequent damage to car and home. With land so expensive today, it pays to use every bit of your property to its best advantage.

What type of shelter should you have for your car? Many homes just have carports. An enclosed garage costs more but has definite advantages. It reduces vandalism and permits you safely to store items such as a bicycle, lawn mower, and tools. It better protects the car from the elements, which can help eliminate starting problems.

Purchase a solid, extra-wide garage door so that there will be no difficulty getting in and out with two cars. You may find one of the comforts of life is an automatic door opener.

GARBAGE RECEPTACLES

Two receptacles are a good idea, considering the volume of trash that accumulates. It helps to surround the immediate area with concrete rather than grass. Be sure there is a porous substance at the bottom so that there is adequate drainage when it rains.

FENCE

If you have a dog or a pool, it is essential to enclose your yard, but you may choose to fence your yard for other reasons as well. Fences can be of wood, brick, or metal. We selected a first-quality cedar wood, which we felt would provide a more pleasant atmosphere than brick or metal. If you use wood, check carefully to see that there are a minimum of knotholes. The fence itself should be solid enough to withstand very strong winds. This can be accomplished by placing the posts close enough together and securing each post in a solid foundation. It also helps to use three, rather than two, rails for support. Keep in mind that labor costs are virtually the same for a shoddy fence as for the finest, but inferior materials will result in a shorter life and labor costs will then be required again. Stick with good quality in fencing as with all your other needs.

FRONT ENTRANCE

The front entrance should be wide enough for two people to walk abreast. Double doors make it easy to move large items in and out, but double doors are hard to screen. A slate floor at the entrance is attractive and easy to maintain.

LIVING ROOM

A spacious living room can be used for entertaining as well as daily activities. If you have children, it may be desirable to have two entertaining areas so that each can be with his or her own friends. Doors should be included that close off the living area and adequate insulation provided to keep down the noise level.

DINING ROOM

A separate dining room provides privacy, but sufficient space should be allowed to accommodate the number of people you usually entertain for dinner. Louvered doors can be closed to separate the living and dining areas. This partition is especially nice for surprise parties, birthdays, and other special events. The living area can be used for cocktails before dinner.

KITCHEN AND BREAKFAST NOOK

Many families like a bright and airy kitchen with an adjoining breakfast nook. Your plans should also include efficient storage and economy of movement. You may wish to put both fluorescent and regular lights in the kitchen. You may want to place your breakfast nook where it can

Figure 5–4   Dining room.

Figure 5–5   Kitchen and breakfast nook.

receive the sunlight in the morning. You can build a little alcove as an added flair, where the light can be lowered and raised as desired.

Our kitchen is a compact area with shelving within easy reaching distance. A storage area is enclosed by a louvered door.

The floors of the kitchen, breakfast nook, utility room, den, and hallways are of a mosaic-like terrazzo. Its appearance is most attractive and the upkeep minimal. However, in checking some homes, I found numerous cracks in terrazzo flooring. This problem can be eliminated by making the floor thick enough (2¼ inches) and having it unbonded, that is, separated from the concrete slab. This type of flooring takes skilled craftsmen and requires considerable time to install.

There are many new, easy-care, attractive flooring materials that are inexpensive to install, such as sheet vinyl, Congoleum, carpet, hardwood floors, and parquet. Remember that darker colors don't show dirt as readily as lighter colors. You may also like a softer composition that will be kinder to the feet and less destructive to breakable objects accidentally dropped.

DEN

The den is the room that receives the most use. For a bright and airy room, use light-colored paneling and a sliding glass door with large, windowed sections.

Ample shelving should be built for books and to display bric-a-brac. As you can see in the photo, double doors close off the den. Beyond the double doors to the left is a center hall closet for guests' coats. Several sliding panel doors were used throughout the house. These pocket doors can be real space-savers, but be sure they are installed properly because they are expensive to repair.

PATIO

The wood fence to the rear of the lot and the walls of neighbors' garages provide privacy in the patio area and a pleasant view from the den. Beyond the sliding glass door in the den, our home includes an eight-foot overhang, which provides protection from the sun and rain.

MASTER BEDROOM

The bedroom wing in our home is located on one side of the house. Four bedrooms are included in this area, as well as two complete baths with shower and tub. This area can be closed off from the rest of the house by two sliding pocket doors.

The master bedroom and bath are at the rear of the house for privacy and quiet. The bath includes a walk-in closet and a large wash basin with drawers to accommodate necessary bath supplies. Sliding

Figure 5–6   View of den looking into breakfast nook.

Figure 5–7   View of den from patio.

79

pocket doors seal off this area from the bedroom, making a nice dressing room. Ample closet space is very important; in planning your home, carefully analyze your storage needs and build accordingly.

STUDY

Either two or three of the other rooms can be used as bedrooms. You may wish to convert the fourth one to a full-time study or sewing room. The closet in the study is of sufficient size to hold a large filing cabinet; built-in shelves give adequate space for reference books. If you were to sell the house, there would be no problem in changing this to another bedroom. You may consider having an extra bedroom exclusively for guests, but space is too valuable today to set aside special areas for this purpose. You can convert the study or the living room into sleeping quarters for friends or relatives.

MAIN BATHROOM

The main bathroom should be situated between two bedrooms. It is helpful to install two wash basins if there is heavy traffic in the bathroom each morning. Provide ample lighting in the bathroom, such as a window and fluorescent lighting. Although a heat light brightens the

Figure 5–8   Study.

Thomas S. Stillman, T & D Photo Co.

Thomas S. Stillman, T & D Photo Co.

Figure 5–9   Main bathroom.

room, there are more energy-efficient means to keep the bathroom warm in the winter. Finally, if the bathroom is a long way from the hot-water heater, it may be energy efficient and convenient to use a hot-water recirculation system, providing instant hot water.

UTILITY ROOM
The utility room is where the washer, dryer, and hot-water heater are located. You should also have a large sink, which can be used for messy jobs, such as cleaning fish. An enclosed half-bath can prove to be a real convenience in this area. The utility room should have a door to seal it off from adjacent rooms.

ATTIC
The attic can be a splendid storage facility, and ample flooring should be installed. Items accumulate rapidly; if you expect to use your attic frequently, it should have adequate height, room, and light.

CLEANING UP
Many building sites are real eyesores and a nightmare for environmentalists. Trash is strewn everywhere with little regard to the neighbors'

Thomas S. Stillman, T & D Photo Co.

Figure 5–10   Attic.

property or people who use the adjacent sidewalk. Materials even may be piled in the street.

You, as builder, can do something from the start to indicate your pride in ownership. A retired naval officer, for example, who did his own subcontracting purchased several trees after buying his lot. He also placed large receptacles at strategic locations on his property. Each sub-contractor was asked to have his men place their debris in those containers. At intervals he had a truck haul away all the rubbish. It cost him $10 to $20 a load, depending on the quantity. He made a point to sweep up the premises daily and neatly arrange the materials. This helped him to keep an accurate inventory and permitted him to instruct his suppliers to furnish additional items before he ran out. As a result, workers made an effort to keep the premises clean and liked working in such surroundings. It also helped keep the injury rate at zero and losses from vandalism to a minimum. Move-in time was speeded up because it meant no massive clean-up job.

There were other advantages as well. He had no insect problem on first moving into his home. Because a surprising amount of debris may be enclosed in walls, attics, and basements, it's little wonder that nests develop and odd creatures make nocturnal visits. Being debris-free also prevented subcontractors from covering up a lot of mistakes.

SUMMARY

The building phase is the action phase. During this period, your prime responsibility is to be on the job site as often as possible. The quality of your home will depend largely upon the amount of personal supervision you provide. You may have the best plans in the world, but it is necessary for you to see that they are used. If you cannot be present, then your spouse or someone else you can depend on should take your place. It is the amount and the depth of personal attention, coupled with sound management principles, that give the subcontracted house a competitive edge in quality and cost. No contractor can afford to provide this caliber of supervision.

You may wish to use a PERT chart and timetable during construction. These can be effective if you have a good working relationship with your subcontractors and suppliers. Help your on-site employees use their time efficiently. This may include running errands for your subcontractors and having suppliers visit you at the building site.

Chapter Six
Checking on What You Have Done

While walking to my office recently, I observed three homes under construction. In each case, the work had come to a standstill. At the first house, the mortar was not available for the bricklayer, so he took another job. At the second house, the electrical inspection had not been made; the contractor had failed to contact the responsible city department. At the third house, there was a conflict between the carpenter and the builder over the terms of payment.

These delays could have been prevented if the builders had taken adequate control measures. The three functions of planning, organizing, and controlling proceed simultaneously and are a continuous process. The process itself follows a repetitive and ongoing pattern of *planning* what you are going to do, *doing* what you planned, and *checking* to see that it is done according to the plan. For example, assume you plan to clean up the premises at 7:30 A.M. While tidying up (doing) you uncover damaged lumber (checking). You then devise a plan for its return and replacement. Concurrently, other subcontractors working for you are performing their various planning, organizing and controlling functions. It is evident that you as manager cannot perform each of these functions in isolation. Think of them as part of your management bag of tools that must be used harmoniously to get the job done efficiently.

To determine the degree of effectiveness of the two major functions of planning and organizing, you must apply certain control techniques. This quantitative and qualitative information permits an insight into the standard of performance and enables the homebuilder to take remedial measures where appropriate. Here are some specific controls you as a homebuilder may use.

ON-THE-SPOT INSPECTIONS

Being present at the job site, you have the opportunity to check both the quality of work and the materials used. For example, you may be particular about the color of paint desired in each room. Your presence will permit you to inform your painter after the first few strokes of the brush that it isn't the proper color. It is much better to discover such a mistake quickly than to find out after the entire interior of the house has been painted.

You can also check, upon delivery, such supplies as material for your fence. If your inspection reveals a number of boards with large knot holes and of inferior quality, you can demand replacements. If the fence is installed before the deficiency is discovered, it is more difficult to convince the subcontractor to replace it.

Being on the job enables you to prevent any unnecessary delays. If a subcontractor is absent, you can call his home or office to find out the reason and can arrange for other work to be accomplished. If supplies are not delivered on schedule, you can take action to obtain them— either by placing a phone call requesting prompt delivery or by picking them up yourself. You also will have a chance to talk with your sub-contractors to recheck schedules and prevent delays.

The significance homebuyers are placing on inspections is apparent from the increasing number of inspection services available in large communities. Potential buyers also are becoming more careful about selecting a home. Many are having new houses checked by qualified inspectors before signing binding contracts. Some inspection services make four to eight inspections during various phases of construction; fees may vary from $100 to $1000 or more, based on the price of home and the number of inspections and guarantees. Imagine how effective your control could be with continual on-the-job inspections instead of those made only four times.

OTHER INSPECTIONS

Visits from loan-agency officials, as well as electrical, plumbing, and other city inspectors, can provide splendid means of checking the quality of workmanship and material. They take a greater interest in making thorough inspections when you are present. Even when they approve the work, it can be helpful to ask their advice on what could have been done to make it better.

If irregularities are found, take prompt action to correct them. This should be accomplished in a friendly working relationship with your subcontractors. Another helpful inspection is visits from friends. Ask their views on workmanship and materials.

An important inspection is made when the house is available for occupancy. You should plan to move in within three days after completion. If necessary, some work can be finished while you are in the house. The advantage of being in the home is that you have a twenty-four-hour check on all aspects of work. Be sure to check *everything* with care. If it is winter time, do not hesitate to try the cooling system.

PENALTIES AND BONUSES

You may wish to include in your contracts with subcontractors appropriate clauses that provide penalties for late completion and extra compensation for work accomplished early. Check closely on the quality of work done to be sure subcontractors do not rush the job to gain the extra compensation.

MEETINGS

Each morning, meet with the subcontractors as soon as they arrive. Discuss what is to be accomplished and any problems that need to be resolved. Before they leave, confirm the time they will be at work the next day. This way, the subcontractors can tell their workers of any changes, so all are informed on matters of common interest and problems that may arise.

Meetings also offer the opportunity to exchange ideas. These skilled craftsmen have many years of experience, and you can acquire considerable knowledge about various aspects of homebuilding. They are proud of their own work and critical of poor workmanship. Having them point out deficiencies enables you to be better armed with facts when requesting corrective action.

To prepare properly for these daily sessions, do your homework the night before. Review your PERT chart, plans, description of materials, timetable, and budget. Their time is valuable, and subcontractors usually work right along with their people. These sessions should be brief; ideally, you should conduct your business while they are working.

Topics that come up frequently include interpretation of the architect's drawing, deadlines, materials needed, inspection requirements, and payments. Try to provide an atmosphere that will encourage the subcontractors to express their views. Comments from workers should also be appreciated. Talk with the subs and their workers during lunch breaks. They are usually a congenial group. Provide a climate that encourages them to present their views on what can be done to make it a better house. For example, one homebuilder discussed changing the pitch of the roof, increasing the size of the breakfast nook, and using a new plastic material. These sessions may help you arrive at sound decisions.

Meeting with workers also provides other benefits. Once I was informed of an article on home construction that appeared in their trade journal. On another occasion, I was told of a house being constructed in the city that was using a new flooring material.

PAYMENT BY CHECK

It is wise to make most payments by check and to obtain necessary receipts. Obviously, you should pay cash only when buying a few soft drinks or several screws, but do keep a record because even these small amounts add up. It is a good idea to endorse the back of the check, indicating the purpose of the payment: "Final payment for painting home at 2311 Oriole, per contract #201."

Prior to return of your monthly statement, you may need to show your loan agency that payment has been made. Your receipt will serve this purpose. It can be valid even if written on a scrap of paper, as long as it is signed by a responsible person in the organization. Take advantage of any discount offered for early payment; otherwise, wait until the due date.

Don't hesitate to stop payment on a check if you find that material is defective or work is not accomplished as promised. It may be the best way to see that appropriate corrective action is taken. Money is the best incentive for getting a job done. Once payments are completed, you have lost your bargaining power. I recommend 10 percent be withheld on major jobs until you make a final inspection.

Never pay in advance. A friend related the following story:

> I made a mistake by paying half of the total swimming pool price to the contractor prior to any work being done. The payment was made the day before the arrival of the workmen with their excavation equipment and trucks. The workers demanded that I pay them in full before they would begin work. I said,

"The contractor has already been paid for your services." Their leader replied, "Yeh, but he doesn't always pay us."

Upon receipt of that news I rushed to the phone and called my bank. Fortunately, I was able to stop payment and learned a good lesson cheap. The pool builder was then informed of the situation. He came to the site promptly and paid the men so they could proceed. Future payments were made only after the work was completed to my satisfaction. And the final 10 percent was withheld until I was sure all of the subcontractors had been paid by the pool builder. Otherwise, I could have been liable for any such debts.

BUDGET

Your budget can serve as a planning and control document. The initial columns of figures indicate the several estimates of what the various items cost. Their total provides you with an indication of the money required to build your home. This information enables you to talk intelligently with your lending agency.

Your estimate, however, does not always coincide with actual costs. In most cases, cost exceeds the amount planned for in the budget. This may be true even though you have price agreements with your subcontractors. Supplies are a different story. There are also changes in plans that can be costly. Still, if you use your budget effectively as a control device, this variation between estimate and actual can be minimized by promptly posting the actual price paid for each item. Then check carefully to see if you have exceeded your estimate and by what amount. The real value of budget control will occur only if you take positive action to correct the problem.

Assume that after the foundation work has been completed, you find your budget estimate has been exceeded by 5 percent. The problem is obvious—you spent too much. You must then decide what to do about it. After obtaining the facts, you proceed to look at alternatives. One solution is to ask your loan agency for more money. A second alternative is to substitute lesser-quality materials on the remaining construction to make up the difference. A third possibility is to eliminate something from the house. From the various alternatives you then can proceed to make a sound decision.

SALES TAX

In maintaining a record of your actual costs, be sure to keep track of any sales taxes. This amount can be reported on your federal income tax if you itemize deductions and is another factor to consider when deciding whether or not to subcontract your own home. It can be an important savings over having your home constructed by a builder or buying a new home. The dollar savings possible is pointed up in this family's experience:

> We realized the importance of having a budget and keeping good records on subcontracting our home when it came time to prepare our Income Tax return and send Uncle Sam his just amount—but not a penny more! The material for our home cost $32,183. The sales tax in our community is 6 percent so we arrived at a figure of over $1900. We are in the 49 percent tax bracket and itemize our deductions. Listing the $1900+ saved us nearly $950—thanks to subcontracting our home.

FILING SYSTEM

A good filing system is a timesaver and can be an effective control technique. If organized properly, it permits you to find records quickly. Such information is essential at times in order to make wise decisions. Assign each subcontractor and supplier an individual file. Checks, budgets, PERT charts, photographs, and so on should be filed separately in alphabetical order for easy reference. Keep your filing system simple.

PERT

PERT is a splendid planning and control document and should be followed with care during the building phase.

Your budget serves as a money control, but PERT permits you to keep your construction on schedule. PERT initially enables you to determine how long it will take to complete the job. It also points out the numerous tasks that can be accomplished concurrently to minimize completion time. If a strike should occur in the cement industry, for example, and your schedule shows it is time to lay the driveway, your PERT chart can assist you in selecting a possible alternative. Regardless of how well conceived, however, a planning document like PERT cannot foresee all eventualities.

PERT is only as valuable as you make it. If you set it up on an unrealistic basis, you are wasting your time.

PHOTOGRAPHS

A camera can be a useful control device. A small one will fit in your pocket, and it enables you to make a permanent record of any potential problem. If there is a question about faulty lumber at the time of delivery, for example, take a picture of it with the company truck in the background, or include in the photo the man who made the delivery.

If you intend to do any future building, photos can be helpful in going over the step-by-step process. An analysis will enable you to make improvements the next time around.

COMMUNICATION

It is extremely important to talk with your workers, suppliers, subcontractors, and other homebuilders. The information you receive can be valuable.

When you give instructions, be sure that what you say is clearly understood. One way to find out is to have the person repeat what you told him. Keep in mind that workers and suppliers use different terms and may interpret things differently. If you have any questions regarding interpretation or misunderstanding, put it in writing.

LEGAL ACTION

Another control measure is positive follow-up action, but take only the necessary amount of action required to get the job done. If a subcontractor or supplier has failed to meet his commitment, you may wish to proceed as follows:

1. Call the person and courteously explain that the work was not satisfactory. Set a time for it to be corrected. By having the contract in writing, you have evidence to remind him of the agreement terms.

2. Make a second phone call firmly explaining that you expect the work to be done, and set a second deadline.

3. Write a letter stating you will take necessary legal action if the work is not done within a specified time. Send copies of letters to appropriate parties such as the Better Business Bureau, a local consumer affairs office, Ralph Nader, and the White House Office of Consumer Affairs. Also send a copy of the complaint to the state licensing board for that specialty.

4. Proceed with the necessary legal action. You may find the small-claims court is sufficient to obtain the amount of damages due you. If not, secure the services of a lawyer. Your chances of being successful in such a situation are improving. In past years most courts sided with builders, but current court rulings are frequently in the homeowner's favor in suits regarding such areas as electrical installation, air-conditioning work, and drainage.

It is wise to take action only for matters of some value. Don't waste your time and energy quibbling over minor points to satisfy your ego. Instead, get on with the job. Once you decide something is important, however, proceed with vigor to gain a fair settlement. In theory, your careful planning and checking on both workers and suppliers should prevent having to take such drastic steps. But it doesn't always work that way. Occasionally someone in whom you have great trust and confidence will let you down.

SUMMARY

Control is an important management tool. Check on what is done to be sure that workmanship and materials meet the standards agreed to in the individual contracts. Examine supplies as they arrive and work as it is completed.

Bills submitted by your subcontractors should be within the limits specified in your written agreements. You should withhold final payments (about 10 percent) until the material or the project can be tested or inspected. It is much easier to secure service before complete payment is made.

PERT is an efficient means of time control. It permits you to revise a schedule as necessary while alternatives are considered.

Chapter Seven
Do You Want a
Swimming Pool?

There are nearly two million swimming pools on the property of home-owners in the United States. In some wealthy residential areas, a permanent pool is in virtually every backyard. The initial cost of a standard-size pool approximates that of a luxury automobile. Smaller pools (10 feet wide, 15 to 20 feet long, 5 to 6 feet deep) are being designed for small lots, town house properties, and cluster housing. The cost of a smaller pool is less than the standard size and it is easier to clean. However, it precludes diving, and active swimming is limited by the size.

Whether or not to build a pool deserves considerable thought. This decision should be arrived at during the planning phase of homebuilding. Here are some of the pros and cons that may help you reach your decision.

ADVANTAGES

Swimming is a delightful and invigorating exercise for every member of the family. A pool allows you to develop athletic skills such as life-saving, scuba diving, and water polo. It can also provide an enjoyable way to entertain relatives and friends. You can barbecue nearby and spend an afternoon or evening of mild exercise and good conversation in a picnic environment.

Financially, a pool can increase the value of your home by more than the original cost of the pool. By building a pool at the time you build your home, you may realize a substantial savings in the initial price as well as interest charges. Furthermore, if you and your family use a swim club or other facilities, there can be dollar and time savings here, too.

There is also satisfaction in knowing that you can do as you please about the pool's use, maintenance, and decor. A pool can be blended into a tastefully landscaped yard that permits a pleasant view from your patio and other rooms. There is also the satisfaction of creating your own design.

DISADVANTAGES

A pool is a heavy initial expense of $10,000 to $25,000, at a time when you are burdened with many other construction costs. In addition to the cost of the pool itself, you must consider the decking, backyard lighting, landscaping, and fencing.

After the pool is built, there will be maintenance expenses which may vary from $500 to $3,500 a year, depending upon how much work you do yourself, the size of the pool, the kind of repairs, where you live, and climatic conditions. Just as an example, here is a summary of our own maintenance costs:

Acid and algicide	$ 42
Chlorine	240
Diatomaceous earth	24
Electricity	365
Pool equipment	112
Repairs	225
Total Annual Cost	$1008

A weekly cleaning service would cost $450 a year and a pool heater adds approximately $80 to the fuel bill. Thus, our yearly expenses could have been increased to over $1500. Keep in mind that the energy shortage will result in rising maintenance costs in the years ahead. Be sure to prepare a budget (a five-year estimate) to determine these costs.

Once your pool is built, you have taken on an additional responsibility. If you wish to have someone else maintain it, you must find a reliable firm and see that the work is done properly. Even with a maintenance contract there is day-to-day upkeep, insurance, and safety precautions which must be taken. A pool can be the cause of numerous, and even fatal, injuries. We are always concerned when youngsters swim in our pool. Be sure to have appropriate insurance coverage, first aid equipment, and a knowledge of artificial respiration.

Another disadvantage is the possibility of financial loss—your pool may be a drawback when you go to sell your home. A number of people don't like them or feel they need one. A factor in making your decision is whether or not pools are prominent in your neighborhood.

Of course, the biggest consideration is whether you will really use and enjoy your pool. If you find that it is a worry, forget it. The novelty wears off quickly and the composition of your family will change over the years. Also, you may prefer the congeniality of a club or public swimming facility.

A MANAGERIAL APPROACH

If you decide to build a swimming pool, follow the same management concepts you used for the construction of a home. Your objective might be "to have a quality swimming pool built within 30 days at a minimum cost." You must plan it wisely, have it built in accordance with your plan, and make adequate checks to ensure construction as specified in the contract. Achieving your objective requires the efficient use of three resources—personnel, money, and materials. Make sound decisions by delineating your objective, determining the resources available, and understanding your managerial functions. In delineating your objective keep in mind building code requirements. Some communities, for example, require solar heating for pools.

SELECTING YOUR LOT

The ideal time to make the decision to have a swimming pool is before you buy your land. It is advantageous to have a pool situated so that it affords privacy. You may consider it important to select a lot where your neighbors could not look directly into your backyard and where buildings facing your patio area are attractive. In selecting your lot, also take into consideration its shape and size. Will its dimensions be adequate for the type of pool you want?

FINANCING YOUR POOL

If you build your swimming pool at the time you construct your home, it becomes part of the total financial package. Thus, if the current mortgage rate is 12 percent, this is what it will cost to finance your pool. If you wait until after the house is completed, you must obtain a home improvement loan. The difference is approximately 2 percent, based on charges at a local savings and loan association. In contrast to the savings and loan 14-percent charge, finance companies advertise real estate loans at 18 percent.

If you select a finance company, your loan usually must be secured by a mortgage to obtain their lower rate; otherwise, it could cost up to 42 percent. Length of payment may be listed as five years, in contrast to the much longer loan period if you build the pool at the time the house is constructed. So if you decide to wait, save your money and pay cash for the pool.

BASIC PLANNING

Once you have determined your financial needs and found a desirable lot, there are other factors to consider. Plan your pool concurrently with the rest of your home and include it in the initial house sketch. To help you develop a suitable drawing, look at a number of other home pools. Current articles and books on the subject can inform you of the latest developments. Be sure to consider your pool as part of the total home picture. That is, relate it to your landscaping, patio, fence, garage, and the house itself. Also, have a bathroom/changing room easily accessible to the pool.

SELECTING A BUILDER

Spend considerable time and study selecting a company to build your pool. Contact experienced people and obtain their views on the quality of construction, costs, time required, and the reliability of the firm. It pays to call your bank, Better Business Bureau, and the local consumer affairs agency. You should also find out if they belong to the National Swimming Pool Institute (2000 K Street, N.W., Washington, D.C. 20006).

Make a point to visit the offices of pool builders. You can get a good idea of the operation by observing their place of work. Also visit homes where pools are under construction and talk with the workers. Note the quality of their workmanship. It requires good supervision and skilled craftsmen to build a quality pool.

Ask pool builders if they will furnish you with a certificate of insurance from a recognized company. The certificate will indicate the kind of insurance, expiration date, and limits of liability. Insurance coverage may include workmen's compensation, employer's liability, bodily injury (except car), property damage, and automobile liability. The certificate will include a statement to the effect that "in the event of cancellation of said policies, the company will make reasonable effort to send notice of such cancellation to the holder at the address shown herein, but the company assumes no responsibility for any mistakes or for failure to give such notice." Another means of protection is to have the company obtain a bond, so that if the work is not in accord with the contract, you will have an insurance agreement covering a stated financial loss.

When you make your selection, determine which firm will give you the best deal, including quality, price, and service. You will need to furnish them with specifications and a preliminary sketch to ensure they are bidding on the type of pool you want. Figure 7–1 is the drawing, based on our initial design, developed by the company we selected.

SPECIFICATIONS

A good sketch and detailed specifications should enable you to receive accurate bids which will be helpful in selecting the firm to build your pool. Let us look at the specifications utilized in my pool. They include four major categories: size, design, construction, and equipment.

Size: 14 to 21 feet wide and 32 feet long; 4 feet at the shallow end to 8 feet at the deepest.

Design: Free form (see sketch in Figure 7-1).

Construction: Pneumatically placed monolithic Gunite; 5 to 10 inches thick; reinforced with ½- and ⅜-inch steel bars; steel bars to be placed 12 inches both ways (vertically and horizontally) in the shallow end and 6 inches both ways in the deep end.

1. Steps: Gunite custom-built steps (three) in shallow end corner.
2. Tile: 6 by 6-inch blue trim around entire pool.
3. Coping: 8-inch brick around entire pool.
4. Deck: None. (We had the subcontractor who prepared our patio and foundation do the decking with the same wash gravel material. Their cost was much lower than the pool company's.)
5. Interior finish: Pure white marble deluxe interior pool finish.
6. Other: Concrete filter slab to support tank and equipment.

Equipment:

1. Filter system: Swimquip model MKW hi-rate diatomaceous with 25 square feet of filter area with stainless steel filter tank, 1 horsepower, 220 volt motor, hair and leaf strainer, face piping, fittings, suction valves, automatic air relief, and pressure gauge.
2. Heater: None. (Provision was made so that a heater could be installed later. Space was left for it next to the filter system and a gas

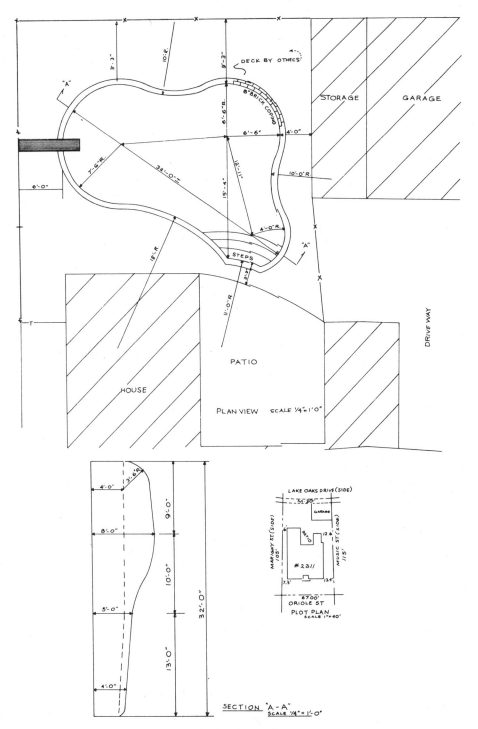

Figure 7–1 Blueprint drawing of a swimming pool.

stub out was installed nearby. A pool heater may vary in price from $500 to $1,000 depending upon size, quality, and installation charges. In this era of energy conservation, it is important to obtain the correct size heater for your pool and one that is most efficient from a cost basis.)

3. Chlorinator: Custom-built tiled chloramatic feeder.

4. Diving board: 8-foot Douglas fir, turquoise color coat with white sand, tread top surface, and stainless steel supports.

5. Ladder: None. (We felt that a ladder cluttered up a small pool and is a needless expense, especially if you have steps.)

6. Vacuum cleaner: 10-inch vacuum cleaner with 30-foot floating hose and 16-foot handle. (There is a vacuum cleaner available that will automatically clean the floor and sides of a pool, but it is expensive—$300 to $400.)

7. Wall brush: 17-inch nylon brush with aluminum bracket and 16-foot handle.

8. Leaf skimmer: Hand skimmer with a plastic screen and 12-foot handle.

9. Test set: Dial-A-Test set with case.

10. Thermometer: None. (If you buy a heater, the thermometer could be a useful item. The hand test suits my needs—if it's too cold, I don't go swimming.)

11. Safety rope: None. (We installed the cycolac cup anchors. If necessary, the safety rope could be purchased later to separate the shallow end from the deep end.)

12. Underwater light: Chrome-plated 500 watt daylight-blue type, complete with lens, bulb, deck box, and switch at filter area.

13. Time clock: Automatic time clock for filtration equipment. (This enables you to regulate the time you wish the pool filter system to operate. It may vary from zero to 24 hours a day.)

14. Fill spout: None. (You may wish to buy a chrome-plated brass one-inch fill spout; it is used to add water to the pool and would have been placed under our diving board. I once bumped my head on a spout at a neighbor's pool because it hangs over the edge. The injury potential and added cost convinced me that it would be better to install a water outlet near the pool and use a hose. This has proved satisfactory. I also use the hose to wash down the deck and water the shrubbery.)

15. Main drain fitting: 8-inch drain frame and grate.

16. Vacuum wall fitting: Vacuum fitting located in skimmer.

17. Return water fitting: Twin-jet returns with whirlpool action.

18. Skimmer: Super-flow self-adjusting type.

19. Other: 135 feet of 4-inch Orangeburg pipe to be installed to

storm sewer drain with three grills. Four gallons of muriatic acid, 40 pounds filter aid, 1 gallon tile cleaner, and 100 pounds of chlorine.

BUILDING PHASE

Begin building your pool after the pilings have been driven. At this point, there will be easy access to your entire lot. If you wait until your home is completed, it might be difficult for the pool builder to work with his equipment. In some situations, this can involve shoveling by hand and removing dirt in wheelbarrows, which will increase the cost of your job considerably. Furthermore, construction of a pool is messy work, and you will have a real clean-up task if your home is already occupied and landscaped.

If you build your pool during the construction of your home, it is important to have some form of temporary fencing to keep stray animals and youngsters out. You should also have insurance to protect you from various types of injuries.

It is important to be present during construction so you can determine if the sketch and specifications are actually being implemented. The following aspects should be observed closely.

Design: Stakes will be placed to indicate the layout of the pool. The layout should conform to your drawing; check to see that it has the proper dimensions. Its location on your property should be in accordance with the plot plan. Review your city and subdivision requirements regarding swimming pools.

Excavation: See that the excavation equipment does not damage sidewalks, neighboring property, or your building material. After the hole has been dug, measure the depth to determine if it complies with the specifications. Trucks will haul away the dirt; if you plan to build up your front yard, make certain that enough topsoil is left to do so. Dirt can also be used for backfill, grading, and terracing. Don't have it hauled away until you are sure you can't use it.

Preparation: Next, workers smooth out the bottom and edges so that it conforms precisely to the pool sketch. Then the main drain is formed up (see Figure 7–2), and a load of shells is placed at the bottom of the pool. Next, steel bars are put in the pool and held in place by ties.

After pipe has been laid from the main drain to an outlet at the top of the pool, concrete is sprayed against the sides.(You may wish to use another type of material for your pool, such as metal, fiberglass, or vinyl; check to find out which is best suited for your area and pocketbook.) Check to see that the floor has approximately five inches and the

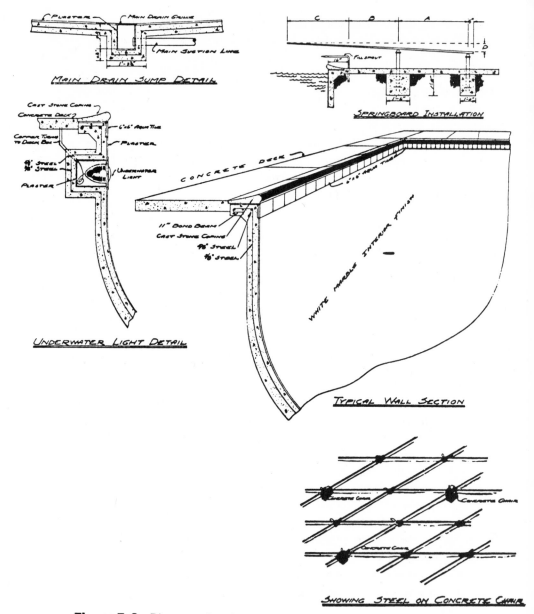

Figure 7–2 Diagrams of pool construction phases.

sides ten inches of concrete. Other tasks include coping, tiling, and installing drainage, electrical equipment, and a filtering system.

The plastering of the pool results in a white interior finish. Once this material is dry, the pool is filled. After the diving board is installed, decking can be completed for the pool area, driveway, and patio.

Thomas S. Stillman, T & D Photo Co.

Figure 7–3 Free-form-designed pool and surroundings.

After your pool is finished, inspect and test the equipment. Be sure that there are no leaks and that final payment is withheld until the city inspectors have given their approval.

SUBCONTRACTING YOUR OWN POOL

You may wish to consider subcontracting your pool in a manner comparable to your home. If so, the procedures outlined in chapters 1 through 6 should be helpful. You would utilize PERT, a planning and building timetable, and other concepts presented. However, I recommend that you do not subcontract your pool if it is being built at the same time as your house because your time can best be employed in the supervision of your entire home, including the pool.

However, if you later decide to add a pool, the subcontracting approach may be appropriate if you have the time to supervise it. A friend of mine built his own home four years ago and decided his above-ground pool was not suitable for his present needs. Six months ago he decided to put in a below-the-ground pool. Here is the experience he related to me:

> About three years ago I bought an above-ground pool, but it proved unsatisfactory for real swimming. Our family then agreed

that we all wanted a quality pool. We have a large lot and wanted a free-form design with a 42-foot length and 20-foot width. A diving board required a depth at the end of 8½ feet. I went to three contractors for bids. Their prices ranged from $19,200 to $22,700. I subcontracted it for $15,780—a savings of nearly 22 percent on the lowest bid. And based on the quality of the workmanship I got, the savings would be closer to 30 percent. I also found the time of year to have the work done had an impact on my price. A slack period made subcontractors more available and agreeable to accepting a lower figure. Here were my costs:

1. Design by draftsman	$ 175
2. Excavation	345
3. Truck to haul away dirt	250
4. Preparation of pool bed to conform to pool sketch, main drain formed, load of shells placed at pool bottom, steel bars put in pool and held by ties, pipe laid from main drain to an outlet at top of pool	2,620
5. Concrete sprayed on pool form	2,090
6. Coping, tiling, and installation of drainage system	1,675
7. Plastering (white marble interior finish)	2,612
8. Electrical equipment and filtering system installed	1,178
9. Heating equipment installed	975
10. Diving board	340
11. Decking completed	2,535
12. Purchase of maintenance equipment (automatic vacuum cleaner, skimmer, brush, and chemicals)	985
Total	$15,780

It took me six weeks to build. I enjoyed doing it and enjoyed saving $3,420, but I would caution people not to undertake such a project unless they can devote the time and understand the responsibilities involved. For the unqualified or naive, there can be costly mistakes which would make subcontracting more expensive than hiring a highly respected pool contractor.

MAINTENANCE

A swimming pool requires considerable care, but this care pays off, giving you an attractive pool and reducing repairs. I recommend that you or a member of your family clean your pool. It is good exercise and alerts you to any problems.

During the swimming season, you will need to add chlorine and acid frequently to maintain clear sparkling water. Check your acid and chlorine content daily, utilizing your test kit. Chlorine and acid can be dangerous, so handle them with care.

Vacuum your pool weekly, clean the tile, skim the pool surface, backwash the filter, wash the deck, and empty the skimmer basket. It is desirable to have your pool inspected each year by a specialist.

A personal daily inspection is also important. Pranksters occasionally toss items over the fence. Eggs are difficult to clean up and the sooner removed the better. Toilet paper rolls can clog the filter system. Copper pennies, nails, and bobby pins cause rust marks if not removed promptly. If rust spots occur, remove them with an abrasive compound.

Ask for advice on how to maintain the equipment and service the pool. You should also receive an instruction manual. Study it with care and go over the procedures several times with the pool representative. *Be sure you understand exactly how everything works.* Mistakes can be costly. For example, if you close off all the valves and turn on the motor, leaks will develop quickly. You should be shown what to do when the filter system loses its prime (that is, doesn't have water in the pipes). Why call a repair man and pay $20 or more per visit when you can do it yourself?

POOL SAFETY

A pool is a delightful form of recreation, but it can be dangerous. Here are some rules which should be established:

1. Never swim alone.
2. Have a life line that can be thrown to a person. We use our garden hose.
3. Don't allow running or horseplay around the pool.
4. Wait at least an hour after eating before swimming.
5. If you have guests, check to see if they can swim. If not, use a safety rope to block off the deep end.

SUMMARY

A swimming pool is a major investment. If you are considering a pool, your research should begin before the lot is purchased. Select a lot that affords some privacy. Prepare a budget (a five year estimate) that includes maintenance costs and energy costs as well as the initial investment.

Prior to obtaining construction bids, it is desirable to prepare specifications and a sketch of your proposed pool. Select a reputable contractor who has adequate financial resources.

It is usually much less expensive to build a pool at the same time that your home is built. If you decide to wait, interest charges for a loan may vary from 10 to 42 percent.

A swimming pool is a continuing responsibility, and it requires a considerable amount of attention. It is preferable to do much of the maintenance yourself; you will save money, and your personal interest will result in a more thorough job.

Chapter Eight
Protecting Your
Property

The best time to consider appropriate security measures for your home is during the planning phase. This will result in lower costs and will provide immediate protection. Unfortunately, most people do not provide adequate protection until a burglary has occurred. Crime is now a major concern in our cities, and the home is a prime target. Approximately $450 million in personal property was stolen last year; only $27 million was recovered. Sixty-five percent of all burglaries occurred at residences, and about three-fourths of those involved forcible entry. Families are disturbed not only by the rising number of burglaries but about their own safety.

This chapter tells what you can do to increase home security. Refer to Figure 8–1, which lists protective measures and their costs.

A MANAGERIAL APPROACH
As a good manager, you should look at all aspects of a security system for your house before deciding what to purchase. Determine what will meet your needs best for the money you can afford to spend. By including requirements in the initial planning of your home, the interest will be at the current first mortgage rate. If you borrow to make such purchases later, the costs may range from 12 to 42 percent.

Security Measure	Cost			
	None	Minor ($1–$20)	Average ($21–$200)	Expensive ($201 and up)
Locks			X	X
Alarm system				X
Marking valuables		X		
Enclosed garage				X
Hardwood or metalclad doors and door jambs				X
Iron doors and windows				X
Police assistance	X			
Neighbors	X			
Dogs			X	X
Guns		X	X	X
Staggered hours	X			
At-home appearance		X		
Store valuables			X	
Photographs		X	X	
Windows secured		X	X	
Outdoor lighting			X	
Fence				X
Wireless equipment			X	X
Alert to tricks	X			
Security checks	X			
Top-secret measures			X	X
Insurance				X
Security during construction		X	X	X
Sitter service				X

Figure 8–1 Protective measures and their relative cost.

A systems approach to security means considering each item in relation to your total home protective needs. Locks, for example, are worthless if you don't have a sound method of checking to be sure they are secured. If you have a fixed amount of money available, you must establish priorities and decide what will meet your requirements best. Security should be viewed as a subsystem of the entire house require-ments. This means you should decide how much to allocate for security in relation to plumbing, electrical equipment, and all other expenses. If you wait to consider protective measures until the home is nearly com-plete, you may have no money to provide such extras as quality locks.

PROTECTIVE MEASURES
Here are some security measures that may be taken to protect your home.

LOCKS
There are a variety of locks for exterior doors, and they provide varying degrees of security. Let us classify them into four major categories.

Key in doorknob: This is the lock that most homes have. It is the easiest to break into and the least expensive. In the construction of spec-ulation homes, builders normally use this type.

Our carpenter showed us how quickly he could enter our home with this type of lock. With a twist of a wrench, he opened the door immediately. He also showed me how to gain entry by inserting the blade of a pocket knife between the latch and the door frame. This particular lock had a trigger bolt that was supposed to prevent such action, but it didn't work.

Our carpenter emphasized that the lock itself might be strong but that it is of little value unless the door has good hinges, is securely encased in a solid frame, and is made of a sturdy material. It takes little effort on the part of a burglar to break the panel of a weak door or knock off the latches and enter your home quickly.

Dead lock: This lock is installed in the face of the door and is available with or without a key. It requires drilling sizable holes in your door and frame. A dead lock normally has a rectangular metal projectile that is inserted into the hole of the frame to lock the door. The longer and larger the projectile, the more difficult it is to pry the door apart. There is no beveled edge or spring mechanism on the dead lock, so a pen knife or credit card cannot open it.

Vertical bolt: This is an auxiliary lock which is screwed onto the door and frame. It prevents a burglar from jimmying the door because it has a pin that fits into a plate, as shown in Figure 8–2. Note the installation instructions for a Yale lock. Unless you are qualified, I would suggest having a locksmith do it.

Special locks: You may wish to consider a lock with an alarm. When a burglar tries to pick it or force entry, the alarm goes off. Pick-proof cylinder locks make it difficult for the professional burglar to open. Bar locks can be purchased to install at the base and top of your doors; to lock them, metal projections are inserted in the ceiling and floor.

There is a wide choice of quality locks available today. Visit several locksmiths and examine their merchandise and talk with security officers at several companies before determining which are best suited to your needs.

ALARM SYSTEM

A burglar-alarm system provides both psychological and physical protection. A potential burglar will see outside your front door an on-off lock device with a red lamp and a warning bell housed in a tamper-proof box. Decals may also be displayed in your window.

In the event of robbery, an alarm is set off when a door or window is entered. The noise may frighten the burglar away and will give you time to notify the police. Emergency switches can be installed in various locations to sound the alarm if you see something suspicious.

In some communities, the house alarm system can be connected directly to police headquarters. In other localities, the home can be tied into the alarm company's office, which in turn will contact the police. For this central hookup there is a monthly charge.

The alarm system should be considered in the plannning phase of homebuilding. It is more reasonable to have it installed during construction, affording you protection the moment you move in.

Alarm systems are expensive. It is important to make certain you are dealing with a reputable firm that will back up its equipment. Prepare your specifications and be precise in your requirements. If possible, obtain three bids based on free estimates. These should be submitted after a study is made of your house plans and alarm-system specifications.

You should also give consideration to an effective fire-alarm system. One type has a fire alarm circuit that sounds a warning horn. You may also install a unit that detects smoke or heat and activates an alarm. By having the combination of heat, smoke, and fire detection, you are in a better position to be warned in time. Such a system is expensive. Instead of a complete fire-alarm system, you may wish to purchase in-

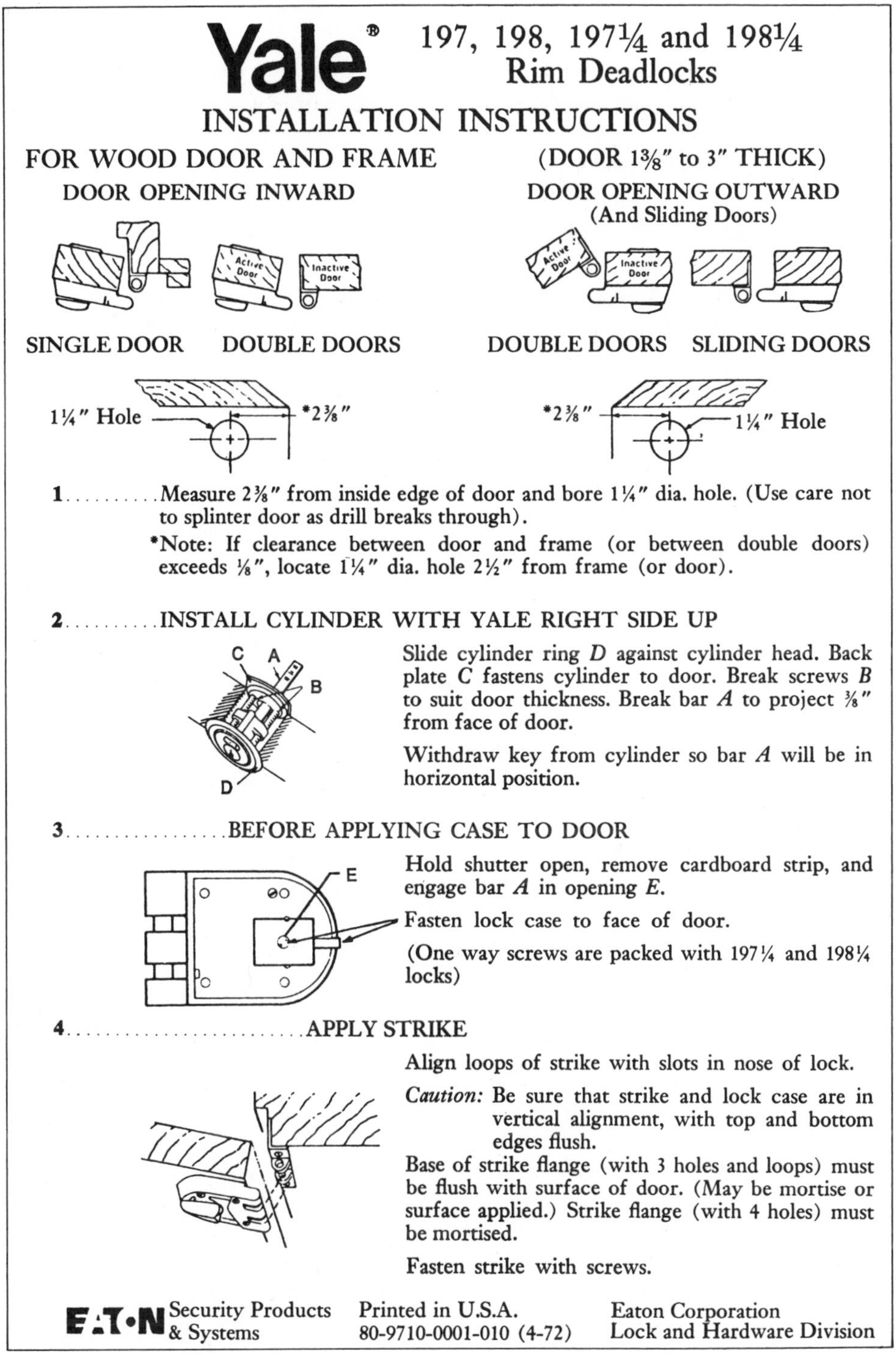

Yale® 197, 198, 197¼ and 198¼ Rim Deadlocks

INSTALLATION INSTRUCTIONS

FOR WOOD DOOR AND FRAME	(DOOR 1⅜" to 3" THICK)
DOOR OPENING INWARD	DOOR OPENING OUTWARD (And Sliding Doors)

SINGLE DOOR   DOUBLE DOORS

DOUBLE DOORS   SLIDING DOORS

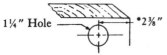

1¼" Hole ———|←——*2⅜"→|

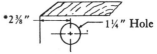

|←*2⅜"→|———— 1¼" Hole

1 . . . . Measure 2⅜" from inside edge of door and bore 1¼" dia. hole. (Use care not to splinter door as drill breaks through).

    *Note: If clearance between door and frame (or between double doors) exceeds ⅛", locate 1¼" dia. hole 2½" from frame (or door).

2 . . . . INSTALL CYLINDER WITH YALE RIGHT SIDE UP

Slide cylinder ring *D* against cylinder head. Back plate *C* fastens cylinder to door. Break screws *B* to suit door thickness. Break bar *A* to project ⅜" from face of door.

Withdraw key from cylinder so bar *A* will be in horizontal position.

3 . . . . BEFORE APPLYING CASE TO DOOR

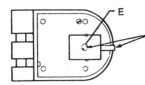

Hold shutter open, remove cardboard strip, and engage bar *A* in opening *E*.

Fasten lock case to face of door.

(One way screws are packed with 197¼ and 198¼ locks)

4 . . . . APPLY STRIKE

Align loops of strike with slots in nose of lock.

Caution: Be sure that strike and lock case are in vertical alignment, with top and bottom edges flush.

Base of strike flange (with 3 holes and loops) must be flush with surface of door. (May be mortise or surface applied.) Strike flange (with 4 holes) must be mortised.

Fasten strike with screws.

E·T·N Security Products & Systems   Printed in U.S.A. 80-9710-0001-010 (4-72)   Eaton Corporation Lock and Hardware Division

Figure 8–2 Sample locks and instructions for installation. Courtesy of Eaton Corporation, Lock and Hardware Division.

dividual fire and smoke detectors for specific rooms. Codes of many communities now require smoke detectors in newly constructed homes.

MARKING VALUABLES

Use an engraving tool to mark your social security number or driver's license number on valuable equipment such as your radio, television, or tape recorder.

Our community has an excellent procedure for identifying property. It is under jurisdiction of the police department and involves the following:

1. Fire stations lend the marking equipment and provide an instruction sheet (Figure 8–3) and a form to list valuables (Figure 8–4).

2. When police department is notified that the valuables have been appropriately marked, they mail the homeowner two sets of decals.

3. The homeowner places the decals on his windows to inform all concerned that his valuables are marked.

4. The completed list of valuables should be placed in your safe-deposit box at the bank. (Include a careful description and serial numbers.)

Figure 8–3 Instruction sheet for marking valuables.

LIST OF VALUABLE ITEMS AND METHODS OF IDENTIFICATION

Tape recorder	Radio
Television	Stereo
Air conditioner	Guns
Camera	Typewriter and business machines
Hub caps of automobile	Wheels of automobile
Lawn mower	Tool box
Kitchen appliances	Repair and garden tools

All items should be marked with the *driver's license* or *social security number* of the head of the home. The marking should be in a place of prominence where it can be easily observed without dismantling the object. This can easily be done on most items without detracting from their decorative appearance. Examples: On the chassis of the rear of a television set; on the inside of a stereo; on the inside or on the outer edge of automobile hub caps.

If an item such as a piece of jewelry cannot easily be marked, a complete description should be made and kept. These types of items should then be placed together on a light background and photographed. The owner should keep two sets of photographs, one which can be supplied to the police if a burglary occurs and the other for identification purposes. Valuable clothing such as fur coats and stoles should be marked with a felt pen in such a place that it would not destroy the attractiveness of the item but still be prominent when viewed by investigators.

**VALUABLE ITEMS THAT A BURGLAR WOULD MOST LIKELY STEAL
FROM MY RESIDENCE**

Item	Make	Year Purchased	Serial Number

After entering all valuable items on this form, place this form in a secure location in order that you may give investigating officers all pertinent data in case of a crime.

Figure 8–4   Form for listing valuables.

ENCLOSED GARAGE

An enclosed garage is a safe place to keep your bicycle, car, and other such equipment. Install necessary locks for each garage door and make daily checks to make sure they are secured.

IRON DOORS AND WINDOWS

Some homeowners today are installing iron grills at their entryways and windows. In some cases this can be attractive, but if used on all windows and entrances it can make a house look like a prison. Grillwork is expensive and requires good locks to be effective.

This method does provide added security, giving the burglar another barrier to penetrate before reaching the interior of the house. If you put an iron door at your front entry only, however, the home is still vulnerable at other entrances and windows. A burglar usually will seek to enter a home at its weakest location. This is why it is so important to consider all aspects of security in devising an effective means of protection.

POLICE ASSISTANCE

The police can be your friend. Make a point to do your part by contacting the police department and asking their views on security measures.

SAFEGUARD YOUR HOME AGAINST CRIMINALS

KEEP outside lights on all night to illuminate all sides of your home.

MAKE sure that the area between the home and detached garage is lighted.

STORE expensive jewelry in a safe deposit box.

IF you leave the house, close the garage door. An open garage door is an open invitation to the daytime burglar.

LEAVE lights on in the house when you are away for the evening.

BEFORE you leave for a vacation, inform the police and a neighbor. Leave window shades and blinds at a normal level and make sure that milk bottles and newspapers do not accumulate at your door. Ask post office to hold mail.

DON'T give keys to strange service men. Separate auto keys and house keys. Check references of maids and cleaning people. Keys are easily duplicated.

LOCK windows and doors—including the side doors—when you retire. Use a supplementary chain lock.

LOCK attic windows. Lock garage too.

PUT a strong short chain on your door.

DON'T leave your door unlocked, even when you're in the house.

KEEP the door chained when a stranger knocks until you are satisfied his purpose is legitimate.

DOUBLE-LOCK your door when you leave.

ALWAYS test your doors to make sure you have locked them before leaving.

SEE that shrubbery that might provide an easy hiding place is kept trimmed.

CHECK thoroughly the references of maids or service people who are given access to your home.

Make sure all screens are secured from the inside.

A DOG provides warning and protection.

TIPS FOR VACATIONERS

STOP all deliveries such as newspapers, milk, and laundry. Ask a neighbor to remove mail from mailbox daily and remove circulars and brochures left at the house.

LOCK all windows and doors securely.

USE a light meter which turns on a lamp and outside lights at dusk.

IF absent for an extended period, arrange to have your lawn mowed, preferably by a relative or trusted neighbor.

NOTIFY police that you will be on vacation, giving address, date and time of departure, and date and time of return.

MARK personal belongings with your driver's license number.

Important Phone Numbers

_____

_____

_____

_____

_____

_____

_____

_____

_____

_____

Figure 8–5 Advice for safeguarding your home.

They may send an officer to your home to offer advice. You may also wish to have a policeman speak on home protection at a neighborhood meeting. He can provide excellent precautions that apply to your specific locality. The meeting will also afford you an opportunity to ask questions (see Figure 8–5).

If you show an interest in the police, they will be more alert to your problems. Cooperation is a two-way street. You may find it helpful to ask them to patrol your area more frequently. In addition to the city protection, your locality may have its own police force. If so, contact this group.

Always call the police when you see any suspicious person, strange vehicle, or unusual action in your neighborhood.

NEIGHBORS

It helps to be friendly with your neighbors. Get to know them and work out some means of mutual cooperation. If you are away, they can look after your property. You can be helpful to them by reporting to the police any suspicious person on their property.

Much more can be accomplished by working as a team than by individual effort. You may find it desirable to organize a group of homeowners to patrol the neighborhood. You may feel a need to hire a private organization to handle the problem. To be effective, any type of arrangement should be worked out with the support and agreement of most neighborhood families.

DOGS

A good dog can be a valuable means of protection; a fierce bark can scare off intruders and will alert members of the family to call the police or turn on the alarm system. For information about a trained watchdog, contact the canine division of your police department. (The police train dogs only for their own use or for other police departments; call a private guard agency if you are interested in buying a trained watchdog.) These animals cost from $150 to $300.

There is the risk, however, that a watchdog may turn on a member of the family. We had a friend who owned a boxer that was extremely loyal to one of his daughters. For some reason, it attacked him one day, tearing a gash in his leg and taking off part of his finger. Fortunately, the daughter drove up at the same moment and called off the dog. If she hadn't arrived, his life would have been in danger.

Dogs can be quite expensive. The initial cost and maintenance for a small size pedigreed in our community is as follows:

Initial Cost		*Annual Cost*	
AKC registration	$ 9	Food	$179
License	12	Toys	14
Initial examination	25	Tags	9
Purchase price	250	Visits to veterinarian	85
	$296		$287

A dog requires daily care. If you take a trip, it means placing him in a kennel or leaving him with a neighbor or relative. This eliminates your home protection during your absence.

GUNS

A rifle or pistol can be an effective means of protection if you know how to shoot it accurately and can reach it on a moment's notice. Some homeowners keep a loaded weapon under their pillow or in a nearby table drawer, but this is very risky. A mistake could be fatal. There is an added danger with your children. In order to preclude their playing with weapons you must put them in a safe place and separate ammunition from the guns. These extra safety measures, however, could mean that the guns would be unavailable if needed in a hurry.

If you do decide to buy a weapon, register it with the police. Check with them to see if it is possible to receive instructions on how to use it properly. Pistols, in particular, require considerable training to be an expert shot. Constant practice is required to keep up your expertise. Perhaps there is a local gun club available that you might wish to join. Your weapon should be cleaned periodically so that it functions when needed.

Weapons are very dangerous and can cause more harm than good. I was an army infantry officer for 23 years, and I have had several close calls as a result of guns being "accidentally fired."

OTHER SUGGESTIONS

Staggered hours: Try not to establish a precise pattern for leaving or returning home, so that people watching your residence will find it difficult to make break-in plans. Robbers much prefer to work an unoccupied house where there is less possibility of being identified or engaged in a fight in which they may be caught, injured, or killed.

At-home appearance: You may wish to turn on your stereo, television, or radio before leaving the house. This gives the impression that someone is at home. At all times, give your home an occupied appearance.

Store valuables: Don't keep valuables at home. If you have heirlooms or other expensive items, keep them in your safe-deposit box at the bank.

Photographs: It is helpful to take pictures of your possessions. Keep one set in the safe-deposit box. Be sure to update your photographs as you acquire additional items. Your memory can play tricks, but your camera will provide solid proof.

Escape routes: Devise a plan to leave your home rapidly in the event of a burglary or fire. Consult your fire department for suggested avenues of escape and what to do in case of fire; they will come to your home to recommend fire prevention measures, including proposals for equipment such as fire extinguishers.

Windows secured: You may want to nail or screw your windows shut to make it more difficult for someone to enter. In the event of fire, however, it could make escape difficult—particularly if you have a multiple-story residence. You may want to keep a screwdriver, hammer, or chair handy in the event it is necessary to open the window.

Outdoor lighting: A good outdoor lighting system can be helpful. Lights may be purchased that come on at dusk and go off at dawn. There is one drawback to this system: it illuminates your home and may bring it to the attention of someone who otherwise might have ignored it.

Enclosed fence: A fence can be another barrier to burglars. A fence however can be a hiding place. Once intruders are in the backyard, they can work unobserved. Shrubbery also can be used as a hiding place if it is too profuse.

Wireless equipment: There are radar devices that can alert you to burglars. This equipment is placed in strategic locations, such as by doors and windows. When a person passes within a certain distance, it sounds an alarm. The advantage over a wired alarm system is that the alarm goes off before the house is broken into, but a friend, animal, or a high wind can also trigger the alarm.

In the wireless monitor system, small radio transmitters are placed on windows and doors and tuned to a master control; if an entry is made, the device sounds an alarm and automatically alerts the alarm company's office, which in turn calls the police.

Be alert to tricks: The following story points out the need to watch for trickery that may result in your home being robbed:

> While a lady was walking downtown, she had her purse snatched. The next day she received a telephone call at home.

The person said, "I found your billfold this morning while walking to the office. It has no money in it, but contains your credit cards and driver's license."

The lady was overjoyed and promised a reward for the return of these items. He said, "I don't have a car, but you could meet me downtown at the Namllits Drug Store. I could take a few minutes off from work to be there at 3 o'clock this afternoon." He described himself well so that there would be no question of mistaken identity.

That afternoon the lady went to Namllits' at the appointed hour. She waited 45 minutes but no one showed up. Upon returning home, she found that her home was robbed. On reporting it to the police, she was informed this trick had been pulled the previous week in another section of town.

Other ruses to gain entry include posing as a policeman, FBI agent, repairman, or mailman. A fake accident and request for help may lure you from your home. It pays to be alert.

Burglars read about funerals, wedding ceremonies, and graduations, and note when the occasion will be held. People who announce their vacation plans in the newspaper or elsewhere also provide good information to robbers.

Security checks: Establish a good security-check system. It doesn't pay to install quality devices and not use them. You can buy the best locks, but if you don't keep them secured they serve no purpose. Establish a workable procedure to ensure that your alarm system is turned on and off as required. Place a sign at each exterior door to remind family members to lock it. Make one person responsible to see that all doors and windows are locked before bedtime.

Top secret measures: The security measures you can develop are limited only by your imagination and finances. These items may include hidden cameras, recording machines, peepholes, eavesdropping devices to pick up conversations on your property, phone monitoring, fingerprinting entryways, trip wires, and other booby traps. The more unknowns you have, the more protection you have against a successful burglary.

INSURANCE

It is important to acquire appropriate insurance from a reputable, first-rate company. Your homeowner's policy may provide you with the needed coverage; read it carefully to be sure.

A homeowner's policy insures your home against fire, lightning, wind, hail, and many other perils. Carry the broadest coverage to include "all physical loss."

Comprehensive personal liability (CPL) insurance is included in the homeowner's policy. This coverage provides protection if you or any member of your household are held legally liable for actions resulting in accidental injuries to others or accidental damage to the property of others. Coverage applies to personal and sports activities and is effective both on and away from the premises and inside and outside the residence.

The following are some situations CPL insurance covers:

1. A deliveryman or a guest is injured in your residence.

2. You accidentally injure someone while engaged in golf, hunting, or horseback riding.

3. One of your children injures a playmate with one of his toys.

4. Your pet bites someone.

5. A fire spreads from your property to the property of others.

The special medical-payment clause and the property-damage clause, which form an integral part of the CPL insurance, do not necessarily require legal liability to be effective. The insured's obligation may be moral rather than legal. Payment under these clauses may be authorized by the insurance company without resorting to a court trial.

Be sure to carry flood insurance if you live in one of the over 3,000 American communities in thirty-one states that qualify with the U.S. Department of Housing and Urban Development. People in these areas may purchase insurance at federally subsidized premium rates. Rates vary with location, so be sure to check for costs with your insurance agent.

The National Flood Insurance Act of 1968 states that "anyone who does not choose to buy flood insurance in a community which is eligible will not be able to get federal financial disaster aid for flood losses that occur after one year from the date his community became eligible to the extent that the loss would have been covered by flood insurance."

Rising costs make it important for you to make annual reappraisals to be sure that you have adequate protection in the event of fire, burglary, or other loss.

SECURITY DURING CONSTRUCTION

Take out appropriate insurance during the construction of your home. If someone is working directly for you, then have coverage in the event of his injury. Also make certain that your subcontractors are properly insured. The following measures can be taken to keep losses at a minimum while building your home:

1. Enclose your garage promptly so that it can serve as a storage area for tools and other materials.

2. Build your home rapidly. The less idle time the better.

3. Order only the amount of supplies needed to accomplish the immediate jobs.

4. Ask your neighbors to keep an eye on the premises.

5. Pay for protection. In one area, much of the vandalism was done by youngsters living in the neighborhood. They turned over paint cans and wrote obscene words on doors and walls. Windows were broken, pipes bent, and materials taken. To combat this theft, a builder asked one of the young toughs to "protect" his property.

A house under construction is a fascinating place for children and draws them like a magnet. You can expect some damage unless there is twenty-four-hour supervision. Some builders hire night watchmen, who come on duty when the subcontractors leave each evening. Losses from vandalism are so great that it is sometimes cheaper to have a person protect construction sites on a continuing basis.

6. Make surprise visits during the weekend and evening hours.

7. Enclose your house as soon as possible. Before installing your permanent doors, your carpenter can nail up plywood sheets each evening.

8. Watch tools. It is important to alert workmen to protect their tools while they are on the job. In some locations, carpenters cannot leave their hammers or saws unguarded for a moment.

A FINAL NOTE

With an alarm system, iron doors and window guards, electronic devices, special locks, watchdogs, elaborate lighting systems, and an arsenal of weapons, you can turn your house into a fortress. But is this the way you want to live? Keep in mind that if someone really wants to enter, he will. No fortress in history has proved to be invulnerable.

On the other hand, you need enough protection to give you a sense of security and peace of mind. This may require enough equipment to discourage an intruder and make him decide it would be easier to go elsewhere.

Remember that security is only as good as you make it. If you fail to lock your doors, turn on your alarm system, or utilize your other security measures, these measures are a wasted expense.

SUMMARY

Determine your security requirements during the planning phase of building your home. You can then allocate a specific amount of money for protective devices that will be within your budget. If you wait, installation costs will be higher, interest charges will be greater, and you will not have protection when you first move in.

A variety of protective measures can be taken. Some, like alarm systems and steel doors, are expensive. Others can be taken for little or no cost. These include neighborhood assistance programs, working with the police, marking valuable items, installing locks yourself, and taking thorough security precautions.

Chapter Nine
How to Keep Your Cool
While Moving

Once your home is available for occupancy, plan to move in as quickly as possible. The slightest delay increases the chance of vandalism, results in extra expenses for living costs, and makes it impossible to check the workmanship and equipment on a twenty-four-hour basis.

With adequate planning, you can make this move into your new home efficiently and economically. The fact that you are subcontracting gives you good control over the completion date and ample time to prepare for a successful move. Your PERT chart and timetable will enable you to determine when the house will be ready, and you can make definite arrangements with the moving company of your choice. The move should be taken into consideration during the planning phase of your home.

If you have made previous moves you no doubt have discovered that each new change of location makes the task of packing, transporting, and unpacking your possessions more difficult. The accumulation of possessions can become a mountainous problem with the passing of time. The best advice is: "If in doubt, pitch it out."

Our numerous moving experiences in the military and academic worlds have varied from outstanding to disastrous. We sometimes relocated only across the street, and sometimes 10,000 miles. Twice we placed our possessions in storage and once we physically moved it all ourselves. Major carriers, government trucks, local carriers, and our family car have all been used at various times.

Good management is of utmost importance. The closer the supervision, the better the move. There is no substitute for personal interest, but this requires a good deal of hard work on your part. For example, when we moved across the street while living in Arlington, Virginia, we had no loss whatsoever, and our expenses were zero. To move 8,000 pounds took three of us two full days, and we had help from several neighbors. But in longer moves where we were unable to adequately supervise the packing, loading, and storage, we had poor results.

MANAGEMENT PROCESS

The management process can be applied successfully to your next move. Let us list each aspect of this process and then discuss them as they pertain to moving.

1. Determine your objective.
2. Plan your move with care.
3. Implement your plan.
4. Check to see if the move is accomplished without damage and within the agreed price.
5. As the "move" manager, make sound decisions by defining your objective; wisely utilizing your resources (personnel, money, materials); and performing the functions of planning, organizing, and controlling within the framework of an effective organization.

OBJECTIVE

Suppose you decide your objective is to move your household goods from city X to city Y upon completion of your home, hiring a major van line to accomplish the shipment economically and efficiently.

As you note, the objective provides answers to the questions of what, when, where, how, and why. Keep in mind that the move objective must be viewed as a subobjective of the entire building project.

PLANNING YOUR MOVE

Adequate planning is absolutely essential for a successful move. Here are some points to consider.

REDUCE HOUSEHOLD POSSESSIONS

During the planning and building of your new home, make periodic examinations of your household possessions and be ruthless in discarding items you may someday use but that you know you never will. Those that have value can be disposed of by advertisement, garage sale, or through a thrift shop. The Salvation Army and Goodwill Industries are delighted to receive a call and will pick up your items. (Contributions to organizations like the Salvation Army and Goodwill are tax deductible.)

Keeping your household possessions to a minimum can reduce your shipping costs markedly and save considerable time and effort on your part in preparing for the move and rearranging everything in your new home.

Consider selling your furnishings at your present location, taking only valuable items with you. Offering to sell your home with the drapes, rugs, basic furniture, and major appliances can be a more attractive deal to some people. If you live in an apartment or rent a house, it may be possible for you to sell the furnishings. Many people like the idea of taking over a tastefully furnished residence and moving in with no concern about decorating.

Reducing your household possessions will enable you to start fresh in your new home. Perhaps the old furnishings will not do justice to the new surroundings. Consider your options, including the cost of buying new furniture. If you decide to purchase new furniture, find out if the lending agency will include it in your mortgage.

SELECT THE BEST METHOD

Use a moving company that has an excellent reputation. This can be checked by asking neighbors and friends who recently used the services of a mover. If possible, obtain estimates of costs from three competent firms for comparison. If you plan to store some of your household goods, visit the warehouse. Consider the alternative of hiring a van and doing the packing and moving yourself. This can be a major undertaking, but for intracity moves or short hauls it can be accomplished at savings in money, time, and breakage.

PROVIDE ADEQUATE FUNDS

In determining your budget requirements, be sure to allow yourself adequate move-in funds—both moving costs (storage and moving) as well as expenses for new furnishings and appliances required when you first enter your new home. If you have to spend time en route, also make an allowance for your own family travel expenses.

There are companies who pay for your entire move and will also guarantee that you do not take a loss in selling your old home. It is

Mayflower

ESTIMATED COST OF SERVICES

REFER TO THIS NUMBER IN ALL COMMUNICATIONS

Order for Service No. ______

NAME OF CARRIER **AERO MAYFLOWER TRANSIT COMPANY, INC.**

ADDRESS OF CARRIER **P.O. Box 107, Indianapolis, Indiana 46206 (317) 639-2451** DATE ______ 19___

NAME OF SHIPPER ______ ADDRESS ______ PHONE ______

SHIPMENT MOVING FROM ______ TO ______

SHIPPER'S DESTINATION CONTACT ______ PHONE ______

PACKING DATE OR PERIOD OF TIME REQUESTED ______

LOADING DATE OR PERIOD OF TIME REQUESTED ______

DELIVERY DATE OR PERIOD OF TIME REQUESTED ______

IMPORTANT NOTICE: This estimate covers only the articles and services listed. It is not a guarantee that the actual charges will not exceed the amount of the estimate. Common carriers are required by law to collect transportation and other incidental charges computed on the basis of rates shown in their lawfully published tariffs, regardless of prior rate quotations or estimates made by the carrier or its agents. Exact charges for loading, transporting, and unloading are based upon the weight of the goods transported, and such charges may not be determined prior to the time the goods are loaded on the van and weighed. Charges for additional services will be added to the transportation charges.

TOTAL ESTIMATED COST $______

I HEREBY ACKNOWLEDGE that I have received from (check one)

______the carrier supplying this estimate

______a carrier supplying another estimate

______other source

Summary of Information for Shippers of Household Goods, Form BOp 103

______
Signature of Shipper or his Representative

If the total tariff charges for the listed articles and services exceed this estimate by more than ten percent, then, upon your request, the carrier must relinquish possession of your shipment upon delivery in advance of the payment of the total amount of tariff charges shown on the bill of lading or freight bill. You are still obligated to pay the balance of the total charges within 15 days. Maximum amount to be paid on delivery of your C.O.D. shipment in cash, certified check or money order is (total estimated cost plus 10 percent):

$______

ESTIMATED COST OF SERVICE (Based on tariff______ MF-I.C.C. NO.______) — ESTIMATED CHARGES

Transportation: Est. wt.______lbs.; ______mi.; @ $______per 100 lbs. $______

Valuation Charge {for liability on part of carrier in excess of that assumed when its lowest rates are charged}

On Transportation: $______ @ 50¢ per $100, or fraction thereof ______

On Storage-in-Transit @ ______¢ per cwt. (10% of monthly storage rate) for each 30 days or fraction thereof ______

Additional transportation charges: (Explain)______ ______

Pickup or delivery for storage in transit ______lbs. @ ______¢ per 100 lbs. ______

Storage in transit at ______lbs. @ ______¢ per 100 lbs. {for each 30 days or fraction thereof} ______

Warehouse handling ______lbs. @ ______¢ per 100 lbs.(one time charge) ______

Extra pickup or delivery at______ ______

Special servicing of appliances______ ______

Hoisting, lowering, or carrying pianos, heavy articles______ (Explain) ______

CONTAINERS (see below)______ ______

Packing (see below)______ ______

Unpacking (see below)______ ______

Labor______man/men for______hrs.; @ ______ (per man per hour) ______

Other services ______ (Explain) ______

COST ESTIMATE ☐ WAS ☐ WAS NOT GIVEN TO SHIPPER

TOTAL ESTIMATED COST: $______

ESTIMATED COST OF CONTAINERS, AND PACKING AND UNPACKING SERVICES	CONTAINERS			PACKING			UNPACKING		
	Estimated Number	Per Each	TOTAL	Estimated Number	Per Each	TOTAL	Estimated Number	Per Each	TOTAL
BARREL, dish-pack, drum, etc.		$	$		$	$		$	$
BOXES, not over 5 cubic feet									
Over 5 not over 8 cubic feet									
CARTONS: Less Than 1½ cubic feet									
1½ cubic feet									
3 cubic feet									
4½ cubic feet									
6 cubic feet									
6½ cubic feet									
Wardrobe Carton									
Crib Mattress Carton									
Mattress Carton, Regular (Not exceeding 54"x75")									
Mattress Carton, King Size (Exceeding 54"x75")									
Mattress Cover (plastic or paper)									
CRATES AND CONTAINERS: (Specially designed for mirrors, paintings, glass or marble tops and similar fragile articles) Gross measurement of crate or container									
	Estimated Container	COSTS	$	Estimated Packing	COSTS	$	Estimated Unpacking	COSTS	$

Remarks______

NOTICE: It is mandatory that the total cubic footage shown on the table of measurements be multiplied by not less than 7 to determine the total estimated weight. Articles not to be shipped should be indicated by a "check mark" in the column provided on the table of measurements.

If the prospective shipper has not previously been furnished with the Summary of Information For Shippers of Household Goods as required by the Interstate Commerce Commission, he should be furnished at this time. (Table of measurements on reverse side)

______ AGENCY ______ SIGNATURE AND TITLE OF ESTIMATOR

Figure 9–1 Sample form for estimating cost of services. Courtesy of Aero Mayflower Transit Company, Inc.

TABLE OF MEASUREMENTS

ARTICLE A B C	ARTICLE	CUFT PER PIECE	NO. OF PIECES	CUBIC FEET	ARTICLE A B C	ARTICLE	CUFT PER PIECE	NO. OF PIECES	CUBIC FEET	ARTICLE A B C	ARTICLE	CUFT PER PIECE	NO. OF PIECES	CUBIC FEET	ARTICLE A B C	ARTICLE	CUFT PER PIECE	NO. OF PIECES	CUBIC FEET
	LIVING AND FAMILY ROOMS					**BEDROOM**					**PORCH, OUTDOOR FUR- NITURE & EQUIPMENT**					**OTHER ITEMS**			
	Bar, Portable	15				Chair, Boudoir	10				Chairs, Porch	10							
	Bench, Fireside or Piano	5				Chair, Straight or Rocker	5				Clothes Line	5							
	Bookcase	20				Chaise Lounge	25				Clothes Dryer Rack	5							
	Bookshelves, Sectional	5				Desk, Small or Winthrop	22				Garden Hose and Tools	10							
	Chair, Arm	10				Dresser or Vanity Bench	3				Glider or Settee	20							
	Chair, Occasional	15				Dresser Doub. (Mr. Mrs.)	50				Ladder, Extension	10							
	Chair, Overstuffed	25				Night Table	5				Lawn Mower (Hand)	5							
	Chair, Rocker	12				Rug, Large or Pad	10				Lawn Mower (Power)	15							
	Chair, Straight	5				Rug, Small or Pad	3				Lawn Mower (Riding)	35							
	Clock, Grandfather	20				Vanity Dresser	20				Leaf Sweeper	5							
	Day Bed	30				Wardrobe, Small	20				Outdoor Child's Slide	10							
	Desk, Small or Winthrop	22				Wardrobe, Large	40				Outdoor Child's Gym	20							
	Desk, Secretary	35										Outdoor Drying Racks	5							
	Fireplace Equipment	5										Outdoor Swings	30							
	Foot Stool	2				**NURSERY**						Picnic Table	20							
	Lamp, Floor or Pole	3				Bathinette	5				Picnic Bench	5							
	Magazine Rack	2				Bed, Youth	30				Porch Chair	10							
	Music Cabinet	10				Chair, Child's	3				Rocker, Swing	15							
	Piano, Baby, Gr. or Upr.	70				Chair, High	5				Roller, Lawn	15							
	Piano, Parlor Grand	80				Chest	12				Rug, Large	7							
	Piano, Spinet	60				Chest, Toy	5				Rug, Small	3							
	Radio, Table	2				Crib, Baby	10				Sand Box	10				**CONTAINERS**			
	Record Player Port.	2				Table, Child's	5				Settee	20				(To Be Packed by Shipper)			
	Rugs, Large Roll or Pad	10				Pen, Play	10				Spreader	1				Barrels	10		
	Rugs, Small Roll or Pad	3				Rug, Large or Pad	10				Table	10				Boxes, Wooden	3		
	Sofa, 2 Cushions	35				Rug, Small or Pad	3				Umbrella	5				Boxes, Wooden	5		
	Sofa, 3 Cushions	50				**KITCHEN**						Wheel Barrow	6				Boxes, Wooden	10		
	Sofa, 4 Cushions	60				Breakfast, Suite Chairs	5									Boxes, Wooden	15		
	Sofa, Sect., per Sect.	30				Breakfast Table	10									Boxes, Wooden	20		
	Stud, Couch or Hideabed	50				Chair, High	5									Carton			
	Tables, Drop'f or Occas.	12				Ironing Board	2				**MISCELLANEOUS**					Less than 1½ cu. ft.			
	Tables, Coffee, End/Nest	5				Kitchen Cabinet	30				Ash or Trash Can	7				1½ cu. ft.			
	Telephone Stand & Chair	5				Roaster	5				Basket (Clothes)	5				3 cu. ft.			
	Television Combination	25				Serving Cart	15				Bicycle	10				4½ cu. ft.			
	TV. or Radio Console	15				Stool	3				Bird Cage & Stand	5				6 cu. ft.			
	Television Table Model	10				Table	5				Card Table	1				6½ cu. ft.			
						Utility Cabinet	10				Cabinet, Filing	20				Wardrobe Furnished			
						Vegetable Bin	3				Carriage, Baby	20				by Carrier	15		
	DINING ROOM										Chairs, Folding	1				**CONTAINERS**			
	Bench, Harvest	10				**APPLIANCES (Large)**					Clothes, Hamper	5				(To Be Packed by Carrier)			
	Buffet	30				Air Conditioner, Window	30				Cot, Folding	10				Barrels	10		
	Cabinet, Corner	20				Dehumidifier	10				Desk, Office	30				Boxes, Wooden	3		
	Cabinet, China	25				Dishwasher	20				Fan	5				Boxes, Wooden	5		
	Chair, Dining	5				Dryer, Electric or Gas	25				Fernery or Plant Stands	10				Boxes, Wooden	10		
	Server	15				Freezer: (Cu. Capacity)					Foot Lockers	5				Boxes, Wooden	15		
	Table, Dining	30				10 or less	30				Garbage Cans	7				Boxes, Wooden	20		
	Tea Cart	10				11 to 15	45				Golf Bag	2				Carton			
	Rugs, Large or Pad	10				16 and over	60				Heater, Gas or Electric	5				Less than 1½ cu. ft.			
	Rugs, Small or Pad	3				Ironer or Mangle	12				Incinerator	10				1½ cu. ft.			
						Range, Electric or Gas	30				Metal Shelves	5				3 cu. ft.			
						Refrigerator (Cu. Capacity)					Ping Pong Table	20				4½ cu. ft.			
						6 cu. ft. or less	30				Pool Table	40				6 cu. ft.			
	BEDROOM					7 to 10 cu. ft.	45				Power Tools	20				6½ cu. ft.			
	Bed, incl. Spring & Mattr.					11 cu. ft. and over	60				Sled	2				Wardrobe Furnished			
	Bed, Double	60				Vacuum Cleaner	5				Step Ladder	5				by Carrier	15		
	Bed, King Size	70				Washing Machine	25				Suitcase	5				**SUB. TOTAL COLUMN 4**			
	Bed, Single or Hollywood	40										Table, Utility	5				**TOTAL COL. 1**			
	Bed, Rollaway	20										Tackle Box	5				**TOTAL COL. 2**			
	Bed, Bunk (set of 2)	70				**PORCH, OUTDOOR FUR- NITURE & EQUIPMENT**					Tool Chest	10				**TOTAL COL. 3**			
	Bookshelves, Sectional	5				Barbecue or Port. Grill	10				Tricycle	5				**TOTAL COL. 4**			
	Bureau, Dresser, Chest of					Bath, Bird	5				Vacuum Cleaner	5							
	Dr'w'rs, Chifrb. or Chifnr.	25				Chairs, Lawn	5				Wagon, Child's	5				**GRAND TOTAL**			
	Cedar Chest	15										Waste Paper Basket	2							
	SUB. TOTAL COLUMN 1					**SUB. TOTAL COLUMN 2**					Work Bench	20							
											Sewing Mach. Portable	5							
											Sewing Mach. Cabinet	10							
											SUB. TOTAL COLUMN 3								

SUMMARY

_____ CU. FT. @ _____ LBS. PER CU. FT. _____ LBS.

ESTIMATED TOTAL WEIGHT _____ LBS.

CODES: A — ARTICLES LOADED B — ARTICLES UN-LOADED C — ARTICLES NOT TO BE SHIPPED

Form R-42 (Rev. 7/72)   (Estimated Cost of Services on Reverse Side)

Figure 9–2 Sample form for estimating cost of services. Courtesy of Aero May-flower Transit Company, Inc.

great if you have this good fortune, but your move can still be more agreeable if you follow sound management concepts.

ESTIMATE MOVING EXPENSES

You should be able to estimate your moving costs with reasonable accuracy. Each carrier you contact will send an estimator to your home to make an estimate of the total charge involved. Be sure to show him everything you plan to send by van so his bid will be accurate, and tell him what extra furnishings you may purchase prior to moving. Well in advance of your move, obtain a copy of the "Estimated Cost of Services." Note in Figure 9–1 the various services that determine the cost of a move: transportation; valuation charge; pickup and delivery for storage in transit; storage in transit; warehouse handling; special servicing of appliances; hoisting, lowering, or carrying pianos and heavy articles; packing and unpacking services; and purchase of barrels, boxes, cartons, mattress covers, crates, and containers.

After studying the table of measurements (Figure 9–2), you may wish to come up with your own estimated total weight. Such an undertaking serves as a check on the estimator and may encourage you to eliminate some of your possessions by sale, donation, and the trash pile.

STORAGE CONSIDERATIONS

If it is necessary to put your furniture in storage, carefully check the warehouse you use. Find out exactly where your furniture will be placed, and if possible, look at it in storage prior to your departure.

You can make storage arrangements with a local warehouse or a major carrier. If you have an agreement with an interstate van line, the terms and conditions of your contract apply to the storage as well as the move. If you use a local warehouse, the terms are whatever you arrange with that firm.

The carrier usually sets a time limit on this temporary storage of no more than 180 days; after that date, it goes into permanent storage, and the warehouse rules apply. This is another reason for completing your home promptly. The longer your possessions remain in storage, the greater the risk of damage or loss.

RECORD POSSESSIONS

Keep an up-to-date record of your possessions. This should include the original cost, year purchased, and the estimate of present value. If losses are sustained, you will then have appropriate evidence to support your claim. Most large moving companies can supply forms for this purpose. See Figure 9–3 for an example of an inventory of household furnishings and personal property.

SUMMARY OF CONTENTS VALUES

Classification	Present Value
Living Room	
Dining Room	
Library or Den	
Bedrooms	
Recreation Room	
Bathrooms	
Musical Instruments	
Furs	
Kitchen, Pantry, Etc.	
Laundry	
Table and Bed Linens	
Porch and Lawn	
Garage and Miscellaneous	
Nursery	
Basement or Utility Room	
Clothing	
Personal Belongings	
Jewelry	
Silverware	
TOTAL	

Name_____

YOUR PERSONAL

Inventory

of

HOUSEHOLD FURNISHINGS
AND PERSONAL PROPERTY

Date_____

In order to protect your household goods sufficiently under the Mayflower Comprehensive Protection Plan, when you move long-distance, it is necessary to know their value accurately. Even though you are not moving long-distance, and therefore do not require this Plan, it is still vitally important for you to have a record of your possessions and their value. It is the only way you can know what insurance coverage you need, and the best way to establish claims in case of loss. We hope this form will be helpful in compiling this record.

AERO MAYFLOWER TRANSIT COMPANY, INC.
INDIANAPOLIS, INDIANA

F-27   LITHO IN U. S. A.

Figure 9–3 Inventory of household furnishings and personal property. Courtesy of Aero Mayflower Transit Company, Inc.

LIVING ROOM

Article	How Many	Year Bought	Cost	Present Value
rs				
es				
nport				
et				
ps				
res				
ors				
o				
an				
o				
k				
ains				
eries				
olace Fittings				
es				
et				
rd Player				
ords				
Conditioner				
AL				

DINING ROOM

Article	How Many	Year Bought	Cost	Present Value
le				
irs				
na Cabinet				
fet				
ver				
Cart				
gs				
pet and Pad				
tains				
peries				
tures				
rors				
ner Sets				
na				
ssware				
TAL				

LIBRARY OR DEN

Article	How Many	Year Bought	Cost	Present Value
Chairs				
Tables				
Desks				
Davenport				
Rugs				
Carpet				
Lamps				
Pictures				
Radio				
Record Player				
Mirrors				
Clock				
Bookcases				
Books				
Curtains				
Draperies				
TV Set				
Typewriter				
Files				
TOTAL				

BEDROOMS

Article	How Many	Year Bought	Cost	Present Value
Beds and Springs				
Mattresses				
Chest				
Chairs				
Vanity				
Dressing Tables				
Clocks				
Rugs				
Carpets				
Lamps				
Pictures				
Bedside Tables				
Toilet Sets				
Curtains				
Draperies				
Sewing Stands				
Cedar Chest				
Radios				
TV Sets				
TOTAL				

RECREATION ROOM

Article	How Many	Year Bought	Cost	Present Value
Chairs				
Tables				
Rugs				
Pictures				
Billiard Table				
Ping Pong Table				
Card Tables				
Curtains				
Books				
Radio				
Lamps				
TV Set				
Bar				
Hi-Fi				
Games				
TOTAL				

KITCHEN, PANTRY, ETC.

Article	How Many	Year Bought	Cost	Pr V
Refrigerator				
Stove				
Deep Freeze				
Kitchen Cabinet				
Floor Covering				
Curtains				
Chairs				
Tables				
Utensils				
Dishes				
Supplies				
Radios				
Dishwasher				
TOTAL				

BATHROOMS

Article	How Many	Year Bought	Cost	Present Value
Cabinet				
Chairs				
Scales				
Clothes Hamper				
Heaters				
TOTAL				

LAUNDRY

Article	How Many	Year Bought	Cost	Pr V
Washer				
Ironer				
Tables				
Chairs				
Electric Irons				
Dryer				
Dehumidifier				
TOTAL				

MUSICAL INSTRUMENTS

Article	How Many	Year Bought	Cost	Present Value
Violin				
Mandolin				
Banjo				
TOTAL				

TABLE AND BED LINENS

Article	How Many	Year Bought	Cost	Pr V
Sheets				
Pillow Cases				
Blankets				
Spreads				
Table Cloths				
Napkins				
Luncheon Sets				
Towels				
Wash Cloths				
Bath Mats				
TOTAL				

FURS

Article	How Many	Year Bought	Cost	Present Value
Coats and Capes				
Neckpieces				
TOTAL				

Figure 9–3 (Continued)

PORCH AND LAWN

Article	How Many	Year Bought	Cost	Present Value
s				
s				
h				
ins				
r				
g				
Set				
serie				
L				

GARAGE AND MISCELLANEOUS

Article	How Many	Year Bought	Cost	Present Value
les				
Mower				
en Tools				
en Hose				
um Sweeper				
ng Machine				
d Tools				
L				

NURSERY

Article	How Many	Year Bought	Cost	Present Value
s				
Covering				
t				
L				

BASEMENT OR UTILITY ROOM

Article	How Many	Year Bought	Cost	Present Value
Bench				
d Tools				
er Tools				
inery				
ed Goods				
L				

CLOTHING

Article	How Many	Year Bought	Cost	Present Value
Men's Suits				
Men's Coats				
Women's Dresses				
Women's Coats				
Children's				
Hats				
Shoes & Boots				
TOTAL				

PERSONAL BELONGINGS

Article	How Many	Year Bought	Cost	Present Value
Golf Equipment				
Tennis Rackets				
Stamp, Coin Collec.				
Fishing Tackle				
Guns				
Luggage				
TOTAL				

JEWELRY

Article	How Many	Year Bought	Cost	Present Value
Watches				
Rings				
Necklaces				
Bracelets				
Brooches				
TOTAL				

SILVERWARE

Article	How Many	Year Bought	Cost	Present Value
Tea Set				
Trays				
Knives				
Forks				
Spoons				
Holloware				
TOTAL				

MOVING CHECKLIST

☐ Change address, get records, trip arrangements.

☐ Collect and sort mail for listing address changes.

☐ Notify post office of move and fill out change of address cards.

☐ Send address change to friends and businesses.

☐ Get all medical and dental records.

☐ Check and clear tax assessments.

☐ Have your W-2s and other tax forms forwarded.

☐ Transfer insurance records, check auto licensing requirements.

☐ Notify school and make arrangements for sending transcripts of school records to new school.

☐ Have letters of introduction written.

☐ Arrange for transfer of jewelry and important documents.

☐ Close charge accounts.

☐ Arrange shipment of pets and any immunization records.

☐ Make travel plans.

☐ Get hotel reservations and make note to reconfirm.

14 Days Before Your Move

☐ Collect all clothing or items to be cleaned or repaired.

☐ Return things borrowed, collect things lent.

☐ Have bank transfer accounts and release safe deposit box.

☐ Arrange to disconnect utility services.

☐ Arrange to connect utility service at new home.

☐ Have farewell parties and visits.

☐ Make arrangements to have heavy appliances serviced for move.

☐ Give away articles you don't plan to take along, give to charitable organizations, get signed receipt for tax purposes.

7 Days Before Your Move

☐ Dispose of all flammables.

☐ Have car inspected and serviced.

☐ Pack suitcases ahead of time.

☐ Select traveling games.

☐ Set things aside to pack in car.

☐ If you haven't made arrangements with your mover to do so, take down curtains, rods, shelves, television antenna if agreement with new owner authorizes this.

☐ Start packing suitcases you can live out of, if necessary, for the first day in your new home.

☐ Line up a baby-sitter for moving day so you can look after moving.

☐ In a special carton, place items you will need in the first few hours in your new home: soap, towels, coffee, cooking pot, etc. Mark this carton with sticker "Load Last—Unload First!"

USE A CHECKLIST

Give consideration to taking actions as indicated in the "Moving Checklist" at both your present and new address. Well in advance of your move, study this checklist with care. There are some excellent suggestions, and you may wish to act on them before and during your move. Without some effective reminder, it is easy to forget something important in the busy days before your departure.

☐ Make up special cartons with "Do not move" for articles to be taken in car.

Day Before Moving

☐ Empty and defrost your refrigerator and freezer and let them air at least 24 hours. Also clean and air your range.
☐ Line up a simple breakfast for next morning that won't require refrigeration or much cooking. Use paper plates.
☐ Finish packing personal belongings, but leave out the alarm clock!
☐ Get a good night's rest.

Moving Day

☐ Be on hand the day of your move, or have someone there authorized to answer questions.
☐ Accompany the van operator while he inventories your possessions to be moved.
☐ Make last-minute check on your appliances to see that they have been serviced.
☐ Sign (and save your copy of) bills of lading and make sure delivery address and place to locate you enroute are correct.
☐ Advise driver exactly how to get to new residence.
☐ Ask that you be advised of final cost. (This will be determined after van is weighed.) Then, if you have not arranged for time payments, make sure you'll have the needed cash, money order, or certified check to pay before van is unloaded at destination (carriers require payment before unloading).
☐ Strip your beds, but leave fitted bottom sheets on your mattresses.
☐ Before leaving house, check each room and closet, make sure windows are down and lights out.

Moving-in Tips

☐ Upon arrival at new location, call the moving agent immediately to leave address and phone number where you can be reached and when so you can make final arrangements for delivery.
☐ Be on hand at unloading and have a plan for placement of your furniture.
☐ Check all electrical fuses. Pennies may have been used as substitutes!
☐ Check the condition of your belongings. If any items are missed or damaged, note this on your inventory sheet and shipping papers; then report such information to your moving agent, who will take care of it for you.
☐ If your utilities haven't been connected, call them for this service, and have them check your appliances for proper operation.

(*Source: Moving Kit,* Copyright 1970, Aero Mayflower Transit Company, Inc.)

CARRY VALUABLES

If possible, take your valuable possessions and heirlooms with you. Be sure to have appropriate insurance. Some people also carry bedding rolls, kitchen utensils, and other necessary items in their car so if the shipment arrives late they will have adequate furnishings to sleep in their home.

HAVE ADEQUATE LOSS PROTECTION

How much protection should you have on your shipment? If you decide not to have additional protection for your household possessions, you will only be paid at a rate of 60 cents per pound per article in the event of damage. If the ten-speed bicycle weighing 25 pounds that you bought for $350 just before you moved was totally damaged during shipment, you would receive $16 and suffer a loss of $334. You can, however, pay an extra amount of money for greater protection. You have two choices: determine the value of your entire shipment or not set a valuation, in which case the mover's maximum liability is automatically $1.25 times the weight of your shipment in pounds. If the net weight totals 5,000 pounds, then you would receive $6,250 in the event of a total loss.

The bill of lading reads as follows:

> Unless the shipper expressly releases the shipment to a value of 60 cents per pound per article, the carrier's maximum liability for loss and damage shall be either the lump sum value declared by the shipper or an amount equal to $1.25 for each pound of weight in the shipment, whichever is greater. The shipment will move subject to the rules and conditions of the carrier's tariff. Shipper hereby releases the entire shipment to a value not exceeding
>
> _____
> (to be completed by the person signing below)
>
> NOTICE: The shipper signing this Request For Service must insert in the space above, in his own handwriting, either his declaration of the actual value of the shipment, or the words "60 cents per pound per article." Otherwise, the shipment will be deemed released to a maximum value equal to $1.25 times the weight of the shipment in pounds.

If your merchandise is lost en route, you receive a cash payment based on the protection you selected. If there is damage, the carrier has the choice of either restoring the article to the same condition when it was taken from your home or paying you the actual value less depreciation.

Keep in mind that your coverage is not called insurance and the Interstate Commerce Commission actually prevents movers from selling insurance. The ICC calls your protection a matter that affects "the liability of the mover for loss or damage to your goods."

READ THE ICC PAMPHLET

The Interstate Commerce Commission (ICC) has prepared a pamphlet entitled "Summary of Information for Shippers of Household Goods."

Every prospective shipper should receive a copy. Although the ICC has made it mandatory for all carriers to provide their customers with copies, an ICC study indicates that about one out of five families who shipped their household goods did not receive a copy.

This booklet lists the following dos and don'ts. Read its entire contents well in advance of your move:

Do

Read this information booklet *entirely*.

Select your household-goods mover with care.

Be sure that agreements between you and the carrier are in writing and on the order for service and the bill of lading.

Examine and make sure that physical inventory record of your household goods is accurate regarding the number of items, condition of furniture, and so on.

Make sure you understand the limited liability of the household-goods carrier.

Schedule your departure and arrival with enough flexibility to allow for possible failure on the part of the carrier to meet his scheduled time exactly.

If you can, accompany your carrier to the weighing station for weighing shipment.

Advise the carrier of a telephone number and/or address where you can be reached en route or at destination.

Request a reweigh of your household goods if you have any reason to believe the weighing is not accurate.

Be certain that everything on the inventory is accounted for *before* the van operator leaves either origin or destination.

File a claim for any loss or damage noted on the delivery papers as soon as possible.

Don't

Believe an estimate is a final cost of your move.

Expect the carrier to provide boxes, cartons, barrels, or other packing materials free of charge.

Expect maid service and appliance service free of charge.

Plan to leave your old residence until the moving company leaves, unless you have a friend or neighbor acting on your behalf.

Fail to make arrangements to have in cash or certified check the maximum amount shown on the order for service unless credit has been arranged for in advance.

Expect your household goods to be unloaded until you have paid at least the maximum amount shown on the order for service

in cash or certified check unless credit has been arranged for
in advance.

Sign any receipt for your household goods until you are certain
that they are all delivered and that any damage has been noted
on the shipping papers.

The ICC has eighty-two offices in major cities throughout the
United States. Each office employs at least two people who are available
to answer your questions and provide other assistance.

IMPLEMENTING YOUR MOVE PLAN

ARRANGE FOR THEIR ARRIVAL

During the packing and moving phase, it is important for you or a member of your family to be present. Plan for the packers' arrival. Have
your household possessions neatly arranged and provide adequate working space for the workers. Items to be packed should be clean and readily available.

Observe the packers' work carefully. You can learn much from
professionals on how best to protect your china and crystal for a safe
move. The next time you may decide to do it yourself.

You may wish to code your containers. Having them clearly
marked will help you place them in the correct room at your new home.
If any breakage occurs while your items are being packed, make a no-
tation on the bill of lading. If the packers indicate that your furniture is
gouged, scratched, or otherwise damaged, and you disagree, state your
disagreement in writing. This written statement will be essential when
submitting your claim.

INSPECT WITH CARE

When the movers start taking furnishings from your residence, you
should have a system of checking each item that is placed in the van.
This check also gives you an opportunity to see if other furnishings are
already aboard. Unless you are able to fill a van, it will normally take
on other household possessions en route in order to have a full load.
This may delay your shipment.

Your personal supervision will normally result in movers taking
greater care. It won't take long to judge if you have a good crew. If
they are sloppy and hurry the job, inform the leader. If it continues,
contact the local office immediately to send a responsible supervisor.

WEIGH YOUR POSSESSIONS

You should receive a bill of lading before the moving van leaves. This is your receipt for your household possessions and will indicate the weight of the van prior to placing your merchandise on it (tare weight). You may wish to follow the van to the weighing station to determine the weight of your load. The weight with your possessions on the van is called the gross weight. Your charge is arrived at by subtracting the tare weight from the gross weight (net weight). Once the net weight has been established, you can call the carrier's local office and obtain the transportation cost of your shipment.

If you have any concern about the accuracy of the weight of your household possessions, you can request that they be weighed again before they're unloaded. In the event there is no marked difference in the weights, you will be required to pay a reasonable charge for the second weighing.

CHECKING ON YOUR MOVE

UNLOADING INSPECTION

The control aspect of your move occurs when the truck arrives and you have the opportunity to check each item. Take time to inspect your possessions with care.

Try to be at your new home before the arrival of the van. If you keep it waiting, you may find that your shipment has been placed in storage, which can be expensive. Find out how long a van will wait before it leaves your residence.

It helps to have a sketch available so your furnishings can be properly placed in the various rooms when the van arrives. Movers get annoyed when you frequently switch furnishings. Check each item as it comes off the van to see if it is damaged. Make appropriate notations on the inventory, delivery receipt, or bill of lading.

If your agreement calls for unpacking, then be sure that all items are removed from the cartons and placed in the various closets, cabinets, and drawers that you designate. Again, make notations of any damage found.

PAYMENT

The movers will be eager to complete unloading, have you sign for the merchandise, and receive payment. Do not make payment for your shipment until you are satisfied all work has been completed in accordance with the contract. Make certain that you have listed all damaged and missing items and it is so stated above your signature. *Don't be rushed.*

Unless you have been given credit by the mover prior to delivery, payment must be made in cash, certified check, money order, traveler's check, or cashier's check.

SUBMITTING A CLAIM

After rechecking for damaged and missing items, submit your claim promptly and follow up to see that you get a fair deal. The ICC states:

> If you need to file a claim, the earlier this is done, the quicker the mover can make settlement. We cannot stress enough that your best proof of claim is notation on the bill of lading, inventory, or delivery receipt at the time of delivery. If you should later discover that an article was lost or damaged and you have proof that such loss or damage was caused by the mover, you can still file a claim for such loss within 9 months after the move. Your claim is much more difficult to process if it is delayed or presented some time after your goods have been delivered.

Because there are variations in claim settlements by major carriers, it is important to check on their performance before making a selection. You may wish to contact the ICC or read articles on the subject in current consumer magazines.

SHORT-DISTANCE MOVE

If you build your home in the community you now live in, you have additional options in deciding how to make such a move. Your choices include employing a large carrier, using a local firm that specializes in short-haul moving, renting a truck and driver, renting the truck and driving it yourself, moving the possessions yourself using family transportation, or a combination of the above.

If you have the time and energy, there is no question that you can save considerable money and do a splendid job by taking on much of the responsibility yourself. The fact that you are building your own home permits you to move in items as soon as you think the house is well secured. But a word of caution: It may be wise not to move many items before you arrive; there is always the possibility of pilferage and theft.

Your automobile can be useful for moving small items. You can then rent a truck and perhaps hire someone to help you move.

Obtain bids from local movers and speak to friends who have used their services. The fact that you will be there to supervise is a major factor in making a successful move.

SUMMARY

To simplify your move and reduce costs, it is desirable to give away furnishings that will not be used later. Eliminate possessions that won't be appropriate for your new house, as well as dust collectors that haven't been used in years.

Have adequate protection for your household possessions while in transit so you will be fully covered for loss. If possible, move your valuables and heirlooms yourself, and under no circumstances ship them with the rest of your things.

Use a management approach in making your move. Determine your objective, plan your move with care, and use your plan. Performing these duties requires supervision—the better the supervision, the more successful the move.

Chapter Ten
Landscaping

Shortly after arriving at your new home, you should begin landscaping. If you have done your planning properly, it should include landscaping. This will permit you to implement the plan when you move in.

WHAT TYPE OF LANDSCAPING IS APPROPRIATE?

Landscaping gives you an opportunity to be creative: it should reflect your personality and be appealing to you. You must take into consideration the possibility of resale, the time available for maintenance, costs involved, and future needs based on the changing composition of your family. If you have a large family, or numerous other interests, you probably will not be able to spend much time keeping the grounds attractive. Simplicity can be accomplished with concrete, artificial grass, and a minimum of shrubs, flowers, and trees.

BUDGET FOR LANDSCAPING

During the planning stage, it is important to budget an adequate amount of money for landscaping. Families often make shortcuts by either failing to consider landscaping or deciding to wait until they are well settled. You can do this, of course, but your property will be unsightly. Good planning will allow you to make your residence attractive from the start.

HOW TO GO ABOUT LANDSCAPING YOUR HOME

There are several approaches you may wish to consider in landscaping your home. Here are some possibilities.

County agents and agricultural extension services can be found in every state. They work with a land-grant university and are paid in part from funds provided by the Department of Agriculture. If a county agent is not nearby, you can write your land-grant university. Some of the free publications available from our local cooperative extension service are entitled: *Enjoy Your Home Grounds, Diseases and Insects of Lawn Grasses, Shrubs for Louisiana Landscapes, Plan Landscapes for the Family,* and *Roses.*

The university or agricultural extension service will also test the soil in your yard to determine what may be needed to improve it (see Figure 10-1).

Talk with neighbors who have attractive yards and find out who is taking care of them. Select the best qualified individual to tend to your grass, shrubs, and flowers. Or contact a professional landscaper and have him prepare a design for your house and give you an estimate of what the entire job will cost. You should try to obtain three bids.

To keep your costs at a minimum, it may be necessary to do it yourself. Landscaping your own property, particularly if you have a small lot, is not a difficult task. You can get splendid ideas from reading available literature and observing attractively landscaped homes.

A NEW LAWN

Your lawn should be established shortly after you move in. This ground cover is important because in the event of heavy rain it will help keep your soil from being washed away. First determine which grass is most appropriate for your area (Figure 10–2 indicates the types of grasses most appropriate for various regions of the United States). It is also advisable to discuss the type of lawn you desire with your county agent and observe the successes and failures of your neighbors. There may be significant soil differences within a community, and you want to be sure your lawn will do well.

The quickest way to have a finished look is to buy sufficient sod to

SOIL TESTING LABORATORY

L. S. U. Agricultural Experiment Station, Baton Rouge 3, Louisiana

NAME	POST OFFICE	DATE OF SAMPLING	LABORATORY NUMBER	SOIL TYPE	SAMPLE IDENTIFICATION
Dr. Richard Stillman	New Orleans, La. 2311 Oriole St.	9-68	10821	s1	

ANALYSIS OF SOIL

		VERY LOW	LOW	MEDIUM	HIGH
Available Phosphorus, (parts per million*)	61				✓
Available Potassium, (parts per million)	110			✓	
Available Calcium, (parts per million)	4000+				✓
Available Magnesium, (parts per million)	380				✓
pH (acidity or alkalinity)	8.7	*alkaline*			
Organic Matter, (per cent)					
Soluble Salts, (per cent)	0.019	✓			

*Parts per million means "pounds per million pounds of soil." An acre of soil 3 ½ inches deep weighs about one million pounds.

RECOMMENDATIONS: - (These are the least amounts of fertilizer that you should use per acre.)

CROP	LIME NEEDED (TONS)	TOTAL NUTRIENTS NEEDED PER ACRE			SUGGESTED FERTILIZER TO MEET THE RECOMMENDATION SEE BACK OF THIS SHEET FOR MORE INFORMATION
		NITROGEN (N)	PHOS-PHATE (P₂O₅)	POTASH (K₂O)	
					_____ lbs. of _____ and _____ lbs. of nitrogen, or use equivalent amounts of other grades or materials. SEE OTHER SIDE.
					_____ lbs. of _____ and _____ lbs. of nitrogen, or use equivalent amounts of other grades or materials. SEE OTHER SIDE.
					_____ lbs. of _____ and _____ lbs. of nitrogen, or use equivalent amounts of other grades or materials. SEE OTHER SIDE.
					_____ lbs. of _____ and _____ lbs. of nitrogen, or use equivalent amounts of other grades or materials. SEE OTHER SIDE.

ADDITIONAL REMARKS: *The salt is not harmful. However, the pH is too high, apply sulfur at the rate of 4 ounces per square yard of surface area and mix well with the soil to lower the pH.*

Figure 10–1 Sample form from soil-testing laboratory.

cover your entire lawn area. This is expensive, however. Instead, you may wish to buy enough sod to cover about one-third of the area, and by distributing it well, the entire lawn will be covered within three months. The most reasonable way is to plant cuttings, but the time needed to complete your lawn will be increased by several months.

If you decide to grow a new lawn yourself, here are some specific steps suggested by Winona Guidry in *Enjoy Your Home Grounds:*

> 1. The first work to do is to level the outdoor area so as to have surface drainage away from the house. If you remove some

INFORMATION ON FERTILIZERS

A complete fertilizer, such as 8-8-8, contains a certain number of pounds of total nitrogen, available phosphate and available potash.

FOR EXAMPLE:	TOTAL NITROGEN (N)	AVAILABLE PHOSPHATE (P₂O₅)	AVAILABLE POTASH (K₂O)
100 lbs. of 8-8-8 contains	8	8	8
100 lbs. of 6-12-6 contains	6	12	6
100 lbs. of 3-12-12 contains	3	12	12

WHEN YOU BUY FERTILIZER- consider the plant food in the bag as well as the price.

Our recommendation lists the minimum grade of fertilizer. You can substitute the following **grades** and **amounts** of fertilizer for those recommended, and obtain the same amounts of plant food.

Instead of using 100 lbs. of these recommended grades,	You could substitute **these amounts** of these fertilizers
8-8-8	80 lbs. of 10-10-10, or 67 lbs. of 12-12-12 or 62 lbs. of 13-13-13
6-12-6	60 lbs. of 10-20-10 or 50 lbs. of 12-24-12
3-12-12	60 lbs. of 5-20-20, or 50 lbs. of 6-24-24
0-14-14	70 lbs. of 0-20-20
5-10-10	83 lbs. of 6-12-12 or 50 lbs. of 10-20-20
5-20-10	72 lbs. of 7-28-14

WHEN YOU NEED NITROGEN, here are the main carriers of nitrogen and their nitrogen contents:

	LBS. NITRATE NITROGEN	LBS. AMMONIA NITROGEN
100 lbs. of anhydrous ammonia contains	————————	82
100 lbs. of urea contains	————————	45
100 lbs. of ammonium nitrate contains	16 ½	16 ½
100 lbs. of "uran" 32 contains	8	24
100 lbs. of ammonium sulfate contains	————————	20
100 lbs. of cyanamid contains	————————	21
100 lbs. of nitrate of soda contains	16	————————

When soils are kept properly limed, each pound of nitrogen from each of these sources gives about the same increase in yield. You should **always** keep your soil limed properly, regardless of the source of nitrogen you use.

of the topsoil, save and use it. Be careful when leveling under trees.

2. Plow, grade, and harrow. You may have to haul soil to fill in low spots.

3. Add organic matter, such as barnyard manure, peat, compost, well-decomposed sawdust, gin trash, or well-rotted rice hulls. For an average 75 × 150 feet, use 1 ton of barnyard manure or equivalent and 150 pounds of 0-12-12 or 0-14-7 fertilizer. If you do not add organic matter, use 150 pounds of 3-12-12 or 6-8-8. Work it well into the soil.

4. Rake until the seedbed is very fine, then roll.

5. You are now ready to seed, sprig, or sod your lawn.

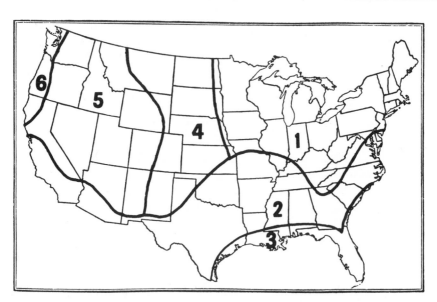

Climatic regions of the U.S. in which the following grasses are suitable for lawns: Region 1. Common Kentucky bluegrass, Merion Kentucky bluegrass, red fescue, and Colonial bentgrass. Tall fescue, bermudagrass, and zoysiagrass in southern portion of the region. Region 2. Bermudagrass and zoysiagrass. Centipedegrass, carpetgrass, and St. Augustinegrass in southern portion of the region with tall fescue and Kentucky bluegrass in some northern areas. Region 3. St. Augustinegrass, bermudagrass, zoysiagrass, carpetgrass, and bahiagrass. Region 4. Nonirrigated areas: Crested wheatgrass, buffalograss, and blue gramagrass. Irrigated areas: Kentucky bluegrass and red fescue. Region 5. Nonirrigated areas: Crested wheatgrass. Irrigated areas: Kentucky bluegrass and red fescue. Region 6. Colonial bentgrass and Kentucky bluegrass.

Figure 10–2 Grasses appropriate for various regions of the U.S. Source: *Better Lawns*, Dept. of Agriculture, Bulletin No. 51.

MAINTAINING YOUR LAWN

Once you have a pretty lawn, how do you go about maintaining it? You can do the work yourself but you will need a lawn mower and edger. It may require cutting once a week in the growing season. A relatively small lawn is easy to maintain and is a splendid form of exercise.

Another solution is to have a gardener take care of your yard. The charge in our area for a weekly visit is $40 to $80 a month. The quality of work ranges from excellent to adequate.

My own view is that there is no substitute for personal attention. It can be argued that your time is valuable and could be better utilized elsewhere. This is true in many cases on a purely monetary basis, but doing your own landscaping can be looked on as a delightful change of pace and relaxation.

A third approach, perhaps in combination with one of the others, is to utilize a lawn care company. Such a firm treats your lawn a specified number of times a year. The yearly cost for doing this work is normally based on the square footage involved. For example, if a lawn covers 5,000 square feet, the charge may vary from $200 to $250. The company would usually make four to five visits during the growing season.

If you decide to use a lawn care company, be sure to obtain all the facts. Points you may wish to determine include: Is the company reliable? Will they do a good job? Do you have the right to terminate the agreement without penalty?

A GARDEN OF YOUR OWN

What about having your own fruit and vegetable garden? With the high cost of living, this can be a great way to save money. It also should be of interest to the health-minded and the environmentalists. This sounds great in theory but can be demanding, discouraging, and expensive in some areas. A neighbor in New Orleans tried a small vegetable garden, specializing in tomatoes. He found, however, that before he could apply protective measures insects had eaten the green fruit. After six months, he gave it up as an impossible task.

In contrast, a friend who lives nearby has successfully kept a garden for years and spends much of his spare time with this hobby. If you are interested, I would suggest you contact your local county agent for advice on maintaining your soil and to learn which crops do well in your locality.

A GARDEN FOR THE CHILDREN

What about a garden for youngsters? Today it is a real challenge to direct their energy toward projects that can be useful in adult life. An appreciation of the soil is certainly a worthwhile undertaking. An interesting article in *South Central Bell Notes* pointed out how to start a small flower garden. This could apply to a vegetable or a fruit garden.

> Looking for something different or unusual to do with your child for coming holidays and vacations? One of the most stimulating things you can do is help your child plan and plant his first garden. Observing how living things grow will be rewarding and exciting.
> A child's first garden should be a small one, about 3' × 6',

with flowers that are easy to grow. First choices should be annuals. They must be planted each year, but the rewards of your youngster's first efforts are almost immediate.

In choosing the flowers to plant, the marigold is a popular choice, with many varieties available. Other favorites are zinnias and petunias. If your child likes flowers for their smell as well as their color, sweet alyssum would be a good choice.

All these plants do well even in poor soil and thrive on lots of sunlight. Most will bloom from seed in six to eight weeks and will last until first frost.

Even a small garden will require weekly care. After preparing the soil, planting, and marking the rows, watering and weeding will keep a youngster busy, but happy and proud as he is rewarded with flowers from his private domain.

OUR INTRODUCTION TO GARDENING

Upon our arrival at the United States Military Academy, a neighbor knocked on our door one evening and said, "My name is Jack Meyer; welcome to West Point." Jack presented us with a bowl of fresh strawberries and a basket of tomatoes.

We spent a delightful evening and learned a great deal about what to expect during our three year tour at the Academy. Before leaving, he told us of a garden plot directly behind our backyard and encouraged us to plant some fruits and vegetables.

The next afternoon, he showed us how to go about it. There were twelve plots being worked by officers who had homes in the area. Jack had one of them and his crops were the most productive. Under his guidance, we started our first garden. Several months later we were eating tomatoes, strawberries, and muskmelon.

The following year, we moved into a house in another area at West Point. We took along some of our strawberry plants and newly found gardening knowledge. There was a sizable area for gardening in back of our new quarters. I rushed out to get started. The soil seemed different but I didn't think much about it—even though no one else was using it. It was rocky in contrast to the rich black earth near our previous house. Shortly after planting my strawberries, I came down with a terrible case of poison ivy. After hospitalization, I tried diligently to achieve results but did not succeed.

LANDSCAPING EXPENDITURES

What should you budget for landscaping? This will vary for each family. You may wish to note initial expenses of one family with an average size lot.

Initial Costs

Grass	$123
Fertilizer	96
Soil (3 loads)	78
Gardener	250
Plants	216
Seeds	31
Edger (electric)	85
Lawnmower (electric)	169
Basic gardening tools (rake, shovel, broom, hoe, trowel, cultivator)	36
Hoses, nozzles, sprinkler	79
Total initial costs	$1163

After the landscaping is complete, there is yearly maintenance. Expenditures will depend upon how much work you do yourself, the size of your yard, where you live, and climatic conditions.

Annual Upkeep

Plants	$78
Seeds	22
Fertilizer	45
Tools	26
Water	29
Repairs	45
Total annual cost	$245

You may wish to keep a running record of your landscaping costs, detailing what you purchase, when, and how much it costs, and total costs to date. If maintaining the yard and garden is a family project, you may want to record who helped with what when, too.

SUMMARY

Landscaping should be considered during the planning stage for your home. In this way you can determine the amount of money required and set it aside for the purpose. It also permits an overview that includes the house, patio, driveway, pool, and lawn. Changes are easy to make at this point, without the pressure of an unfinished lot and the mess it entails.

Determine the type of grass, trees, shrubs, and flowers that are best suited to your area. Contact your county agent or land grant university—either can be of great help at no expense to you. They can provide you with pamphlets on all aspects of landscaping, as well as help you to estimate costs.

Chapter Eleven
Maintenance, Repairs,
Improvements

Give consideration to the upkeep of your new home shortly after you are settled. Good maintenance will reduce your need for repairs. As the house grows older, expenditures for repairs will increase. Make plans for later additions while building your home. A neighbor, for example, built his home when he needed only one bedroom. To conserve limited funds, he completed the first floor, including the master bedroom and decided to finish the second floor after the first child arrived, making certain that the structure would support a second floor. In these times of high inflation and the energy shortage, such an approach should be given serious consideration.

MAINTENANCE

Maintaining your house means keeping it in a certain condition or position of efficiency and good repair. If you have done a quality job in building your home, your maintenance should be minimal.

As you look at your present home, are you faced with sizable repair bills because of poor quality construction? Have you contributed to this expense by failing to keep your premises and equipment in good shape?

Preventive maintenance, taking proper care of your equipment before it breaks down, can forestall many major repairs. The advantages are twofold: you are able to use the equipment longer and it reduces your repair bills. The key to it all is that you must buy good equipment initially and have it properly installed. The best maintenance will be wasted if construction is poor and the equipment inferior. If this is true, your best solution is to replace it.

Maintenance will be increased considerably by poor planning. For example, at a nearby home completed last year, the owner wanted a patio that would be well protected. The architect devised a rectangular area surrounded on three sides by the house and on one side by the garage, completely enclosing the area except for the open ceiling. Upon seeing it finished, the owner was delighted. But this happiness was short-lived. After the first heavy rain, the patio was flooded. No drainage had been provided and the only way to remove the water was to bail it out. The lowest estimate to remedy the situation was $1950.

From a maintenance standpoint, there is an advantage to planning and building your own home. Your presence enables you to check on the quality and ask questions about keeping the equipment in good condition. Make a point to find out from the experts how best to take care of your roof, rugs, floors, air conditioning, and other items. Proper maintenance can extend their life considerably.

TOOLS AND STORAGE

To maintain your equipment properly, you need adequate tools and a satisfactory place to store them. When planning your home, provide adequate space for this purpose. My recommendation is to use space within an enclosed garage, basement, or utility room. You may wish to purchase a small shed that could be located in your backyard. A 12 x 18-foot lawn building costs $500 to $900 and can store considerable equipment. Extra items designed for this building include shelving, tool rack, pegboard, and work bench.

Arrange your tools neatly and keep them in first class condition by cleaning and oiling them frequently. Tools are expensive and should be protected. If they're in a garage, keep it locked. Buy only the necessary items to do your maintenance and repair jobs satisfactorily. The cost of quality tools, including a box, for the routine tasks varies between $200 and $300.

RECORD KEEPING

The file system you developed in the planning stage of your home should include folders for maintenance, repairs, and home improvements. Keep warranties and instructions on how to care for your equip-

Item	Frequency of Maintenance	Date Last Completed
Dishwasher	_____	_____
Flooring	_____	_____
Heating and cooling	_____	_____
Painting, exterior	_____	_____
Oven	_____	_____
Painting, interior	_____	_____
Refrigerator	_____	_____
Termite inspection	_____	_____

Figure 11-1   Checklist of items and frequency of maintenance.

ment. You also may wish to devise a checklist (see Figure 11-1) that could serve as a reminder to see that these items are properly maintained. Include such items as the heating and cooling unit, floors, fence, refrigerator, oven, dishwasher, termite inspection, and painting.

MAINTAINING YOUR COOLING UNIT

Central air conditioning is an expensive investment in warm areas, both in original cost and in upkeep. For it to perform economically, the system must be kept operating efficiently. After you have a quality unit installed, what steps must be taken to maintain it? One local utility advises its customers as follows:

> Clean or replace filter at least every month during the summer. Dirty filters put an added strain on your air conditioning and on your cooling bills too, so keep them clean.
>
> Set thermostat at highest setting that keeps you comfortable—and leave it there. The lower the setting, the longer your unit will run and the more it will cost to operate.
>
> Keep windows and doors closed—unnecessary opening of windows and doors lets in outside air that must be cooled and dehumidified.
>
> Keep hot sunlight out—use draperies, awnings, shutters, or shades to keep the sun out.
>
> Have system checked annually—a check of the mechanical operation of your system by a qualified serviceman is important for efficient, economical operation.[1]

[1] "How the Weather Usually Means Higher Public Service Bills," *Homemaking*, New Orleans Public Service, June 1973, p. 3.

PAINTING

If you paint your own home you can save money, but it requires considerable hard work and time. If the interior needs painting, work in one room at a time over an extended period so that it does not become a major undertaking.

Last year, I found it necessary to paint the outside of our house. We first checked on three firms that specialized in home painting and had a good reputation in the community. Their prices varied from $825 to $1580. I then went to several job sites where painting was in progress; and after observing their work, I talked to several men about working for me in their spare time. Two came to my home and gave me estimates. In one case, I was told the job would cost $9.50 an hour if I supplied all the equipment, including brushes and paint. The second individual wanted to supply his own paint and equipment; his price was $12 an hour.

I next went to a first class paint company and priced brushes and paint. I also received good advice on the essential preparation prior to painting.

Painting the exterior of my house appeared to be a major project. Fortunately, my older son offered to paint if I would do the necessary preparation. It sounded like a great idea, but this preparation was more than I bargained for. It took considerable time and effort.

You may be interested in the following price comparison that influenced my do-it-yourself decision.

Painting contractors	$825–$1580
Painters	$576–$ 660
Our family	$126*

*Cost for brushes, sandpaper, paints, mildew remover, rollers, masking tape, etc.

It is very important to buy quality paint, brushes, and materials. We bought the best grade paint at $12 per gallon. The price differential is minor and this extra cost is recouped in a long-lasting, better-looking paint.

As indicated previously, my job was the preparation. This required removing the flaked paint. Fortunately, the paint on the house required very little sanding, but our gates required sandpapering, caulking, puttying, securing loose nails, and removing mildew. The final preparatory step was to protect the brick, windows, doorknobs, shrubs, and driveway from paint splotches. Old sheets, newspapers, and masking tape did the trick. It is much easier to take these protective measures than to remove unwanted paint.

Painting requires good management. You want to make certain that the preparatory work, including purchasing the necessary equipment and cleaning up the area, has been done properly. You must also see that a first class job is accomplished.

REPAIRS

If you want to get an item repaired promptly and properly, you may find it pays to do it yourself. Today's life style has brought a multitude of marvelous gadgets and equipment to many households. But how often have you heard:

"The stupid thing won't work!"

"Broken? I just bought it yesterday!"

"That serviceman promised to be here last week. What happened?"

A partial solution is the utilization of a very available resource—yourself. There used to be a belief in some quarters that white-collar employees do not do blue-collar work. Such a philosophy meant that the college graduate didn't dirty his lily-white hands. Times have changed, but there are still a goodly number in our society who make no effort to discover how useful their hands can be in making repairs.

It might be prudent to learn the basics of repairing electrical items, maintaining your car, handling a power mower without getting hurt, painting your home, or taking care of an outboard motor.

If you want the peace of mind of getting things done, it's a good idea to learn more about how to do it yourself. The benefits are not only the money saved and the physical exercise, but also the mental satisfaction of being able to do things yourself—and, in many cases, to do them better than the professional because of personal interest and pride.

From time to time you will have to replace an item, regardless of how well you maintain your equipment and how fine the quality. Things wear out. Your own conscientious inspection system should enable you to estimate when a replacement is needed. This will permit you more easily to sell, trade, or replace the item while it is working.

In considering replacements, keep in mind that new and better products constantly are being made available to the public. Keep abreast of the latest advances not only for their convenience but also in the event that you decide to sell your home.

Before making a change, check carefully into the newest equipment available. In making replacements it is important not only to select fine material but also to secure the subcontractor with the skill to do the best job at the most economical price. This is well illustrated by the experience of one homeowner I know:

> My garage was ten years old last year, and I had had no previous trouble with it. However, at that time, I saw water dripping from the corner of my garage roof after a heavy rain. I checked it out and it appeared to be a leak in my roof. I contacted three roofers for bids. Two told me I needed a complete new roof and gutters at costs ranging from $1250 to $1645. The third said that my gutters were rusted out due to water standing in them. He added that I needed a sheet-metal man and not a roofer. He said, "I could do the job for $363 and that would include putting in an extra downspout and all new gutters, but this is not my specialty."
>
> I then contacted a sheet-metal man who was highly recommended and was a respected member of the local Better Business Bureau. He informed me that the standing water in my gutters was due to the improper slope of the gutters. The water was not draining off into the downspouts located on two of the roof's corners. This master craftsman said that thirty feet of the garage's gutter needed to be replaced and the remaining twenty feet only required recoating with a tar-base material that would prevent rusting. No extra downspout was required. He agreed to complete this job, including removal of the old gutters from the premises, for $168.
>
> The sheet-metal man used 26-gauge galvanized steel gutters to replace my rusted ones. This 26-gauge metal is heavier, stronger and of better quality than the standard 28-gauge found in many homes. He reported seeing 26-gauge gutters still in good shape after forty to fifty years of use. He further advised me not to paint the new gutters for six months because they needed to be weathered. If done immediately after installation, the paint would not properly adhere to the metal and would peel off. I have had no further trouble with my garage during the past year. It sure saved me money and I learned a lot by getting the expert to do the job.

HOME IMPROVEMENTS

Assume that you want to make a major improvement in your home. If you have, for instance, initially built your home and completed only the first floor, you may now decide to finish the upstairs, or you may want to add an enclosed garage, den, or extra bedroom. These improvements can best be accomplished if they have been considered during the planning stage.

Once you decide to make a major improvement, follow the steps outlined earlier in this book. Take time to plan exactly what you want. The time to allow for your home improvement project is during the planning stage. I was speaking with a successful contractor last week. He related the importance of making changes no later than during the blueprint stage:

> You can take an eraser to correct a rough drawing. Even if your design is finalized, you can modify it and a new set will cost only $50 to $75. But it really becomes expensive when the building is underway. Recently we contracted to add a new wing to an old house. The foundation had been poured. The framing, bricking, plumbing, and electrical wiring were also completed. At this point, the housewife decided to move her sink one foot to the right. She thought we were cheating her when our estimate indicated it would cost $1,200. I told her this change meant I had to contact the subcontractors involved for their changes. Numerous modifications would have to be made. If this was not done, the plumbing fixture would go right through the window. The electrician would have to modify his wiring. I needed to call back the carpenter to change the cupboards, etc. She finally realized her mistake in not taking greater time to plan her kitchen.

Adequate planning also means checking with care before selecting a firm to make a major improvement in your home. Try to obtain three estimates and secure a written contract.

People are usually given contracts at the most inopportune time— just before they are asked to sign them. A contract should be studied with care well in advance of closing the deal. If necessary, let your lawyer look it over.

A good friend of mine who failed to read his contract can tell you his sad experience:

> We decided to add a guest house in our backyard. I found the name of a contractor in the phone book and proceeded to call the owner of what I will call "Goodluck Industries." That evening he came to our house and quoted a price of $14,700. I signed the contract with the understanding that work would begin within 30 days. A week prior to his starting, I became concerned and proceeded to check him out with the BBB. To my dismay, I found that the owner of "Goodluck Industries" was a fraud. He never finished a job. But the contract specified that in the event of cancellation, I must pay a penalty of $1,470 even though no work was ever done. I went to my lawyer and after much effort, including threatening legal action, I bluffed my way out of it. But the time expended cost me $7,000 in lost business.

Here are seven excellent suggestions to prevent being taken in a home improvement swindle.

1. Get bids from several reliable contractors. Best sources of information on reliability are the Better Business Bureau (checking under both firm's name and contractor's name) and references from customers. Call the Remodelers Council and inquire about the arbitration provisions in their contracts. If this is important to you, make sure your contractor agrees to it.

2. Get it in writing, including details on work to be performed, guarantees, and specifications of materials to be used. Total cost and schedule of payments should also be in the contract. The most advantageous contract for the consumer reserves a substantial final payment to ensure that all work will be completed. Never make an advance payment for a special price or permit use of your home for advertising.

3. Do not sign contracts with door-to-door salesmen. Do not allow people to "inspect" your roof or heating system or your home for termite damage unless you have called them. Unnecessary work has been done and some homes actually damaged by roving "specialists."

4. Be wary of package deals which include financing. Shop as carefully for your money as you do for your contractor. Think twice before agreeing to mortgages; investigate FHA loans.

5. Make sure your contractor has a building permit.

6. Never sign a completion certificate until all work has been completed to your satisfaction.

7. For additional information, read: Chapter II, "How to Avoid Swindles on Home Improvements" in *Consumer Swindles and How to Avoid Them;* "Home Improvements for Love of Money" in the January 1973 issue of *Money;* and Better Business Bureau publications, including "Tips on Home Improvements" and Safeguard Bulletins 5 and 12.[2]

Effective home planning takes future improvement projects into consideration. In making these improvements, use the same management concepts you did in building your home. This will enable you to do a better job at a lower cost.

SUMMARY

One of the best ways to keep maintenance to a minimum is to design and build your house with low upkeep as a priority, using quality, low-

[2] Nell Weekly, "How to Avoid Being 'Had,' " *New Orleans Times-Picayune,* May 6, 1973.

maintenance materials for construction. Once built, your investment will benefit from a regular program of periodic inspection and prompt repair.

When repair time arrives, determine if you can do the job yourself. Read instructions with care. If you need help, obtain the services of a reliable firm.

New items for the home are being developed each year. Before you make significant repairs on old equipment, examine new products that may do a better job at a lower cost. They will also add to the value of your house, and make it more salable.

Epilogue

Do-it-yourself subcontracting has worked for many people, including myself. Since publication of the first edition, many readers have informed me of their own successful experiences. But subcontracting may not be your cup of tea. You may decide to use a contractor to build your home instead of doing this job yourself. But do remember to provide him enough free supervision to minimize any misunderstandings.

Another approach was recently suggested by a friend. "You busted your gut—for what? We looked at a home last Friday and moved in Monday. It was three years old, landscaped, ideal for our needs, and in perfect condition. All we had to do was settle in." My friend's solution may be a better answer for many—at least it's a lot simpler.

Don't kid yourself about your interest or abilities in managing your own subcontracting. Building your own home is a big project and there are potential risks. So examine your own limitations before starting such a venture, and familiarize yourself with the current building codes and zoning restrictions. Do not try it if you doubt your ability to handle the managerial and financial matters involved in subcontracting.

Let's assume that, after weighing the alternatives of buying a home or hiring a contractor, you decide to build. Successfully managing the building of your own home will require a conscientious effort and a lot of hard work. But the satisfaction you gain from finishing the project, in my view, makes it all worthwhile.

Appendix A
Sample Architectural Drawings

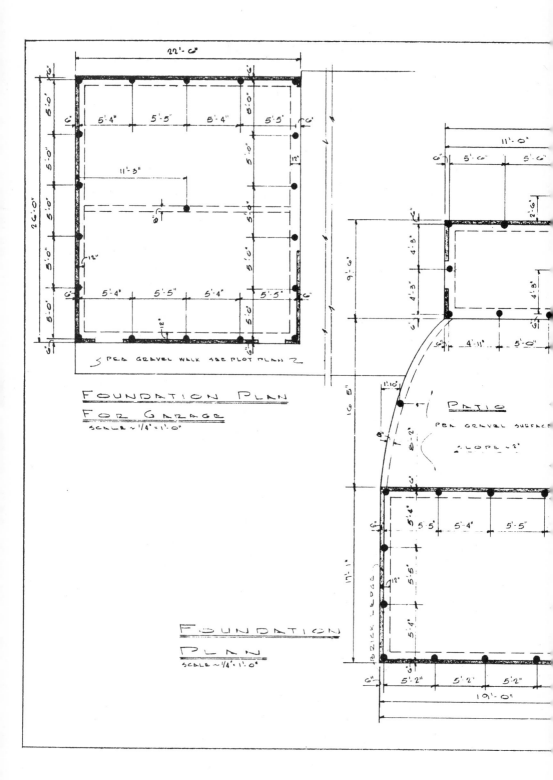

22'-0"

6'-0"

5'-0"

5'-0"

26'-0"

5'-0"

5'-0"

5'-4" 5'-5" 5'-4" 5'-5"

6" 6"

11'-3"

12"

12"

5'-0" 5'-0" 5'-0" 5'-0"

12"

5'-4" 5'-5" 5'-4" 5'-5"

6" 6"

PEA GRAVEL WALK SEE PLOT PLAN

FOUNDATION PLAN

FOR GARAGE

SCALE ~ 1/4" = 1'-0"

11'-0"

6" 5'-0" 5'-0"

2'-0"

4'-3"

9'-0"

4'-3"

6" 4'-11" 5'-0"

1'-10"

0"

PATIO

PEA GRAVEL SURFACE

SLOPE ~ 2"

FOUNDATION

PLAN

SCALE ~ 1/4" = 1'-0"

5'-4" 5'-5" 5'-4" 5'-5"

6"

5'-5"

12"

17'-1"

BRICK LEDGE

5'-4"

6" 5'-2" 5'-2" 5'-2"

19'-0"

158

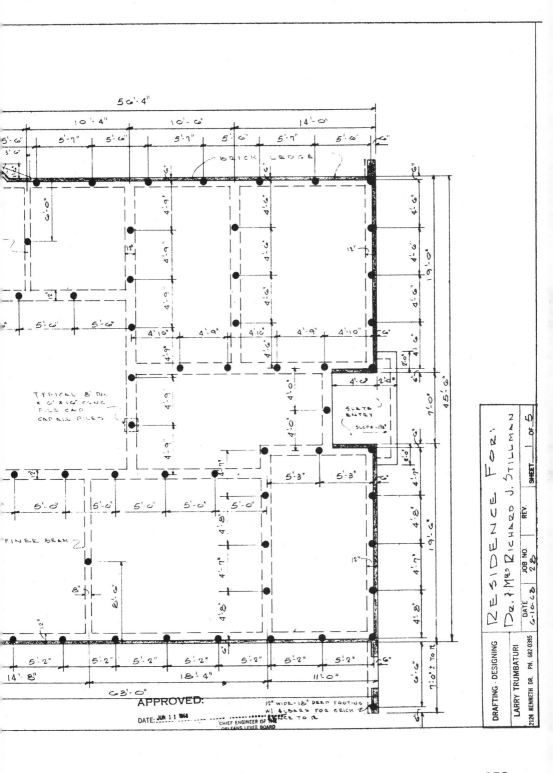

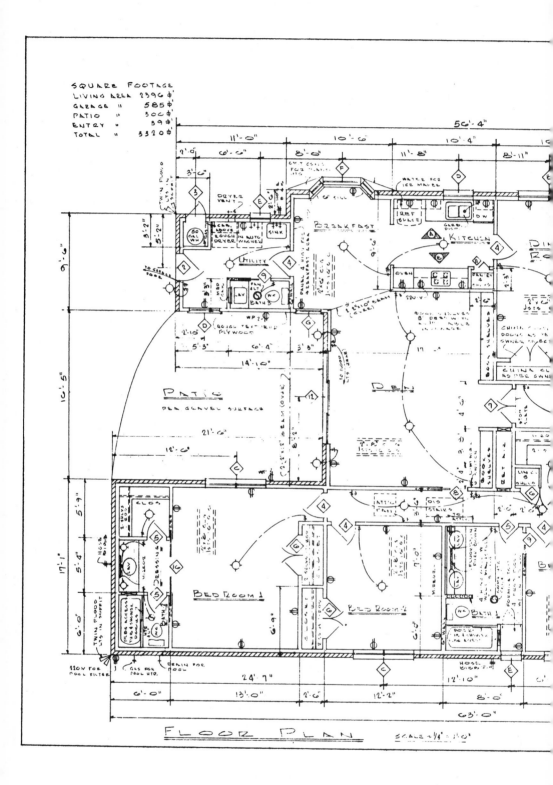

FLOOR PLAN   SCALE = 1/4" = 1'-0"

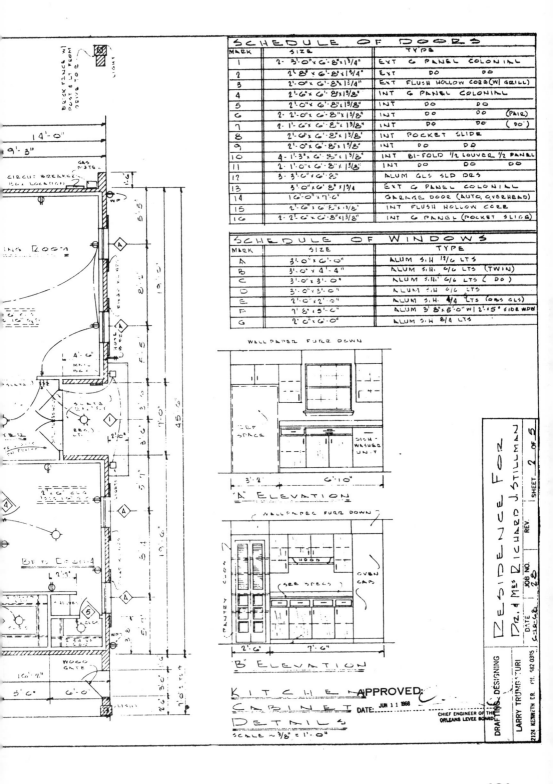

SCHEDULE OF DOORS

MARK	SIZE	TYPE
1	2-3'-0"x6'-8"x1 3/4"	EXT 6 PANEL COLONIAL
2	2'-8"x6'-8"x1 3/4"	EXT DO DO
3	2'-0"x6'-8"x1 3/4"	EXT FLUSH HOLLOW CORE (W/ GRILL)
4	2'-6"x6'-8"x1 3/8"	INT 6 PANEL COLONIAL
5	2'-0"x6'-8"x1 3/8"	INT DO DO
6	2-2'-0"x6'-8"x1 3/8"	INT DO DO (PAIR)
7	2-1'-0"x6'-8"x1 3/8"	INT DO DO (DO)
8	2'-0"x6'-8"x1 3/8"	INT POCKET SLIDE
9	2'-0"x6'-8"x1 3/8"	INT DO DO
10	4-1'-3"x6'-8"x1 3/8"	INT BI-FOLD 1/2 LOUVER 1/2 PANEL
11	2-1'-0"x6'-8"x1 3/8"	INT DO DO DO
12	3-3'-0"x6'-8"	ALUM GLS SLD DRS
13	3'-0"x6'-8"x1 3/4	EXT 6 PANEL COLONIAL
14	16'-0"x7'-0"	GARAGE DOOR (AUTO. OVERHEAD)
15	2'-6"x6'-8"x1 3/8"	INT FLUSH HOLLOW CORE
16	2-2'-6"x6'-8"x1 3/8"	INT 6 PANEL (POCKET SLIDE)

SCHEDULE OF WINDOWS

MARK	SIZE	TYPE
A	3'-0"x6'-0"	ALUM S.H 12/6 LTS
B	3'-0"x4'-4"	ALUM S.H. 6/6 LTS (TWIN)
C	3'-0"x3'-0"	ALUM S.H. 6/6 LTS (DO)
D	3'-0"x3'-0"	ALUM S.H 6/6 LTS
E	2'-0"x2'-0"	ALUM S.H. 4/4 LTS (OBS GLS)
F	7'-8"x5'-0"	ALUM 3'-8"x5'-0" W/ 2'-15° SIDE WDW
G	2'-0"x6'-0"	ALUM S.H 8/4 LTS

WALLPAPER FURR DOWN

REF SPACE

DISH-WASHER UNIT

3'-4" 6'-10"

"A" ELEVATION

WALLPAPER FURR DOWN

HOOD

SEE SPECS

OVEN CAB

2'-6" 7'-6"

"B" ELEVATION

KITCHEN CABINET DETAILS

SCALE ~ 3/8" = 1'-0"

APPROVED

DATE: JUN 11 1968

CHIEF ENGINEER OF THE ORLEANS LEVEE BOARD

RESIDENCE FOR Mr. & Mrs. RICHARD J. STILLMAN

SHEET 2 OF 5

REV. JOB NO. 28 DATE 6-10-68

DRAFTING · DESIGNING

LARRY TRUMPATURI

2124 KENNETH DR. PH. 582-0315

161

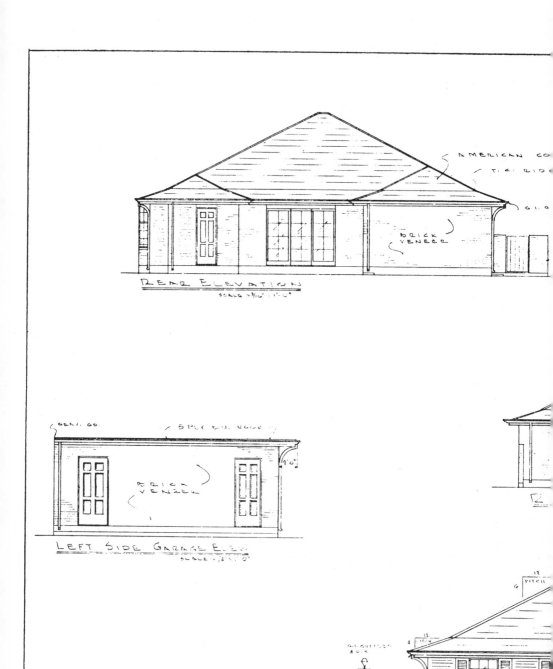

REAR ELEVATION
SCALE 3/16" = 1'-0"

AMERICAN CO

T.C. RID

G.I. G

BRICK
VENEER

GRAV. GO.

5 PLY B.U. ROOF

BRICK
VENEER

LEFT SIDE GARAGE ELEV.
SCALE 1/4" = 1'-0"

2'-0"

12
PITCH
6

G.I. GUTTER
4 O.C.

12
4

HIGH
5'-0" MAX

BRICK VENEER
4 O.C.

FRONT E

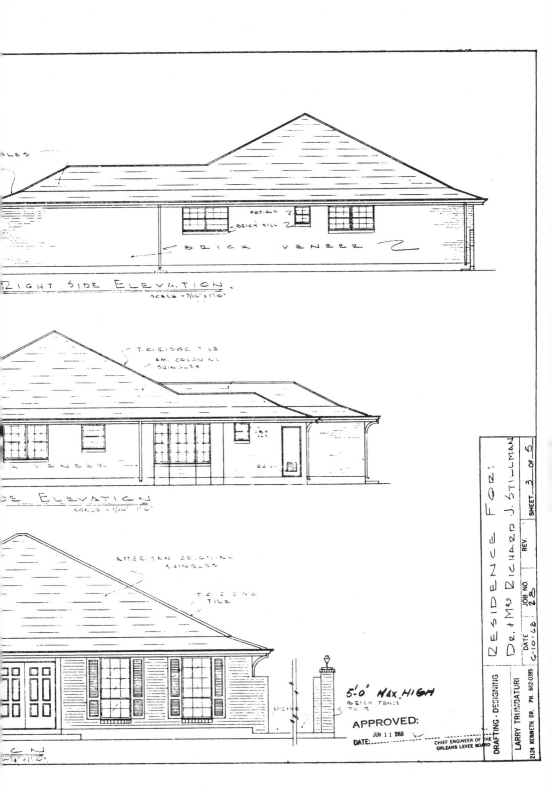

RIGHT SIDE ELEVATION
SCALE = 3/16" = 1'-0"

BRICK SILL

BRICK VENEER

T.C. RIDGE TILE
AM. COLONIAL
SHINGLES

ELEVATION
SCALE = 3/16" = 1'-0"

AMERICAN COLONIAL
SHINGLES

T.C. RIDGE
TILE

5'-0" MAX. HIGH
BRICK FENCE
TO R.

DRIVE

APPROVED:
JUN 1 1 1968
DATE: ....
CHIEF ENGINEER OF THE
ORLEANS LEVEE BOARD

RESIDENCE FOR:
DR. & MRS. RICHARD J. STILLMAN

SHEET 3 OF 5

REV.

JOB NO. 28

DATE 6-10-68

DRAFTING · DESIGNING

LARRY TRIMBATURI

2124 KENNETH DR.   PH. 662-0385

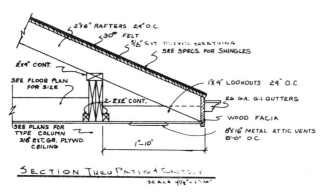

2"x6" RAFTERS 24" O.C.
30# FELT
5/8" EXT. PLYWD. SHEATHING
SEE SPECS. FOR SHINGLES
2"x4" CONT.
SEE FLOOR PLAN FOR SIZE
1"x4" LOOKOUTS 24" O.C.
2-2"x6" CONT.
26 GA. G.I. GUTTERS
WOOD FACIA
SEE PLANS FOR TYPE COLUMN
3/8 EXT. GR. PLYWD. CEILING
8"x16" METAL ATTIC VENTS 8'-0" O.C.
1"-10"

SECTION THRU PATIO & ENTRY
SCALE 1 1/2" = 1'-0"

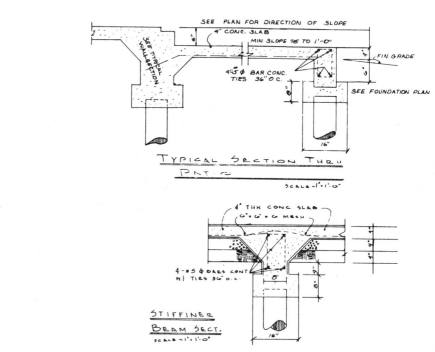

SEE PLAN FOR DIRECTION OF SLOPE
4" CONC. SLAB
MIN. SLOPE 1/8 TO 1'-0"
6"
SEE TYPICAL WALL SECTION
FIN GRADE
4-#5 ∅ BAR CONC. TIES 36" O.C.
SEE FOUNDATION PLAN
8"
16"

TYPICAL SECTION THRU PATIO
SCALE - 1" = 1'-0"

4" THK CONC SLAB
6"x6" - 6 MESH
4-#5∅ BARS CONT W/ TIES 36" O.C.
6"
6"
16"

STIFFINER BEAM SECT.
SCALE - 1" = 1'-0"

164

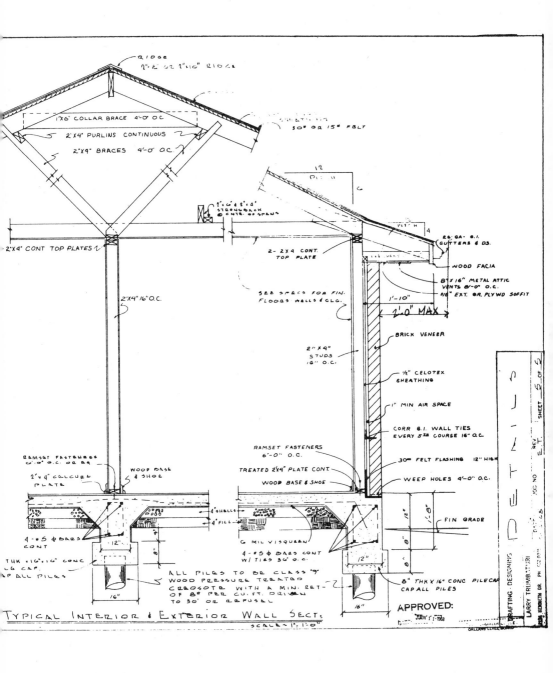

2"x2" or 2"x10" RIDGE

1"x6" COLLAR BRACE 4'-0" O.C.

2"x4" PURLINS CONTINUOUS

2"x4" BRACES 4'-0" O.C.

SHEATHING
30# OR 15# FELT

1"x6"x4'-0" STRONGBACK @ CENTR. OF SPANS

12 PITCH

PITCH

2"x4" CONT TOP PLATES

2 - 2 x 4 CONT. TOP PLATE

26 GA. G.I. GUTTERS & D.S.

WOOD FACIA

8"x16" METAL ATTIC VENTS 8'-0" O.C.

3/8" EXT. GR. PLYWD SOFFIT

1'-10"

2'-0" MAX

2"x4" 16" O.C.

SEE SPECS FOR FIN. FLOORS WALLS & CLG.

BRICK VENEER

2"x4" STUDS 16" O.C.

1/2" CELOTEX SHEATHING

1" MIN AIR SPACE

CORR. G.I. WALL TIES EVERY 5TH COURSE 16" O.C.

RAMSET FASTENERS 6'-0" O.C. OR 2/4

RAMSET FASTENERS 6'-0" O.C.

WOOD BASE & SHOE

TREATED 2x4" PLATE CONT.

30# FELT FLASHING 12" HIGH

2"x4" CONT. SILL PLATE

WOOD BASE & SHOE

WEEP HOLES 4'-0" O.C.

FIN GRADE

4" SHELLS

4" FILL

4 - #5 Ø BARS CONT

6 MIL VISQUEEN

4 - #5 Ø BARS CONT W/ TIES 36" O.C.

THK x16"x16" CONC LG CAP CAP ALL PILES

ALL PILES TO BE CLASS "A" WOOD PRESSURE TREATED CREOSOTE WITH A MIN. RET- OF 8# PER CU. FT. DRIVEN TO 30' OR REFUSAL

8" THK x 16" CONC PILECAP CAP ALL PILES

12"

16"

12"

16"

TYPICAL INTERIOR & EXTERIOR WALL SECT.

SCALE ~ 1":1'-0"

APPROVED:

JUNE 1 1968

type

DRAFTING DESIGNING

LARRY TRUMBAUURI

308 KENNETH DR. PH. 523-7708

DATE

JOB NO.

REV

E.T.

SHEET 5 OF 5

DETAIL

165

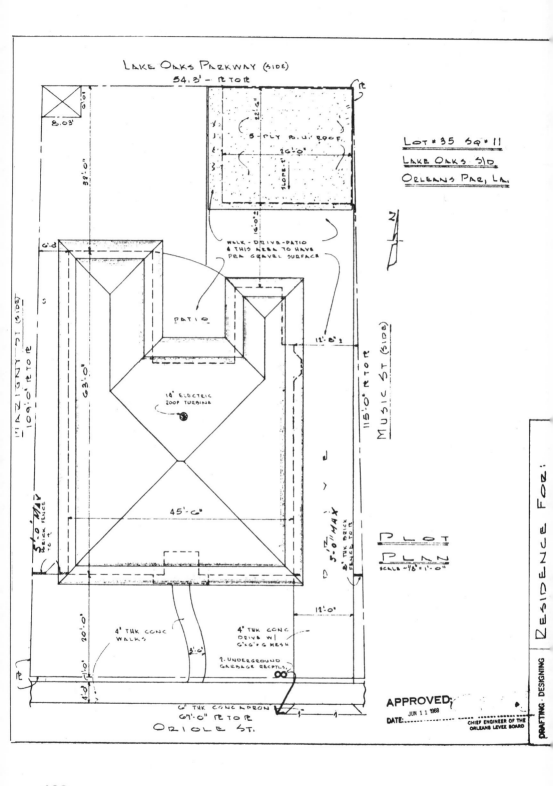

LAKE OAKS PARKWAY (SIDE)
54.3' - RTO R

LOT # 35 SQ # 11
LAKE OAKS S/D
ORLEANS PAR, LA.

5-PLY B.U. ROOF
22'-6"
26'-0"
SLOPE 2"
16'-0"

8.03'
32'-0"
6'-0"

WALK - DRIVE - PATIO
& THIS AREA TO HAVE
PEA GRAVEL SURFACE

N

PATIO

14" ELECTRIC
ROOF TURBINE

MAZIGNY ST (SIDE)
109'-0" RTO R

MUSIC ST (SIDE)
115'-0" RTO R

63'-0"

12'-8"±

45'-0"

5'-0" MAX
BRICK FENCE
TO C

5'-0" MAX
8" THK BRICK
FENCE TO C

PLOT
PLAN
SCALE ~1/8" = 1'-0"

12'-0"

20'-0"

4" THK CONC
WALKS

4" THK CONC
DRIVE W/
6"x6" G MESH

3'-6"

? UNDERGROUND
GARBAGE RECPTLS.

4'-0"

6" THK CONC APRON
67'-0" RTO R
ORIOLE ST.

APPROVED:
JUN 1 1 1968
DATE:
CHIEF ENGINEER OF THE
ORLEANS LEVEE BOARD

DRAFTING · DESIGNING | RESIDENCE FOR:

166

Appendix B
Sample Description of Materials

U. S. DEPARTMENT OF HOUSING AND URBAN DEVELOPMENT
FEDERAL HOUSING ADMINISTRATION
For accurate register of carbon copies, form
may be separated along above fold. Staple
completed sheets together in original order.

☐ Proposed Construction **DESCRIPTION OF MATERIALS** No. _____
(To be inserted by FHA or VA)

☐ Under Construction

Property address _____ City _____ State _____

Mortgagor or Sponsor _____ _____
(Name)   (Address)

Contractor or Builder _____ _____
(Name)   (Address)

INSTRUCTIONS

1. For additional information on how this form is to be submitted, number of copies, etc., see the instructions applicable to the FHA Application for Mortgage Insurance or VA Request for Determination of Reasonable Value, as the case may be.
2. Describe all materials and equipment to be used, whether or not shown on the drawings, by marking an X in each appropriate check-box and entering the information called for in each space. If space is inadequate, enter "See misc." and describe under item 27 or on an attached sheet. THE USE OF PAINT CONTAINING MORE THAN ONE PERCENT LEAD BY WEIGHT IS PROHIBITED.
3. Work not specifically described or shown will not be considered unless required, then the minimum acceptable will be assumed. Work exceeding minimum requirements cannot be considered unless specifically described.
4. Include no alternates, "or equal" phrases, or contradictory items. (Consideration of a request for acceptance of substitute materials or equipment is not thereby precluded.)
5. Include signatures required at the end of this form.
6. The construction shall be completed in compliance with the related drawings and specifications, as amended during processing. The specifications include this Description of Materials and the applicable Minimum Property Standards.

1. EXCAVATION:
Bearing soil, type _____

2. FOUNDATIONS:
Footings: concrete mix _____; strength psi _____ Reinforcing _____
Foundation wall: material _____ Reinforcing _____
Interior foundation wall: material _____ Party foundation wall _____
Columns: material and sizes _____ Piers: material and reinforcing _____
Girders: material and sizes _____ Sills: material _____
Basement entrance areaway _____ Window areaways _____
Waterproofing _____ Footing drains _____
Termite protection _____
Basementless space: ground cover _____; insulation _____; foundation vents _____
Special foundations _____
Additional information: _____

3. CHIMNEYS:
Material _____ Prefabricated (make and size) _____
Flue lining: material _____ Heater flue size _____ Fireplace flue size _____
Vents (material and size): gas or oil heater _____; water heater _____
Additional information: _____

4. FIREPLACES:
Type: ☐ solid fuel; ☐ gas-burning; ☐ circulator (make and size) _____ Ash dump and clean-out _____
Fireplace: facing _____; lining _____; hearth _____; mantel _____
Additional information: _____

5. EXTERIOR WALLS:
Wood frame: wood grade, and species _____ ☐ Corner bracing. Building paper or felt _____
Sheathing _____; thickness _____; width _____; ☐ solid; ☐ spaced _____ o. c.; ☐ diagonal; _____
Siding _____; grade _____; type _____; size _____; exposure _____"; fastening _____
Shingles _____; grade _____; type _____; size _____; exposure _____"; fastening _____
Stucco _____; thickness _____"; Lath _____; weight _____ lb.
Masonry veneer _____ Sills _____ Lintels _____ Base flashing _____
Masonry: ☐ solid ☐ faced ☐ stuccoed; total wall thickness _____"; facing thickness _____"; facing material _____
Backup material _____; thickness _____"; bonding _____
Door sills _____ Window sills _____ Lintels _____ Base flashing _____
Interior surfaces: dampproofing, _____ coats of _____; furring _____
Additional information: _____
Exterior painting: material _____; number of coats _____
Gable wall construction: ☐ same as main walls; ☐ other construction _____

6. FLOOR FRAMING:
Joists: wood, grade, and species _____; other _____; bridging _____; anchors _____
Concrete slab: ☐ basement floor; ☐ first floor; ☐ ground supported; ☐ self-supporting; mix _____; thickness _____";
reinforcing _____; insulation _____; membrane _____
Fill under slab: material _____; thickness _____". Additional information: _____

7. SUBFLOORING: (Describe underflooring for special floors under item 21.)
Material: grade and species _____; size _____; type _____
Laid: ☐ first floor; ☐ second floor; ☐ attic _____ sq. ft.; ☐ diagonal; ☐ right angles. Additional information: _____

8. FINISH FLOORING: (Wood only. Describe other finish flooring under item 21.)

LOCATION	ROOMS	GRADE	SPECIES	THICKNESS	WIDTH	BLDG. PAPER	FINISH
First floor							
Second floor							
Attic floor ___ sq. ft.							

Additional information: _____

9. PARTITION FRAMING:
Studs: wood, grade, and species _____ size and spacing _____ Other _____
Additional information: _____

10. CEILING FRAMING:
Joists: wood, grade, and species _____ Other _____ Bridging _____
Additional information: _____

11. ROOF FRAMING:
Rafters: wood, grade, and species _____ Roof trusses (see detail): grade and species _____
Additional information: _____

12. ROOFING:
Sheathing: wood, grade, and species _____ ; ☐ solid; ☐ spaced _____ " o.c.
Roofing _____ ; grade _____ ; size _____ ; type _____
Underlay _____ ; weight or thickness _____ ; size _____ ; fastening _____
Built-up roofing _____ ; number of plies _____ ; surfacing material _____
Flashing: material _____ ; gage or weight _____ ; ☐ gravel stops; ☐ snow guards
Additional information: _____

13. GUTTERS AND DOWNSPOUTS:
Gutters: material _____ ; gage or weight _____ ; size _____ ; shape _____
Downspouts: material _____ ; gage or weight _____ ; size _____ ; shape _____ ; number _____
Downspouts connected to: ☐ Storm sewer; ☐ sanitary sewer; ☐ dry-well. ☐ Splash blocks: material and size _____
Additional information: _____

14. LATH AND PLASTER
Lath ☐ walls, ☐ ceilings: material _____ ; weight or thickness _____ Plaster: coats _____ ; finish _____
Dry-wall ☐ walls, ☐ ceilings: material _____ ; thickness _____ ; finish _____ ;
Joint treatment _____

15. DECORATING: (Paint, wallpaper, etc.)

Rooms	Wall Finish Material and Application	Ceiling Finish Material and Application
Kitchen _____		
Bath _____		
Other _____		

Additional information: _____

16. INTERIOR DOORS AND TRIM:
Doors: type _____ ; material _____ ; thickness _____
Door trim: type _____ ; material _____ Base: type _____ ; material _____ ; size _____
Finish: doors _____ ; trim _____
Other trim (item, type and location) _____
Additional information: _____

17. WINDOWS:
Windows: type _____ ; make _____ ; material _____ ; sash thickness _____
Glass: grade _____ ; ☐ sash weights; ☐ balances, type _____ ; head flashing _____
Trim: type _____ ; material _____ Paint _____ ; number coats _____
Weatherstripping: type _____ ; material _____ Storm sash, number _____
Screens: ☐ full; ☐ half; type _____ ; number _____ ; screen cloth material _____
Basement windows: type _____ ; material _____ ; screens, number _____ ; Storm sash, number _____
Special windows _____
Additional information: _____

18. ENTRANCES AND EXTERIOR DETAIL:
Main entrance door: material _____ ; width _____ ; thickness _____ ". Frame: material _____ , thickness _____ "
Other entrance doors: material _____ ; width _____ ; thickness _____ ". Frame: material _____ ; thickness _____ "
Head flashing _____ Weatherstripping: type _____ ; saddles _____
Screen doors: thickness _____ "; number _____ ; screen cloth material _____ Storm doors: thickness _____ "; number _____
Combination storm and screen doors: thickness _____ "; number _____ ; screen cloth material _____
Shutters: ☐ hinged; ☐ fixed. Railings _____ , Attic louvers _____
Exterior millwork: grade and species _____ Paint _____ ; number coats _____
Additional information: _____

19. CABINETS AND INTERIOR DETAIL:
Kitchen cabinets, wall units: material _____ ; lineal feet of shelves _____ ; shelf width _____
Base units: material _____ ; counter top _____ ; edging _____
Back and end splash _____ Finish of cabinets _____ ; number coats _____
Medicine cabinets: make _____ ; model _____
Other cabinets and built-in furniture _____
Additional information: _____

20. STAIRS:

Stair	Treads		Risers		Strings		Handrail		Balusters	
	Material	Thickness	Material	Thickness	Material	Size	Material	Size	Material	Size
Basement _____										
Main _____										
Attic _____										

Disappearing: make and model number _____
Additional information: _____

21. SPECIAL FLOORS AND WAINSCOT:

	LOCATION	MATERIAL, COLOR, BORDER, SIZES, GAGE, ETC.	THRESHOLD MATERIAL	WALL BASE MATERIAL	UNDERFLOOR MATERIAL
FLOORS	Kitchen				
	Bath				

	LOCATION	MATERIAL, COLOR, BORDER, CAP. SIZES, GAGE, ETC.	HEIGHT	HEIGHT OVER TUB	HEIGHT IN SHOWERS (FROM FLOOR)
WAINSCOT	Bath				

Bathroom accessories: ☐ Recessed; material _____; number _____; ☐ Attached; material _____; number _____

Additional information: _____

22. PLUMBING:

FIXTURE	NUMBER	LOCATION	MAKE	MFR'S FIXTURE IDENTIFICATION NO.	SIZE	COLOR
Sink						
Lavatory						
Water closet						
Bathtub						
Shower over tub△						
Stall shower△						
Laundry trays						

△☐ Curtain rod △☐ Door ☐ Shower pan: material _____

Water supply: ☐ public; ☐ community system; ☐ individual (private) system. ★

Sewage disposal: ☐ public; ☐ community system; ☐ individual (private) system. ★

★ Show and describe individual system in complete detail in separate drawings and specifications according to requirements.

House drain (inside): ☐ cast iron; ☐ tile; ☐ other _____ House sewer (outside): ☐ cast iron; ☐ tile; ☐ other _____

Water piping: ☐ galvanized steel; ☐ copper tubing; ☐ other _____ Sill cocks, number _____

Domestic water heater: type _____; make and model _____; heating capacity _____

_____ gph. 100° rise. Storage tank: material _____; capacity _____ gallons.

Gas service: ☐ utility company; ☐ liq. pet. gas; ☐ other _____ Gas piping: ☐ cooking; ☐ house heating.

Footing drains connected to: ☐ storm sewer; ☐ sanitary sewer; ☐ dry well. Sump pump; make and model _____

_____; capacity _____; discharges into _____

23. HEATING:

☐ Hot water. ☐ Steam. ☐ Vapor. ☐ One-pipe system. ☐ Two-pipe system.

☐ Radiators. ☐ Convectors. ☐ Baseboard radiation. Make and model _____

Radiant panel: ☐ floor; ☐ wall; ☐ ceiling. Panel coil: material _____

☐ Circulator. ☐ Return pump. Make and model _____; capacity _____ gpm.

Boiler: make and model _____ Output _____ Btuh.; net rating _____ Btuh.

Additional information: _____

Warm air: ☐ Gravity. ☐ Forced. Type of system _____

Duct material: supply _____; return _____ Insulation _____, thickness _____ ☐ Outside air intake.

Furnace: make and model _____ Input _____ Btuh.; output _____ Btuh.

Additional information: _____

☐ Space heater; ☐ floor furnace; ☐ wall heater. Input _____ Btuh.; output _____ Btuh.; number units _____

Make, model _____ Additional information: _____

Controls: make and types _____

Additional information: _____

Fuel: ☐ Coal; ☐ oil; ☐ gas; ☐ liq. pet. gas; ☐ electric; ☐ other _____; storage capacity _____

Additional information: _____

Firing equipment furnished separately: ☐ Gas burner, conversion type. ☐ Stoker: hopper feed ☐; bin feed ☐

Oil burner: ☐ pressure atomizing; ☐ vaporizing _____

Make and model _____ Control _____

Additional information: _____

Electric heating system: type _____ Input _____ watts; @ _____ volts; output _____ Btuh.

Additional information: _____

Ventilating equipment: attic fan, make and model _____; capacity _____ cfm.

kitchen exhaust fan. make and model _____

Other heating, ventilating. or cooling equipment _____

24. ELECTRIC WIRING:

Service: ☐ overhead; ☐ underground. Panel: ☐ fuse box; ☐ circuit-breaker; make_____ AMP's _____ No. circuits _____

Wiring: ☐ conduit; ☐ armored cable; ☐ nonmetallic cable; ☐ knob and tube; ☐ other _____

Special outlets: ☐ range; ☐ water heater; ☐ other _____

☐ Doorbell. ☐ Chimes. Push-button locations _____ Additional information: _____

25. LIGHTING FIXTURES:

Total number of fixtures_____ Total allowance for fixtures, typical installation, $_____

Nontypical installation _____

Additional information: _____

26. INSULATION:

LOCATION	THICKNESS	MATERIAL, TYPE, AND METHOD OF INSTALLATION	VAPOR BARRIER
Roof			
Ceiling			
Wall			
Floor			

HARDWARE: (make, material, and finish.) _____

SPECIAL EQUIPMENT: (State material or make, model and quantity.   Include only equipment and appliances which are acceptable by local law, custom and applicable FHA standards.   Do not include items which, by established custom, are supplied by occupant and removed when he vacates premises or chattles prohibited by law from becoming realty.) _____

27. MISCELLANEOUS: (Describe any main dwelling materials, equipment, or construction items not shown elsewhere; or use to provide additional information where the space provided was inadequate.   Always reference by item number to correspond to numbering used on this form.) _____

PORCHES:

TERRACES:

GARAGES:

WALKS AND DRIVEWAYS:
Driveway: width _____; base material _____; thickness _____"; surfacing material _____; thickness _____"
Front walk: width _____; material _____; thickness _____". Service walk: width _____; material _____; thickness _____"
Steps: material _____; treads _____"; risers _____". Cheek walls _____

OTHER ONSITE IMPROVEMENTS:
(Specify all exterior onsite improvements not described elsewhere, including items such as unusual grading, drainage structures, retaining walls, fence, railings, and accessory structures.)

LANDSCAPING, PLANTING, AND FINISH GRADING:
Topsoil _____" thick: ☐ front yard; ☐ side yards; ☐ rear yard to _____ feet behind main building.
Lawns (seeded, sodded, or sprigged): ☐ front yard _____; ☐ side yards _____; ☐ rear yard _____
Planting: ☐ as specified and shown on drawings; ☐ as follows:

_____ Shade trees, deciduous, _____" caliper.	_____ Evergreen trees. _____' to _____', B & B.
_____ Low flowering trees, deciduous, _____' to _____'	_____ Evergreen shrubs. _____' to _____', B & B.
_____ High-growing shrubs, deciduous, _____' to _____'	_____ Vines, 2-year _____
_____ Medium-growing shrubs, deciduous, _____' to _____'	
_____ Low-growing shrubs, deciduous, _____' to _____'	

IDENTIFICATION.—This exhibit shall be identified by the signature of the builder, or sponsor, and/or the proposed mortgagor if the latter is known at the time of application.

Date _____   Signature _____

Signature _____

Appendix C
Sample Mortgage

Source: Courtesy of M. R. Toups, President, Greater New Orleans Homestead.

Sale of Property

BY

Greater New Orleans Homestead Association

TO

UNITED STATES OF AMERICA

STATE OF LOUISIANA

CITY OF NEW ORLEANS

═══════

BE IT KNOWN, That on this

day of   , in the year nineteen

hundred and

Before me,

a Notary Public in and for the City of New Orleans, in the Parish of Orleans, and State of Louisiana, aforesaid, duly commissioned and qualified, and in the presence of the witnesses hereinafter named and undersigned,

PERSONALLY CAME AND APPEARED:

herein acting for and representing the

GREATER NEW ORLEANS HOMESTEAD ASSOCIATION

a duly incorporated institution of this State, domiciled in this City, created by act before John Janvier, Notary, dated June 19, 1909, recorded in the Mortgage Office of this Parish in Book 950, Folio 297 et seq., amended by an act passed before Jacob D. Dresner, Notary Public, on September 17, 1924, recorded in Mortgage Office Book 1305, Folio 456, also amended by an act passed before Jacob D. Dresner, Notary Public, on June 17, 1926, recorded in Mortgage Office Book 1338, Folio 141, and amended by an act passed before Jacob D. Dresner, Notary Public, on October 13, 1937, recorded in Mortgage Office Book 1536, Folio 354, herein and hereunto authorized by a Resolution of the Board of Directors of said Association, adopted at a meeting of said Board, a copy of which resolution is hereto annexed for reference and made part hereof, which said appearer declared that for the consideration and on the terms and conditions hereinafter expressed, he does, by these presents, in said capacity, grant, bargain, sell, convey, transfer, assign, and set over unto

here present, accepting and purchasing for   heirs and assigns, and acknowledging delivery and possession thereof, the following described property, together with all the buildings and improvements thereon, and all rights, ways, privileges, servitudes, appurtenances, and prescriptions, liberative and acquisitive, thereunto belonging or in anywise appertaining, to-wit:

173

Being the same property which was acquired by said Association, by purchase from

as per act passed before me, Notary, on the   day of   19   , registered in the Con-

veyance Office of this City, in Book   Folio

    1. This sale is made and accepted for and in consideration of the price and sum of

                                               Dollars, ($), and, to represent
the said amount the purchaser has made and subscribed a certain promissory note for the sum of $
drawn by the purchaser to the order of said Association, payable on demand at its office, dated this day and bearing interest at the rate of   (%) per cent per annum from date until paid. The principal and
interest on the aforesaid note are payable monthly, in advance, on the first day of each month hereafter, in monthly installments of not less than

Dollars ($), until the whole of said principal sum is paid. All interest is to be calculated monthly by the
use of the three hundred and sixty day interest tables, and charged for each day in the month, on any balance of the
principal sum remaining due and unpaid, in accordance with the charter and by-laws of the Association; provided, that
if the borrower shall at any time be in arrears for as much as   days in the making of the stipulated monthly payments required under the terms of this act, including the additional payments hereinafter set forth, the interest rate hereinabove stipulated shall during delinquency be automatically increased by the addition of interest at the rate of
                  per cent (%), per annum.

    2. And the said promissory note, after having been paraphed "Ne Varietur" by me, notary, in order to identify the
same herewith, has been delivered unto said association through its undersigned officer who hereby acknowledges the
receipt thereof.

    3. The aforesaid monthly payments shall be made by the purchaser and accepted by the Association as dues on ac-
count of the monthly reduction shares in the Association, subscribed to by the purchaser, and herein assigned and given
in pledge to the Association.

    4. In addition to the monthly payments hereinabove stipulated, the purchaser is bound and obligated to pay each
month, in advance, a sum equal to one-twelfth (1/12th), of the total taxes, paving installments, special assessments, and
insurance premiums, of each current year, bearing against the above described property. In the event the amount of the annual
taxes, paving installments, special assessments, or insurance premiums, for any current year, is not available, the Association shall be privileged to make an estimate of the amount of said taxes, insurance premiums, paving installments, or special
assessments, based upon the previous year's assessment, rates, and previous charges. The estimate, so made, may be
corrected from year to year, at the Association's option, whenever the proper assessment or rates are available. In the event
insurance is effected for three years, one-thirty-sixth (1/36th) of the premiums instead of one-twelfth (1/12th) shall be
added to the monthly payment.

    5. In the event the purchaser shall promptly make the herein stipulated monthly payments, and shall punctually
comply with the obligations of this act, the Association will, when either the taxes, paving installments, or insurance
premiums become due, advance, for the purpose of paying these items, an amount not to exceed the total payments made
by the purchaser during the twelve months previous to the time of the maturities of the items herein specified that are
in excess of the monthly payments of principal and interest due on account of the note. Provided that, if the Association
shall have advanced, during the twelve (12) month period aforesaid any amount for the payment of either taxes, paving
installments, special assessments, or insurance premiums, this amount may be deducted from the amount so paid by the
purchaser to the Association before making any further advance. Any amount advanced or owing may at the discretion of the
Association be added to and become part of the indebtedness due on account of the note, and shall be secured by this
mortgage and vendor's lien.

    6. And in order to secure the payment of said promissory note in principal and interest, according to its tenor and
to the provisions herein contained and set forth in the Charter and By-Laws of the Association, and also in order to
secure the faithful performance of all of the obligations contained herein and the reimbursement and payment of all taxes,
insurance premiums, paving and other assessments, costs, fees, and expenses hereinafter set out, the purchaser does, by
these presents, specially mortgage, affect and hypothecate unto and in favor of said GREATER NEW ORLEANS
HOMESTEAD ASSOCIATION, its legal successors, representatives and assigns, in addition to the vendor's lien and
privilege specially granted and retained on said property, the said hereinabove described property, which said purchaser
agrees not to sell, alienate, encumber, remove, waste, or destroy to the prejudice of this act.

    7. And in order still further to secure said indebtedness the said purchaser does, by these presents, assign and pledge
to said Association all the installments now paid and to be paid, on   Monthly Reduction shares of the capital
stock of said Association, standing in the said purchaser's name on the Books of the Association, and represented by Certificate No.   , Installment Book No.   which is delivered to said Association through its undersigned
officer, who hereby acknowledges receipt and delivery of same; and the said pledge is hereby made under all the terms and
provisions of said above-mentioned Charter and By-Laws.

METHOD OF APPLYING PAYMENTS:

8. The purchaser further covenants and agrees, and is specially bound and obligated as follows:

That the monthly payments, made and accepted as dues on the aforesaid shares, together with any and all additional payments, as herein specified, shall be added together, and the aggregate amount thereof shall be paid by the purchaser each month, in advance, in a single payment, and shall be applied by the Association in the following manner:

(a) To the payment of interest on the aforesaid note, at the rate hereinabove stipulated, on any balance of the principal remaining due and unpaid.

(b) To the re-payment of any amount which the Association shall have advanced for the payment of taxes, paving assessments, insurance premiums, special assessments, transfer fees, repairs, costs, attorney's and notarial fees, and expenses of any nature, together with interest thereon at the same rate as that charged on the principal sum.

(c) The balance, if any, to be applied to the reduction of the principal sum.

The above order of imputation may be changed at the discretion of the Association, or the remainder after payment of interest, may be credited in such manner as the Association may determine.

(d) Any deficiency in the amount of the aggregate monthly payment shall constitute a default under this act.

9. The balance due on the aforesaid note shall, at any time, be the amount of the face of said note, plus any amount which may have been advanced by or due to the Association, on account of taxes, insurance premiums, assessments, transfer fees, paving assessments, repairs, costs, attorney's and notarial fees, and/or expenses of any nature, together with interest thereon at the same rate as hereinabove stipulated, minus such sums as shall have been applied against the borrower's indebtedness.

10. That he will promptly pay all taxes, assessments, water rates, and other governmental or municipal charges, fines, or impositions, for which provision has not been made herein, and promptly deliver the official receipt therefor to the Association. If the purchaser fails to make such payments the Association is hereby authorized at its option to make them, and any sums so advanced shall bear interest at the same rate as, and become a part of, the principal debt from the date of payment, and shall be secured by the pledge and mortgage herein granted and by the vendor's lien herein retained.

11. That sums advanced by the Association for the payment of any taxes, special assessments, premiums of insurance, or any other charges against the property, or for any expense or cost whatsoever shall bear interest at the same rate as, and become a part of, the principal debt from the date of payment, and the reimbursement thereof shall be secured by the pledge and mortgage herein granted and the vendor's lien herein retained.

INSURANCE:

12. That he will insure and keep the building and improvements now existing, or hereafter erected, on said grounds, constantly insured, in such sums as the Association may require, against loss by fire, windstorm, tornado, and such other risks as the Association may hereafter require, in some good and solvent company or companies (which company or companies must be acceptable to the Association) until full and final payment of all the indebtedness hereunder, and will transfer and deliver the policy or policies of such insurance or insurances, and their renewals, to the Association, or assigns; in default of which the Association, or assigns, is hereby authorized, at its option, to avail itself of the rights hereinafter set forth, or to cause such insurance to be made and effected at the cost, charge, and expense of said purchaser.

13. That if the property covered hereby, or any pert thereof, shall be damaged or destroyed by fire or other hazard against which insurance is held, the amounts due by any insurance company shall, to the extent of the indebtedness then remaining unpaid, be paid to the Association, and, when so paid, may, at its option, be applied to the debt or be used for the repairing or rebuilding of the said property.

14. The purchaser also agrees in the event of loss, not to make settlement with any Insurance Company without the approval of the Association and hereby employs its Building Expert to adjust any loss, the fee to be paid by the Insurance Company, if such fee is provided for in the policy. If the policy does not provide for such fee, then the purchaser shall pay said fee.

REPAIRS:

15. The purchaser agrees to keep the property in good repair; that failure to do so within ten days after written notification by the Association to the purchaser, at his last known address, shall ipso facto mature the entire balance due said Association by the purchaser and shall authorize executory process by the Association under the general terms and provisions relating to executory process as herein provided; or if the Association prefers, the purchaser hereby authorizes said Association without putting in default to cause necessary repairs to be made at the purchaser's expense, and charge same plus the cost of supervision to the purchaser's obligation.

REIMBURSEMENT FOR ADVANCES:

16. The said purchaser hereby authorizes said Association to reimburse itself from any credits or pledges, including paid up stock or optional payment shares, in its possession and belonging to said purchaser, for all payments due it and for all payments or advances made by it by reason of non-payment by said purchaser of any obligations due hereunder, including attorney's and notary's fees, and costs.

ASSIGNMENT OF RENTS:

17. In the event of violation of any of the terms, conditions, or covenants of this act, such violation shall ipso facto effect an assignment of the leases and rents to said Association and the purchaser hereby authorizes the Association to collect, by legal process, if necessary, rentals due by tenants of the purchaser occupying the property hereinabove described and to have delinquent tenants evicted. After deducting the cost and/or eviction, the net proceeds shall be credited to the purchaser, and the purchaser hereby specially agrees that when the account is delinquent, payments thereon may be credited in the manner the Association deems best.

CONDITIONS MATURING NOTE:

18. That in the event the purchaser should violate any of the conditions of this act, or should fail promptly to perform any obligation hereunder or be in arrears for a period of 13 weeks even if the purchaser shall have made prior payments in excess of the amount required, or upon the happening of any one or more of the events or conditions listed below, the entire balance due by the purchaser to the Association shall ipso facto, without demand, notice, or putting in default, immediately become due, exigible and payable, together with interest, taxes, premiums of insurance, attorney's and notarial fees, advances and all costs, expenses and other charges, whatsoever, the said purchaser hereby confessing judgment in favor of said Association and its assigns, for the full amount of said promissory note together with all interest, taxes, premiums of insurance, attorney's and notarial fees, advances, and all costs, expenses, and other charges whatsoever:

(a) Insolvency of the purchaser, application by the purchaser to be adjudicated a bankrupt, or the institution of involuntary bankruptcy proceedings against him, or the institution by or against the purchaser of any proceedings for the appointment of a receiver or syndic, or the filing of any proceeding seeking reorganization if the purchaser be a corporation; the purchaser hereby agreeing that the happening of any one or more of the incidents herein enumerated will not in any way enjoin, hinder or delay any legal proceedings which the Association has the right to institute under the provisions of this act; and the purchaser further agrees that no Order of any Court in any of the above enumerated proceedings will be sought to enjoin, hinder or delay the proceedings which the Association has the right to institute under the provisions of this act.

(b) The recordation or registry of any lien or claim, or the institution of any legal proceedings to enforce any lien or claim against the property; or if the property be seized or levied upon by an officer of court.

(c) Death or dissolution of the purchaser.

(d) The cancellation of any insurance covering the property, for whatever reason, if the purchaser fail immediately to replace said insurance in a company or companies satisfactory to the Association; or upon the inability of the purchaser to procure insurance protection required under the terms of this act;

(e) The use of the property for any unlawful purpose;

(f) The making of any repairs, additions, or alterations to the buildings or improvements on the ground herein conveyed, or allowing of any work to be done whereby any lien or privilege could result against the property, or in case of the actual or threatened alteration, repair or addition to, demolition or removal of any building on the property herein mortgaged, without previously obtaining the written consent of the Association;

(g) The sale or transfer of the property without the written consent of the Association.

19. The purchaser acknowledges and agrees that all of the provisions of this deed are of its essence; that any violation of any of the terms hereof; shall ipso facto mature the obligation of the purchaser and shall authorize said Associa ion to proceed by executory or any other process in accordance with the terms of this deed governing the procedure when executory or other process may be resorted to; and that the Association would not have made the present sale to the purchaser unless all of said provisions were agreed to by the purchaser.

175

20. That in the event of any default or the violation of the conditions of this act, or the happening of any one or more of the events hereinabove mentioned, the Association shall have the right, without the necessity of demand or of putting in default, to cause the property herein described, together with all the improvements thereon, to be seized and sold under executory or other process issued by any competent court, or may proceed to the enforcement of its rights in any other manner provided by law, and the property may be sold with or without appraisement, at the option of the Association, to the highest bidder for cash, the purchaser hereby waiving the benefit of all laws relative to the appraisement of property seized and sold under executory or other process.

21. In the event of sale of said property under executory or other legal process said Association shall have the option of causing said property to be offered and sold by the Sheriff at the Sheriff's Sale, in parcels or as a whole.

22. That if legal proceedings are instituted for the recovery of any amount due hereunder, or if any claim hereunder is placed in the hands of an attorney for collection, the purchaser agrees to pay the fees of the attorney at law employed for that purpose, and such fees are hereby fixed at _____ per centum (%) of the amount due, the minimum attorney's fee to be twenty-five dollars.

23. The Association may, at any time, without notice, release all or a part of the mortgaged premises from the lien or effects of this mortgage, grant an extension, or deferment of the time of payment for any indebtedness secured hereby, or release from liability any one or more parties that have become liable for the payment of said indebtedness secured hereby, without affecting the personal liability of the purchaser, or any other party liable, or hereafter becoming liable, for the payment of any of the indebtedness secured by this mortgage.

24. Upon application by the purchaser, or any future owner of the property hereinabove described, to the Association, for a reduction in the amount of the monthly payments, the Association shall have the right, through any of its designated officers, or committee, as its Board of Directors may authorize, to act on such matters. In case of such reduction, the certificate of any officer of the Association, under its seal, shall at all times, be conclusive and authentic evidence of the amount of the required monthly payment and of its having been fixed by competent authority.

25. It is hereby agreed and understood by and between the parties hereto that if the said purchaser shall make the herein stipulated payments promptly and punctually, then and in that case, the principal of said note shall not become exigible until the value of said shares of stock shall become equal to the amount of said indebtedness with all interest and costs that may be due upon the same, at the happening of which event, said stock and said indebtedness shall cancel each other, the stock and indebtedness being alike extinguished and thereupon it shall be the duty of any officer of said Association, to cancel said stock and give to said purchaser full receipt and acquittance, as well as to surrender to said purchaser the said abovementioned promissory note.

26. If at any time before the value of the purchaser's stock shall be equal to the purchaser's indebtedness, the said purchaser should desire to pay, settle, and cancel said indebtedness, said purchaser shall have the right to surrender to the Association in part payment of such indebtedness at their cash value, the shares herein pledged in this Association provided said purchaser pays in cash the balance of such indebtedness and, then it shall be the duty of any officer of said Association to cancel said stock and to give and render to said purchaser a proper receipt and acquittance as well as to surrender said note to said purchaser.

27. To have and to hold the said property and appurtenances to the said purchaser, said purchaser's heirs and assigns to their proper use and behoof forever.

28. The Association declares that this sale is made without warranty, not even for the return of the purchase price; but, the said Association subrogates the said purchaser to all the rights and actions of warranty and otherwise, which the said Association has or may have against all former owners of said property, fully authorizing the said purchaser to exercise the said rights and actions in the same manner as said Association itself might or could have done, the whole without recourse.

29. And the said Association declares that the fact that it does not warrant the title of said property is not to be construed as casting any doubt or cloud upon the title, for the reason that the property is vested in said Association temporarily only, and merely for the purpose of obtaining the security of a vendor's lien mortgage in accordance with the special provisions of the law of Louisiana governing Building and Loan Associations.

30. This sale and mortgage is made to the purchaser in consideration of his membership in the Association and the member-purchaser agrees that the Charter and By-Laws of said Association are and shall be binding upon him and do by reference form a part of this contract, and he further agrees that any amendment to the said Charter or By-Laws of the said Association, properly and regularly adopted, shall be likewise binding upon him and so long as any part of the obligation hereunder created shall be unpaid, said amendments to the Charter and By-Laws shall become and form a part of this contract to the same extent as if the same were written in extenso herein.

31. The purchaser agrees that the failure of the Association to exercise any of its rights, privileges, or options, at any time, is an indulgence granted to him and shall not constitute a waiver of its rights to exercise the same at any other time. Nothing, in this act contained, shall be construed so as to limit any right or remedy granted or available to the Association under any provision of law, or its charter and by-laws.

32. The covenants herein contained shall bind, and the benefits and advantages shall inure to, the respective heirs, executors, administrators, successors, and assigns of the parties hereto. Whenever used, the singular number shall include the plural, the plural the singular, and the use of any gender shall be applicable to all genders.

33. It is agreed that the right herein given to said Association to pay taxes, effect insurance, collect rents, make repairs, or any other right granted herein, shall not be construed as obligating said Association to do any or all of these things, or making it liable in any manner for its not doing any or all of them.

34. The production of Mortgage, Conveyance, and United States District and Circuit Court Certificates is hereby waived by the parties hereto, who relieve and release me, Notary, from all responsibility and liability in the premises for such nonproduction.

35. The purchaser waives and renounces in favor of the vendor, and any future holder of said note, any and all homestead rights in and to the above property which he has or may have under the Constitution and laws of the State of Louisiana.

36. Any paving or other lien or assessment chargeable against the herein conveyed property is assumed by the purchaser. All the taxes on the said property, up to and including those due and exigible in the year 19 , are paid, as will appear by reference to the vendor's act of purchase hereinabove mentioned. The taxes for 19 , are assumed by the present purchaser.

THUS DONE AND PASSED at my office in the City of New Orleans, on the day, month and year first above written, in the presence of the undersigned competent witnesses, who have hereunto signed their names with the appearers and me, Notary, after reading of the whole.

GREATER NEW ORLEANS HOMESTEAD ASSOCIATION

WITNESSES:

By: ....
President.

Appendix D
Inflation Tables and
Compound Interest
Tables

Table D-1 Inflation Projection
Annual Devaluation of $1 at 1 to 20 Percent Rates of Inflation Over 1 to 50 Years

Period	1%	2%	3%	4%	5%	6%	7%	8%	9%	10%
1	.9901	.9804	.9709	.9615	.9524	.9433	.9346	.9259	.9174	.9091
2	.9803	.9612	.9426	.9246	.9070	.8900	.8734	.8573	.8417	.8264
3	.9706	.9423	.9151	.8890	.8638	.8396	.8163	.7938	.7722	.7513
4	.9610	.9238	.8884	.8548	.8227	.7921	.7629	.7350	.7084	.6830
5	.9515	.9057	.8626	.8219	.7835	.7473	.7130	.6805	.6499	.6209
6	.9420	.8880	.8375	.7903	.7462	.7050	.6663	.6302	.5963	.5645
7	.9327	.8706	.8131	.7600	.7107	.6651	.6227	.5835	.5470	.5132
8	.9235	.8535	.7894	.7307	.6768	.6274	.5820	.5403	.5019	.4665
9	.9143	.8368	.7664	.7026	.6446	.5919	.5440	.5002	.4604	.4241
10	.9053	.8203	.7441	.6756	.6139	.5584	.5083	.4632	.4224	.3855
11	.8963	.8043	.7224	.6496	.5847	.5268	.4751	.4289	.3875	.3505
12	.8874	.7885	.7014	.6246	.5568	.4970	.4440	.3971	.3556	.3186
13	.8787	.7730	.6810	.6006	.5303	.4688	.4150	.3677	.3262	.2897
14	.8700	.7579	.6611	.5775	.5051	.4423	.3878	.3405	.2992	.2633
15	.8613	.7430	.6419	.5552	.4810	.4173	.3624	.3152	.2745	.2394
16	.8528	.7284	.6232	.5340	.4581	.3936	.3387	.2191	.2519	.2176
17	.8444	.7142	.6050	.5134	.4363	.3714	.3166	.2703	.2311	.1978
18	.8360	.7002	.5874	.4936	.4155	.3503	.2959	.2502	.2120	.1799
19	.8277	.6864	.5703	.4746	.3957	.3305	.2765	.2317	.1945	.1635
20	.8195	.6730	.5537	.4564	.3769	.3118	.2584	.2145	.1784	.1486
21	.8114	.6598	.5375	.4388	.3590	.2942	.2415	.1987	.1637	.1351
22	.8034	.6468	.5219	.4220	.3418	.2775	.2257	.1839	.1502	.1228
23	.7954	.6342	.5067	.4057	.3256	.2618	.2110	.1703	.1378	.1117
24	.7876	.6217	.4919	.3901	.3101	.2470	.1971	.1577	.1264	.1015
25	.7798	.6095	.4776	.3751	.2953	.2330	.1842	.1460	.1160	.0923
26	.7720	.5976	.4637	.3607	.2812	.2198	.1722	.1352	.1064	.0839
27	.7644	.5859	.4502	.3468	.2678	.2074	.1609	.1252	.0976	.0763
28	.7568	.5744	.4371	.3335	.2551	.1956	.1504	.1159	.0895	.0693
29	.7493	.5631	.4243	.3207	.2430	.1846	.1406	.1073	.0822	.0630
30	.7419	.5521	.4120	.3083	.2314	.1741	.1314	.0994	.0754	.0573
31	.7346	.5412	.4000	.2965	.2204	.1643	.1228	.0920	.0691	.0521
32	.7273	.5306	.3883	.2851	.2100	.1550	.1147	.0852	.0634	.0474
33	.7201	.5202	.3770	.2741	.1999	.1462	.1072	.0789	.0582	.0431
34	.7130	.5100	.3660	.2636	.1904	.1380	.1002	.0730	.0534	.0391
35	.7060	.5000	.3554	.2534	.1813	.1301	.0937	.0676	.0490	.0356
36	.6990	.4902	.3450	.2437	.1727	.1227	.0875	.0626	.0449	.0323
37	.6920	.4806	.3350	.2343	.1644	.1158	.0818	.0580	.0412	.0294
38	.6852	.4712	.3252	.2253	.1566	.1092	.0765	.0537	.0378	.0267
39	.6784	.4619	.3158	.2166	.1491	.1031	.0715	.0497	.0347	.0243
40	.6717	.4529	.3066	.2083	.1420	.0972	.0668	.0460	.0318	.0221
41	.6650	.4440	.2976	.2003	.1353	.0917	.0624	.0426	.0292	.0201
42	.6584	.4353	.2890	.1926	.1288	.0865	.0583	.0395	.0268	.0183
43	.6519	.4268	.2805	.1852	.1227	.0816	.0545	.0365	.0246	.0166
44	.6454	.4184	.2724	.1780	.1169	.0770	.0509	.0338	.0226	.0151
45	.6391	.4102	.2644	.1712	.1113	.0727	.0476	.0313	.0207	.0137
46	.6327	.4022	.2567	.1646	.1060	.0685	.0445	.0290	.0190	.0125
47	.6265	.3943	.2493	.1583	.1010	.0647	.0416	.0269	.0174	.0113
48	.6203	.3865	.2420	.1523	.0961	.0610	.0389	.0249	.0160	.0103
49	.6141	.3790	.2350	.1463	.0916	.0575	.0363	.0230	.0147	.0094
50	.6080	.3715	.2281	.1407	.0872	.0543	.0339	.0213	.0134	.0085

Table D–1 (continued)

Period	11%	12%	13%	14%	15%	16%	17%	18%	19%	20%
1	.9009	.8929	.8850	.8772	.8696	.8621	.8547	.8475	.8403	.8333
2	.8116	.7972	.7831	.7695	.7561	.7432	.7305	.7182	.7062	.6944
3	.7312	.7118	.6931	.6750	.6575	.6407	.6244	.6086	.5934	.5787
4	.6587	.6355	.6133	.5921	.5718	.5523	.5337	.5158	.4987	.4823
5	.5935	.5674	.5428	.5194	.4972	.4761	.4561	.4371	.4190	.4019
6	.5346	.5066	.4803	.4556	.4323	.4104	.3898	.3704	.3521	.3349
7	.4817	.4523	.4250	.3996	.3759	.3538	.3332	.3139	.2959	.2791
8	.4339	.4039	.3762	.3506	.3269	.3050	.2848	.2660	.2487	.2326
9	.3909	.3606	.3329	.3075	.2843	.2630	.2434	.2255	.2090	.1938
10	.3522	.3220	.2946	.2697	.2472	.2267	.2080	.1911	.1756	.1615
11	.3173	.2875	.2607	.2366	.2149	.1954	.1778	.1619	.1476	.1346
12	.2858	.2567	.2307	.2076	.1869	.1685	.1520	.1372	.1240	.1122
13	.2575	.2292	.2042	.1821	.1625	.1452	.1299	.1163	.1042	.0935
14	.2320	.2046	.1807	.1597	.1413	.1252	.1110	.0985	.0876	.0779
15	.2090	.1827	.1599	.1401	.1229	.1079	.0949	.0835	.0736	.0649
16	.1883	.1631	.1415	.1229	.1069	.0930	.0811	.0708	.0618	.0541
17	.1696	.1456	.1252	.1078	.0929	.0802	.0693	.0600	.0520	.0451
18	.1528	.1300	.1108	.0946	.0808	.0691	.0592	.0508	.0437	.0376
19	.1377	.1161	.0981	.0830	.0703	.0596	.0506	.0431	.0367	.0313
20	.1240	.1037	.0868	.0728	.0611	.0514	.0433	.0365	.0308	.0261
21	.1117	.0926	.0768	.0638	.0531	.0443	.0370	.0309	.0259	.0217
22	.1007	.0826	.0680	.0560	.0462	.0382	.0316	.0262	.0218	.0181
23	.0907	.0738	.0601	.0491	.0402	.0329	.0270	.0222	.0183	.0151
24	.0817	.0659	.0532	.0431	.0349	.0284	.0231	.0188	.0154	.0126
25	.0736	.0588	.0471	.0378	.0304	.0245	.0197	.0160	.0129	.0105
26	.0663	.0525	.0417	.0331	.0264	.0211	.0169	.0135	.0109	.0087
27	.0597	.0469	.0369	.0291	.0230	.0182	.0144	.0115	.0091	.0073
28	.0538	.0419	.0326	.0255	.0200	.0157	.0123	.0097	.0077	.0061
29	.0485	.0374	.0289	.0224	.0174	.0135	.0105	.0082	.0064	.0051
30	.0437	.0333	.0256	.0196	.0151	.0116	.0090	.0070	.0054	.0042
31	.0394	.0298	.0226	.0172	.0131	.0100	.0077	.0059	.0046	.0035
32	.0355	.0266	.0200	.0151	.0114	.0087	.0066	.0050	.0038	.0029
33	.0320	.0238	.0177	.0132	.0099	.0075	.0056	.0042	.0032	.0024
34	.0288	.0212	.0157	.0116	.0086	.0064	.0048	.0036	.0027	.0020
35	.0260	.0189	.0139	.0102	.0075	.0055	.0041	.0030	.0023	.0017
36	.0234	.0169	.0123	.0090	.0065	.0049	.0035	.0026	.0019	.0014
37	.0210	.0151	.0109	.0078	.0058	.0041	.0030	.0022	.0016	.0012
38	.0190	.0135	.0096	.0069	.0049	.0036	.0026	.0019	.0013	.0010
39	.0171	.0120	.0085	.0060	.0043	.0031	.0022	.0016	.0011	.0008
40	.0154	.0107	.0075	.0053	.0037	.0026	.0019	.0013	.0010	.0007
41	.0139	.0096	.0067	.0046	.0032	.0023	.0016	.0011	.0008	.0006
42	.0125	.0086	.0059	.0041	.0028	.0020	.0014	.0010	.0007	.0005
43	.0112	.0076	.0052	.0036	.0025	.0017	.0012	.0008	.0006	.0004
44	.0101	.0068	.0046	.0031	.0021	.0015	.0010	.0007	.0005	.0003
45	.0091	.0061	.0041	.0027	.0019	.0013	.0009	.0006	.0004	.0003
46	.0082	.0054	.0036	.0024	.0016	.0011	.0007	.0005	.0003	.0002
47	.0074	.0049	.0032	.0021	.0014	.0009	.0006	.0004	.0003	.0002
48	.0067	.0043	.0028	.0019	.0012	.0008	.0005	.0004	.0002	.0002
49	.0060	.0039	.0025	.0016	.0011	.0007	.0005	.0003	.0002	.0001
50	.0054	.0035	.0022	.0014	.0009	.0006	.0004	.0003	.0002	.0001

Table D–2   Inflation Projection
Devaluation of $1 Invested Annually at 1 to 20 Percent
Rates of Inflation Over 1 to 50 Years

Period	1%	2%	3%	4%	5%	6%	7%	8%	9%	10%
1	.9901	.9804	.9709	.9615	.9524	.9434	.9346	.9259	.9174	.9091
2	1.9704	1.9416	1.9135	1.8861	1.8594	1.8334	1.8080	1.7833	1.7591	1.7355
3	2.9410	2.8839	2.8286	2.7751	2.7232	2.6730	2.6243	2.5771	2.5313	2.4868
4	3.9020	3.8077	3.7171	3.6299	3.5460	3.4651	3.3872	3.3121	3.2397	3.1699
5	4.8534	4.7135	4.5797	4.4518	4.3295	4.2124	4.1002	3.9927	3.8896	3.7908
6	5.7955	5.6014	5.4172	5.2421	5.0757	4.9173	4.7665	4.6229	4.4859	4.3553
7	6.7282	6.4720	6.2503	6.0021	5.7864	5.5824	5.3893	5.2064	5.0329	4.8684
8	7.6517	7.3255	7.0197	6.7327	6.4632	6.2098	5.9713	5.7466	5.5348	5.3349
9	8.5660	8.1622	7.7861	7.4353	7.1078	6.8017	6.5152	6.2469	5.9952	5.7590
10	9.4713	8.9826	8.5302	8.1109	7.7217	7.3601	7.0236	6.7101	6.4176	6.1446
11	10.3676	9.7868	9.2526	8.7605	8.3064	7.8869	7.4987	7.1390	6.8052	6.4951
12	11.2551	10.5753	9.9540	9.3851	8.8633	8.3838	7.9427	7.5361	7.1607	6.8137
13	12.1337	11.3484	10.6350	9.9856	9.3936	8.6527	8.3577	7.9038	7.4869	7.1033
14	13.0037	12.1062	11.2961	10.5631	9.8986	9.2950	8.7455	8.2442	7.7861	7.3667
15	13.8651	12.8493	11.9379	11.1184	10.3797	9.7122	9.1079	8.5595	8.0607	7.6061
16	14.7179	13.5777	12.5611	11.6523	10.8378	10.1059	9.4467	8.8514	8.3125	7.8237
17	15.5623	14.2919	13.1661	12.1657	11.2741	10.4773	9.7632	9.1216	8.5436	8.0215
18	16.3983	14.9920	13.7535	12.6593	11.6896	10.8270	10.0591	9.3719	8.7556	8.2014
19	17.2260	15.6785	14.3238	13.1339	12.0853	11.1581	10.3356	9.6036	8.9501	8.3649
20	18.0456	16.3514	14.8775	13.5903	12.4622	11.4700	10.5940	9.8181	9.1285	8.5136
21	18.8570	17.0112	15.4150	14.0292	12.8212	11.7641	10.8355	10.0168	9.2922	8.6487
22	19.6604	17.6580	15.9369	14.4511	13.1630	12.0416	11.0612	10.2007	9.4424	8.7715
23	20.4558	18.2922	16.4436	14.8568	13.4886	12.3034	11.2722	10.3711	9.5802	8.8832
24	21.2434	18.9139	16.9355	15.2470	13.7986	12.5504	11.4693	10.5288	9.7066	8.9847
25	22.0232	19.5235	17.4131	15.6221	14.0939	12.7834	11.6536	10.6748	9.8226	9.0770
26	22.7952	20.1210	17.8768	15.9828	14.3752	13.0032	11.8258	10.8100	9.9289	9.1609
27	23.5600	20.7069	18.3270	16.3296	14.6430	13.2105	11.9867	10.9352	10.0266	9.2372
28	24.3164	21.2813	18.7641	16.6631	14.8981	13.4062	12.1371	11.0511	10.1161	9.3066
29	25.0658	21.8444	19.1885	16.9837	15.1411	13.5908	12.2777	11.1584	10.1983	9.3696
30	25.8077	22.3965	19.6004	17.2920	15.3724	13.7648	12.4090	11.2578	10.2736	9.4269
31	26.5423	22.9377	20.0004	17.5885	15.5923	13.9291	12.5319	11.3498	10.3428	9.4790
32	27.2696	23.4683	20.3888	17.8736	15.8023	14.0840	12.6465	11.4349	10.4062	9.5264
33	27.9897	23.9886	20.7658	18.1476	16.0026	14.2302	12.7538	11.5139	10.4644	9.5694
34	28.7027	24.4986	21.1318	18.4112	16.1929	14.3681	12.8540	11.5869	10.5178	9.6086
35	29.4086	24.9986	21.4872	18.6646	16.3742	14.4982	12.9477	11.6546	10.5668	9.6441
36	30.1075	25.4888	21.8323	18.9083	16.5469	14.6209	13.0352	11.7172	10.6118	9.6765
37	30.7995	25.9695	22.1672	19.1426	16.7113	14.7368	13.1170	11.7752	10.6529	9.7059
38	31.4847	26.4406	22.4925	19.3679	16.8679	14.8460	13.1935	11.8289	10.6908	9.7326
39	32.1630	26.9026	22.8082	19.5845	17.0170	14.9491	13.2649	11.8786	10.7255	9.7569
40	32.8347	27.3555	23.1148	19.7928	17.1591	15.0463	13.3317	11.9246	10.7574	9.7790
41	33.4997	27.7995	23.4124	19.9931	17.2944	15.1380	13.3941	11.9672	10.7866	9.7991
42	34.1581	28.2348	23.7014	20.1856	17.4232	15.2245	13.4524	12.0067	10.8134	9.8174
43	34.8100	28.6616	23.9819	20.3708	17.5459	15.3062	13.5069	12.0432	10.8379	9.8339
44	35.4555	29.0800	24.2543	20.5488	17.6628	15.3832	13.5579	12.0771	10.8605	9.8491
45	36.0945	29.4902	24.5187	20.7200	17.7741	15.4559	13.6055	12.1084	10.8812	9.8628
46	36.7272	29.8923	24.7754	20.8847	17.8801	15.5243	13.6500	12.1374	10.9002	9.8753
47	37.3537	30.2866	25.0247	21.0429	17.9811	15.5890	13.6916	12.1643	10.9176	9.8866
48	37.9740	30.6731	25.2667	21.1951	18.0772	15.6500	13.7305	12.1891	10.9336	9.8969
49	38.5881	31.0521	25.5017	21.3415	18.1688	15.7076	13.7668	12.2122	10.9482	9.9063
50	39.1961	31.4236	25.7298	21.4822	18.2559	15.7619	13.8007	12.2335	10.9617	9.9148

Table D-2 (continued)

Period	11%	12%	13%	14%	15%	16%	17%	18%	19%	20%
1	.9009	.8928	.8849	.8772	.8696	.8621	.8547	.8475	.8403	.8333
2	1.7125	1.6900	1.6681	1.6467	1.6257	1.6052	1.5852	1.5656	1.5465	1.5278
3	2.4437	2.4018	2.3611	2.3216	2.2832	2.2459	2.2096	2.1743	2.1399	2.1065
4	3.1024	3.0373	2.9745	2.9137	2.8550	2.7982	2.7432	2.6901	2.6386	2.5887
5	3.6959	3.6048	3.5172	3.4331	3.3522	3.2743	3.1993	3.1272	3.0576	2.9906
6	4.2305	4.1114	3.9975	3.8887	3.7844	3.6847	3.5892	3.4976	3.4098	3.3255
7	4.7122	4.5637	4.4226	4.2883	4.1604	4.0386	3.9224	3.8115	3.7057	3.6046
8	5.1461	4.9676	4.7988	4.6389	4.4873	4.3436	4.2072	4.0776	3.9544	3.8372
9	5.5370	5.3282	5.1316	4.9464	4.7716	4.6065	4.4506	4.3030	4.1633	4.0310
10	5.8892	5.6502	5.4262	5.2161	5.0188	4.8332	4.6586	4.4941	4.3389	4.1925
11	6.2065	5.9377	5.6869	5.4527	5.2337	5.0286	4.8364	4.6560	4.4865	4.3271
12	6.4923	6.1944	5.9176	5.6603	5.4206	5.1971	4.9884	4.7932	4.6105	4.4392
13	6.7499	6.4235	6.1218	5.8424	5.5831	5.3423	5.1183	4.9095	4.7147	4.5327
14	6.9819	6.6282	6.3025	6.0021	5.7245	5.4675	5.2293	5.0081	4.8023	4.6106
15	7.1909	6.8109	6.4624	6.1422	5.8474	5.5755	5.3242	5.0916	4.8759	4.6755
16	7.3792	6.9739	6.6039	6.2651	5.9542	5.6685	5.4053	5.1624	4.9377	4.7296
17	7.5488	7.1196	6.7291	6.3729	6.0472	5.7487	5.4746	5.2223	4.9897	4.7746
18	7.7016	7.2497	6.8399	6.4674	6.1280	5.8178	5.5339	5.2732	5.0333	4.8122
19	7.8393	7.3658	6.9380	6.5504	6.1982	5.8775	5.5845	5.3162	5.0700	4.8435
20	7.9633	7.4694	7.0247	6.6231	6.2593	5.9288	5.6278	5.3527	5.1009	4.8696
21	8.0751	7.5620	7.1015	6.6870	6.3125	5.9731	5.6648	5.3837	5.1268	4.8913
22	8.1757	7.6446	7.1695	6.7429	6.3587	6.0113	5.6964	5.4099	5.1486	4.9094
23	8.2664	7.7184	7.2296	6.7921	6.3988	6.0442	5.7234	5.4321	5.1668	4.9245
24	8.3481	7.7843	7.2829	6.8351	6.4338	6.0726	5.7465	5.4509	5.1822	4.9371
25	8.4217	7.8431	7.3200	6.8729	6.4641	6.0971	5.7662	5.4669	5.1951	4.9476
26	8.4880	7.8957	7.3717	6.9061	6.4906	6.1182	5.7831	5.4804	5.2060	4.9563
27	8.5478	7.9425	7.4085	6.9352	6.5135	6.1364	5.7975	5.4919	5.2151	4.9636
28	8.6016	7.9844	7.4412	6.9607	6.5335	6.1520	5.8099	5.5016	5.2228	4.9697
29	8.6501	8.0218	7.4701	6.9830	6.5509	6.1656	5.8204	5.5098	5.2292	4.9747
30	8.6938	8.0552	7.4956	7.0027	6.5660	6.1772	5.8294	5.5168	5.2347	4.9798
31	8.7331	8.0850	7.5183	7.0199	6.5791	6.1872	5.8371	5.5227	5.2392	4.9824
32	8.7686	8.1116	7.5383	7.0350	6.5905	6.1959	5.8437	5.5277	5.2430	4.9854
33	8.8005	8.1353	7.5560	7.0482	6.6005	6.2034	5.8493	5.5320	5.2462	4.9878
34	8.8293	8.1566	7.5717	7.0599	6.6091	6.2098	5.8541	5.5356	5.2489	4.9898
35	8.8552	8.1755	7.5856	7.0700	6.6167	6.2153	5.8582	5.5386	5.2512	4.9915
36	8.8786	8.1924	7.5978	7.0790	6.6231	6.2201	5.8617	5.5412	5.2531	4.9929
37	8.8996	8.2075	7.6087	7.0868	6.6288	6.2242	5.8647	5.5434	5.2547	4.9941
38	8.9186	8.2210	7.6183	7.0937	6.6337	6.2278	5.8673	5.5452	5.2561	4.9951
39	8.9357	8.2330	7.6268	7.0997	6.6380	6.2309	5.8695	5.5468	5.2572	4.9959
40	8.9510	8.2438	7.6344	7.1050	6.6418	6.2335	5.8713	5.5482	5.2582	4.9966
41	8.9649	8.2534	7.6410	7.1097	6.6450	6.2358	5.8729	5.5493	5.2590	4.9972
42	8.9774	8.2619	7.6469	7.1138	6.6478	6.2377	5.8743	5.5502	5.2596	4.9976
43	8.9886	8.2696	7.6521	7.1173	6.6503	6.2394	5.8755	5.5510	5.2602	4.9980
44	8.9988	8.2764	7.6568	7.1205	6.6524	6.2409	5.8765	5.5517	5.2607	4.9984
45	9.0079	8.2825	7.6609	7.1232	6.6543	6.2421	5.8773	5.5523	5.2611	4.9986
46	9.0161	8.2880	7.6645	7.1257	6.6559	6.2432	5.8781	5.5528	5.2614	4.9989
47	9.0235	8.2928	7.6677	7.1278	6.6573	6.2442	5.8787	5.5532	5.2617	4.9991
48	9.0302	8.2972	7.6705	7.1296	6.6585	6.2450	5.8792	5.5536	5.2619	4.9992
49	9.0362	8.3010	7.6730	7.1312	6.6596	6.2457	5.8797	5.5539	5.2621	4.9993
50	9.0416	8.3045	7.6752	7.1326	6.6605	6.2463	5.8801	5.5541	5.2623	4.9994

Table D-3 Value of $1 Compounded Annually at Rates of Return from 1 to 20 Percent

Year	1%	2%	3%	4%	5%	6%	7%	8%	9%	10%
1	1.01	1.02	1.03	1.04	1.05	1.06	1.07	1.08	1.09	1.10
2	1.02	1.04	1.06	1.08	1.10	1.12	1.15	1.17	1.19	1.21
3	1.03	1.05	1.09	1.13	1.16	1.19	1.23	1.26	1.30	1.33
4	1.04	1.08	1.13	1.17	1.22	1.26	1.31	1.36	1.41	1.46
5	1.05	1.10	1.16	1.22	1.28	1.34	1.40	1.47	1.54	1.61
6	1.06	1.13	1.19	1.27	1.34	1.42	1.50	1.59	1.68	1.77
7	1.07	1.15	1.23	1.32	1.41	1.50	1.61	1.71	1.83	1.95
8	1.08	1.17	1.27	1.37	1.48	1.59	1.72	1.85	1.99	2.14
9	1.09	1.20	1.31	1.42	1.55	1.69	1.84	2.00	2.17	2.36
10	1.10	1.22	1.34	1.48	1.63	1.79	1.97	2.16	2.37	2.59
11	1.12	1.24	1.38	1.54	1.71	1.90	2.11	2.33	2.58	2.85
12	1.13	1.27	1.43	1.60	1.80	2.01	2.25	2.52	2.81	3.14
13	1.14	1.29	1.47	1.67	1.89	2.13	2.41	2.72	3.07	3.45
14	1.15	1.32	1.51	1.73	1.98	2.26	2.58	2.94	3.34	3.80
15	1.16	1.35	1.56	1.80	2.08	2.40	2.76	3.17	3.64	4.18
16	1.17	1.37	1.61	1.87	2.18	2.54	2.95	3.43	3.97	4.60
17	1.18	1.40	1.65	1.95	2.29	2.69	3.16	3.70	4.33	5.05
18	1.20	1.43	1.70	2.03	2.41	2.85	3.38	4.00	4.72	5.56
19	1.21	1.46	1.75	2.11	2.53	3.03	3.62	4.32	5.14	6.12
20	1.22	1.49	1.81	2.19	2.65	3.21	3.87	4.66	5.60	6.73
21	1.23	1.52	1.86	2.28	2.79	3.40	4.14	5.03	6.11	7.40
22	1.25	1.55	1.92	2.37	2.93	3.60	4.43	5.44	6.66	8.14
23	1.26	1.58	1.97	2.46	3.07	3.82	4.74	5.87	7.26	8.96
24	1.27	1.61	2.03	2.56	3.23	4.05	5.07	6.34	7.91	9.85
25	1.28	1.64	2.09	2.67	3.39	4.29	5.43	6.85	8.62	10.84
26	1.30	1.66	2.15	2.77	3.56	4.55	5.81	7.40	9.40	11.92
27	1.31	1.69	2.22	2.88	3.73	4.82	6.21	7.99	10.25	13.11
28	1.32	1.72	2.29	3.00	3.92	5.11	6.65	8.63	11.17	14.42
29	1.33	1.76	2.36	3.12	4.12	5.42	7.12	9.06	12.17	15.86
30	1.35	1.79	2.43	3.24	4.32	5.74	7.61	9.51	13.27	17.45
31	1.36	1.83	2.50	3.37	4.54	6.09	8.15	10.27	14.46	19.20
32	1.38	1.87	2.58	3.51	4.77	6.45	8.72	11.09	15.76	21.12
33	1.39	1.90	2.65	3.65	5.00	6.84	9.33	11.98	17.18	23.23
34	1.40	1.94	2.73	3.79	5.25	7.25	9.98	12.94	18.73	25.55
35	1.42	1.98	2.81	3.95	5.52	7.69	10.68	13.98	20.41	28.11
36	1.43	2.02	2.90	4.10	5.79	8.15	11.43	15.09	22.25	30.92
37	1.45	2.06	2.99	4.27	6.08	8.64	12.23	16.30	24.25	34.01
38	1.46	2.10	3.08	4.44	6.39	9.15	13.08	17.60	26.44	37.41
39	1.47	2.14	3.17	4.62	6.71	9.70	14.00	19.01	28.82	41.15
40	1.49	2.19	3.26	4.80	7.04	10.29	14.98	20.53	31.41	45.26
41	1.50	2.25	3.36	4.99	7.39	10.90	16.02	23.46	34.24	49.78
42	1.52	2.30	3.46	5.19	7.76	11.56	17.14	25.34	37.32	54.76
43	1.53	2.34	3.56	5.40	8.15	12.25	18.34	27.37	40.68	60.24
44	1.55	2.40	3.67	5.62	8.55	13.00	19.63	29.55	44.34	66.26
45	1.56	2.44	3.78	5.84	8.99	13.76	21.00	31.92	48.33	72.89
46	1.58	2.49	3.89	6.07	9.43	14.60	22.47	34.47	52.68	80.18
47	1.60	2.54	4.01	6.32	9.90	15.47	24.04	37.23	57.42	88.20
48	1.61	2.59	4.13	6.57	10.40	16.39	25.73	40.21	62.59	97.02
49	1.63	2.64	4.26	6.83	10.92	17.38	27.53	43.43	68.22	106.72
50	1.64	2.69	4.38	7.12	11.47	18.42	29.46	46.90	74.36	117.40

Table D-3 (continued)

Year	11%	12%	13%	14%	15%	16%	17%	18%	19%	20%
1	1.11	1.12	1.13	1.14	1.15	1.16	1.17	1.18	1.19	1.20
2	1.23	1.25	1.28	1.30	1.32	1.35	1.37	1.39	1.41	1.44
3	1.37	1.41	1.44	1.48	1.52	1.56	1.60	1.64	1.69	1.73
4	1.52	1.57	1.63	1.69	1.75	1.81	1.87	1.94	2.00	2.07
5	1.69	1.76	1.84	1.93	2.01	2.10	2.19	2.29	2.39	2.49
6	1.87	1.97	2.08	2.20	2.31	2.44	2.57	2.70	2.83	2.99
7	2.08	2.21	2.35	2.50	2.66	2.83	3.00	3.19	3.38	3.58
8	2.30	2.48	2.66	2.85	3.06	3.29	3.51	3.76	4.02	4.30
9	2.56	2.77	3.00	3.25	3.52	3.80	4.11	4.44	4.79	5.16
10	2.84	3.11	3.40	3.71	4.05	4.41	4.81	5.23	5.69	6.19
11	3.15	3.48	3.84	4.23	4.65	5.12	5.62	6.17	6.78	7.43
12	3.50	3.90	4.34	4.82	5.35	5.94	6.59	7.28	8.06	8.92
13	3.88	4.36	4.90	5.49	6.15	6.89	7.70	8.60	9.60	10.69
14	4.31	4.89	5.54	6.26	7.08	7.99	9.00	10.15	11.41	12.84
15	4.79	5.47	6.25	7.14	8.14	9.27	10.54	11.97	13.59	15.41
16	5.31	6.13	7.07	8.14	9.36	10.75	12.33	14.13	16.17	18.49
17	5.90	6.87	7.99	9.28	10.76	12.47	14.43	16.67	19.24	22.19
18	6.54	7.69	9.03	10.57	12.38	14.46	16.88	19.67	22.90	26.62
19	7.26	8.61	10.20	12.06	14.23	16.78	19.74	23.21	27.25	31.95
20	8.06	9.65	11.52	13.74	16.37	19.46	23.10	27.39	32.43	38.34
21	8.94	10.80	13.02	15.67	18.82	22.57	27.03	32.32	38.60	46.01
22	9.93	12.10	14.72	17.86	21.65	26.19	31.63	38.14	45.92	55.21
23	11.03	13.55	16.63	20.36	24.89	30.38	37.00	45.00	54.64	66.25
24	12.24	15.18	18.79	23.21	28.63	35.24	43.30	53.10	65.03	79.50
25	13.59	17.00	21.23	26.46	32.92	40.87	50.66	62.67	77.39	95.40
26	15.08	19.04	23.99	30.16	37.86	47.41	59.27	73.94	92.10	114.48
27	16.74	21.33	27.11	34.39	43.54	55.00	69.34	87.26	109.59	137.37
28	18.58	23.88	30.64	39.20	50.07	63.80	81.13	102.97	130.41	164.84
29	20.62	26.75	34.62	44.69	57.58	74.00	94.93	121.50	155.19	197.81
30	22.89	29.96	39.12	50.95	66.22	85.84	111.01	143.37	184.68	237.38
31	25.41	33.56	44.20	58.08	76.15	99.56	129.94	169.18	219.77	284.85
32	28.21	37.58	49.95	66.21	87.57	115.52	152.03	199.63	261.51	341.82
33	31.31	42.09	56.44	75.48	100.71	134.00	177.89	235.56	311.20	410.19
34	34.75	47.14	63.78	86.05	115.81	155.44	208.12	277.96	370.33	492.22
35	38.58	52.80	72.07	98.09	133.18	180.31	243.50	328.00	440.70	590.67
36	43.82	59.14	81.44	111.83	153.16	209.17	285.00	387.04	524.43	708.80
37	47.53	66.23	92.03	127.48	176.13	242.63	333.33	456.70	624.08	850.56
38	52.76	74.18	103.99	145.33	202.55	281.45	390.00	538.91	742.65	1020.67
39	58.56	83.08	117.51	165.67	232.94	326.49	456.30	635.91	883.75	1224.81
40	65.00	93.05	132.79	188.87	267.88	378.72	533.87	750.38	1051.67	1469.78
41	72.15	104.22	150.04	215.33	308.04	439.32	624.63	885.45	1251.48	1763.72
42	80.09	116.72	169.55	245.47	354.25	509.61	730.81	1044.83	1489.27	2116.47
43	88.90	130.73	191.59	279.84	407.39	591.14	855.05	1232.90	1772.23	2539.76
44	98.67	146.42	216.50	319.02	468.50	685.73	1000.41	1454.82	2108.95	3047.72
45	109.53	164.00	244.64	363.68	538.77	795.44	1170.48	1716.68	2509.65	3657.26
46	121.58	183.67	276.44	414.59	619.58	922.71	1369.46	2025.69	2986.48	4388.71
47	134.95	205.71	312.38	472.64	712.52	1070.35	1602.27	2390.31	3553.92	5266.46
48	149.80	230.40	352.99	538.81	819.40	1241.60	1874.65	2820.57	4229.16	6319.75
49	166.28	258.04	398.88	614.24	942.31	1440.26	2193.35	3328.27	5032.70	7583.70
50	184.60	289.00	450.73	700.23	1083.66	1670.70	2566.21	3927.36	5988.91	9100.44

**Table D–4 Compounded Growth of $1 Invested Annually at 1 to 20
Percent Over 1 to 50 Years**

Year	1%	2%	3%	4%	5%	6%	7%	8%	9%	10%
1	1.00	1.00	1.00	1.00	1.00	1.00	1.00	1.00	1.00	1.00
2	2.01	2.02	2.03	2.04	2.05	2.06	2.07	2.08	2.09	2.10
3	3.03	3.06	3.09	3.12	3.15	3.18	3.21	3.25	3.28	3.31
4	4.06	4.12	4.18	4.25	4.31	4.37	4.44	4.51	4.57	4.64
5	5.10	5.20	5.31	5.42	5.53	5.64	5.75	5.87	5.98	6.11
6	6.15	6.31	6.47	6.63	6.80	6.98	7.15	7.34	7.52	7.72
7	7.21	7.43	7.66	7.90	8.14	8.39	8.65	8.92	9.20	9.49
8	8.29	8.58	8.89	9.21	9.55	9.90	10.26	10.64	11.03	11.44
9	9.37	9.75	10.16	10.58	11.03	11.49	11.98	12.49	13.02	13.58
10	10.46	10.95	11.46	12.01	12.58	13.18	13.82	14.49	15.19	15.94
11	11.57	12.17	12.81	13.49	14.21	14.97	15.78	16.65	17.56	18.53
12	12.68	13.41	14.19	15.03	15.92	16.87	17.89	18.98	20.14	21.38
13	13.81	14.68	15.62	16.63	17.71	18.88	20.14	21.50	22.95	24.52
14	14.95	15.97	17.09	18.29	19.60	21.01	22.55	24.21	26.02	27.98
15	16.10	17.29	18.60	20.02	21.58	23.28	25.13	27.15	29.36	31.77
16	17.26	18.64	20.16	21.82	23.66	25.67	27.89	30.32	33.00	35.95
17	18.43	20.01	21.76	23.70	25.84	28.21	30.84	33.75	36.97	40.54
18	19.61	21.41	23.41	25.65	28.13	30.91	34.00	37.45	41.30	45.60
19	20.81	22.84	25.12	27.67	30.54	33.76	37.38	41.45	46.02	51.16
20	22.02	24.30	26.87	29.78	33.07	36.79	41.00	45.76	51.16	57.28
21	23.24	25.78	28.68	31.97	35.72	39.99	44.86	50.42	56.76	64.00
22	24.47	27.30	30.54	34.25	38.51	43.39	49.01	55.46	62.87	71.40
23	25.72	28.85	32.45	36.62	41.43	47.00	53.44	60.89	69.53	79.54
24	26.97	30.42	34.43	39.08	44.50	50.82	58.18	66.76	76.79	88.50
25	28.24	32.03	36.46	41.65	47.73	54.86	63.25	73.11	84.70	98.35
26	29.53	33.67	38.55	44.31	51.11	59.16	68.68	79.95	93.32	109.18
27	30.82	35.34	40.71	47.08	54.67	63.71	74.48	87.35	102.72	121.10
28	32.13	37.05	42.93	49.97	58.40	68.53	80.70	95.34	112.97	134.21
29	33.45	38.79	45.22	52.97	62.32	73.64	87.35	103.97	124.14	148.63
30	34.78	40.57	47.58	56.09	66.44	79.06	94.46	113.28	136.31	164.49
31	36.13	42.38	50.00	59.33	70.76	84.80	102.07	123.35	149.58	181.94
32	37.49	44.23	52.50	62.70	75.30	90.89	110.22	134.21	164.04	201.14
33	38.87	46.11	55.08	66.21	80.06	97.34	118.93	145.95	179.80	222.25
34	40.26	48.03	57.73	69.86	85.07	104.18	128.26	158.63	196.98	245.48
35	41.66	49.99	60.46	73.65	90.32	111.43	138.24	172.32	215.71	271.02
36	43.08	51.99	63.28	77.60	95.84	119.12	148.91	187.10	236.12	299.13
37	44.51	54.03	66.17	81.70	101.63	127.27	160.34	203.07	258.38	330.04
38	45.95	56.11	69.16	85.97	107.71	135.90	172.56	220.31	282.63	364.04
39	47.41	58.24	72.23	90.41	114.10	145.06	185.64	238.94	309.07	401.45
40	48.89	60.40	75.40	95.03	120.80	154.76	199.63	259.06	337.88	442.59
41	50.37	62.61	78.66	99.83	127.84	165.04	214.61	280.78	369.29	487.85
42	51.88	64.86	82.02	104.82	135.23	175.95	230.63	304.24	403.53	537.64
43	53.40	67.16	85.48	110.01	142.99	187.50	247.78	329.58	440.84	592.40
44	54.93	69.50	89.05	115.41	151.14	199.76	266.12	356.95	481.52	652.64
45	56.48	71.89	92.72	121.03	159.70	212.74	285.74	386.50	525.86	718.90
46	58.04	74.33	96.50	126.87	168.68	226.51	306.75	418.43	574.19	791.79
47	59.63	76.82	100.40	132.94	178.11	241.10	329.22	452.90	626.86	871.97
48	61.22	79.35	104.40	139.26	188.02	256.56	353.27	490.13	684.28	960.17
49	62.83	81.94	108.54	145.83	198.43	272.96	379.00	530.34	746.86	1057.19
50	64.46	84.58	112.80	152.67	209.34	290.33	406.53	573.77	815.08	1163.91

Year	11%	12%	13%	14%	15%	16%	17%	18%	19%	20%
1	1.00	1.00	1.00	1.00	1.00	1.00	1.00	1.00	1.00	1.00
2	2.11	2.12	2.13	2.14	2.15	2.16	2.17	2.18	2.19	2.20
3	3.34	3.37	3.41	3.44	3.47	3.51	3.54	3.57	3.61	3.64
4	4.71	4.78	4.85	4.92	4.99	5.07	5.14	5.22	5.29	5.37
5	6.23	6.35	6.48	6.61	6.74	6.88	7.01	7.15	7.30	7.44
6	7.91	8.12	8.32	8.54	8.75	8.98	9.21	9.44	9.68	9.93
7	9.78	10.09	10.40	10.73	11.07	11.41	11.77	12.14	12.52	12.92
8	11.86	12.30	12.76	13.23	13.73	14.24	14.77	15.33	15.90	16.50
9	14.16	14.78	15.42	16.09	16.79	17.52	18.28	19.09	19.92	20.80
10	16.72	17.55	18.42	19.34	20.30	21.32	22.39	23.52	24.71	25.96
11	19.56	20.65	21.81	23.05	24.35	25.73	27.20	28.76	30.40	32.15
12	22.71	24.13	25.65	27.27	29.00	30.85	32.82	34.93	37.18	39.58
13	26.21	28.03	29.98	32.09	34.35	36.79	39.40	42.22	45.24	48.50
14	31.10	32.39	34.88	37.58	40.50	43.67	47.10	50.82	54.84	59.20
15	34.41	37.28	40.42	43.84	47.58	51.66	56.11	60.97	66.26	72.04
16	39.19	42.75	46.67	50.98	55.72	60.93	66.65	72.94	79.85	87.44
17	44.50	48.88	53.74	59.12	65.08	71.67	78.98	87.07	96.02	105.93
18	50.40	55.75	61.73	68.39	75.84	84.14	93.40	103.74	115.26	128.11
19	56.94	63.44	70.75	78.97	88.21	98.60	110.28	123.41	138.17	154.74
20	64.20	72.05	80.95	91.03	102.44	115.38	130.03	146.62	165.42	186.68
21	72.27	81.70	92.47	104.77	118.81	134.84	153.14	174.02	197.85	225.02
22	81.21	92.50	105.49	120.44	137.63	157.41	180.17	206.34	236.44	271.03
23	91.15	104.60	120.20	138.30	159.28	183.60	211.80	244.48	282.36	326.23
24	102.17	118.16	136.83	158.66	184.17	213.97	248.81	289.49	337.01	392.23
25	114.41	133.33	155.62	181.87	212.79	249.21	292.10	342.60	402.04	471.98
26	128.00	150.33	176.85	208.33	245.71	290.08	342.76	405.27	479.43	567.32
27	143.08	169.37	200.84	238.50	283.57	337.50	402.03	479.22	571.52	681.85
28	159.82	190.70	227.95	272.89	327.11	392.50	471.38	566.48	681.11	819.22
29	178.40	214.58	258.58	312.09	377.17	456.30	552.51	669.44	811.52	984.00
30	199.02	241.33	293.20	356.79	434.75	530.31	647.44	790.94	966.71	1181.88
31	221.91	271.29	332.32	407.74	500.96	616.16	758.50	934.32	1151.39	1419.26
32	247.32	304.85	376.52	465.82	577.10	715.75	888.45	1103.49	1371.15	1704.11
33	275.53	342.43	426.46	532.04	664.67	831.27	1040.48	1303.12	1632.67	2045.93
34	306.84	384.52	482.90	607.52	765.37	965.27	1218.37	1538.69	1943.88	2456.12
35	341.59	431.66	546.68	693.57	881.17	1120.71	1426.50	1816.65	2314.21	2948.34
36	380.17	484.46	618.75	791.67	1014.35	1301.03	1669.99	2144.65	2754.91	3539.00
37	422.98	543.60	700.19	903.51	1167.50	1510.19	1954.89	2531.68	3279.35	4247.81
38	470.51	609.83	792.21	1031.00	1343.63	1752.82	2288.22	2988.39	3903.42	5098.38
39	523.27	684.01	896.20	1176.34	1546.17	2034.27	2678.22	3527.30	4646.07	6119.05
40	581.83	767.09	1013.70	1342.03	1779.10	2360.76	3134.52	4163.21	5529.83	7343.86
41	646.83	860.14	1146.48	1530.91	2046.95	2739.48	3668.39	4913.59	6581.50	8813.63
42	718.98	964.36	1296.53	1746.23	2355.00	3178.79	4293.02	5799.04	7832.98	10577.35
43	799.07	1081.08	1466.08	1991.71	2709.25	3688.40	5023.83	6843.86	9322.25	12693.83
44	887.92	1211.81	1657.67	2271.54	3116.63	4279.55	5878.88	8076.76	11094.47	15233.59
45	986.64	1358.23	1874.16	2590.56	3585.13	4965.27	6879.29	9531.58	13203.42	18281.31
46	1096.17	1522.22	2118.81	2954.24	4123.90	5760.72	8049.77	11248.26	15713.07	21938.57
47	1217.75	1705.88	2395.25	3368.84	4743.48	6683.43	9419.23	13273.95	18699.55	26327.29
48	1352.70	1911.59	2707.63	3841.47	5456.00	7753.78	11021.50	15664.26	22253.47	31593.74
49	1502.50	2141.98	3060.62	4380.28	6275.40	8995.39	12896.15	18484.82	26482.63	37913.49
50	1668.77	2400.02	3459.51	4994.52	7217.72	10435.65	15089.50	21813.09	31515.34	45497.19

Appendix E
Mortgage Tables
(10, 11, and 12%)

Find out from your lending institution precisely what the monthly payments will be (interest and principal) on the home you subcontract. These charges vary among lending firms. I suggest you itemize cost in a format similar to that shown in the tables that follow. In arriving at your total yearly payments, be sure to add in all other costs such as insurance and taxes. There may also be points charged that would appear in the first year's expenses.

You will note in the tables that the final payments are less than the others. This indicates that the mortgagee is paying a slightly higher rate of interest than the stated rate over the term of the loan. I recommend you determine the exact amount of interest paid, principal paid, total payment, and balance due for each monthly payment *prior* to obtaining a home loan so that you will know the specific payments you will be making. Notice that there is very little reduction in the amount of principal owed over the first several years of your loan. Your payments for the first several years are almost entirely interest (profit for the lending institution) and you still owe nearly the entire amount of principal (and you are building up very little equity in your home). Few people stay in the same house for the life of the mortgage. These tables provide you with an excellent picture of the large principal amount still due if you sell your home in the first few years after purchasing it. There may also be a penalty for prepayment of your mortgage.

There is yet another point to investigate. The mortgage payments may differ depending on the way interest and monthly payments are computed. Interest may be charged on a 365-day year, but payments may be computed on a 360-day basis. This method makes the Annual Percentage Rate (APR) higher than if it were based on charging interest on 360 days and also computing payments on a 360-day basis. The latter method makes the APR equal to the stated interest rate. For example, a $100,000 loan for 30 years at 10 percent interest charged over 365 days would require a monthly mortgage payment of $877.58. However, the same loan computed over 360 days would result in a mortgage payment of $887.90—a difference of $10.48 per month. Over the 30-year period, this amounts to an additional $3,772.80.

Table E-1 Monthly Payments on a $100,000 Loan at 10% Interest Over a Thirty Year Period
(Monthly payment per $1,000 = $8.78)

I Number of Monthly Payments		II Interest Paid	III Principal Paid	IV Total Payment	V Total Principal Due (Balance)
	1	$ 833	$ 45	$ 878	$99,955
	2	833	45	878	99,910
	3	833	45	878	99,865
	4	832	46	878	99,819
	5	832	46	878	99,773
	6	831	47	878	99,726
	7	831	47	878	99,679
	8	831	47	878	99,632
	9	830	48	878	99,584
	10	830	48	878	99,536
	11	829	49	878	99,487
	12	829	49	878	99,438
1st Year	Total	$9,974	$562	$10,536	
	13	$ 829	$ 49	$ 878	$99,389
	14	828	50	878	99,339
	15	828	50	878	99,289
	16	827	51	878	99,238
	17	827	51	878	99,187
	18	827	51	878	99,136
	19	826	52	878	99,084
	20	826	52	878	98,032
	21	825	53	878	98,979
	22	825	53	878	98,926
	23	824	54	878	98,872
	24	824	54	878	98,818
2nd Year	Total	$9,916	$620	$10,536	
	25	$ 823	$ 55	$ 878	$98,763
	26	823	55	878	98,708
	27	823	55	878	98,653
	28	822	56	878	98,597
	29	822	56	878	98,541
	30	821	57	878	98,484
	31	821	57	878	98,427
	32	820	58	878	98,369
	33	820	58	878	98,311
	34	819	59	878	98,252
	35	819	59	878	98,193
	36	818	60	878	98,133
3rd Year	Total	$9,851	$685	$10,536	
	37	$ 818	$ 60	$ 878	$98,073
	38	817	61	878	98,012
	39	817	61	878	97,951
	40	816	62	878	97,889
	41	816	62	878	97,827
	42	815	63	878	97,764
	43	815	63	878	97,701
	44	814	64	878	97,637
	45	814	64	878	97,573
	46	813	65	878	97,508
	47	813	65	878	97,443
	48	812	65	878	97,377
4th Year	Total	$9,780	$756	$10,536	

Table E–1 (continued)

I Number of Monthly Payments		II Interest Paid	III Principal Paid	IV Total Payment	V Total Principal Due (Balance)
	49	$ 811	$ 67	$ 878	$97,310
	50	811	67	878	97,243
	51	810	68	878	97,175
	52	810	68	878	97,107
	53	809	69	878	97,038
	54	809	69	878	96,969
	55	808	70	878	96,899
	56	807	71	878	96,828
	57	807	71	878	96,757
	58	806	72	878	96,685
	59	806	72	878	96,613
	60	805	73	878	96,540
5th Year	Total	$9,699	$837	$10,536	
	61	$ 805	$ 73	$ 878	$96,467
	62	804	74	878	96,393
	63	803	75	878	96,318
	64	803	75	878	96,243
	65	802	76	878	96,167
	66	801	77	878	96,090
	67	801	77	878	96,013
	68	800	78	878	95,935
	69	799	79	878	95,856
	70	799	79	878	95,777
	71	798	80	878	95,697
	72	797	81	878	95,616
6th Year	Total	$9,612	$924	$10,536	
	73	$ 797	$ 81	$ 878	$95,535
	74	796	82	878	95,453
	75	795	83	878	95,370
	76	795	83	878	95,287
	77	794	84	878	95,203
	78	793	85	878	95,118
	79	793	85	878	95,033
	80	792	86	878	94,947
	81	791	87	878	94,860
	82	791	87	878	94,773
	83	790	88	878	94,685
	84	789	89	878	94,596
7th Year	Total	$9,516	$1,020	$10,536	
	85	$ 788	$ 90	$ 878	$94,506
	86	788	90	878	94,416
	87	787	91	878	94,325
	88	786	92	878	94,233
	89	785	93	878	94,140
	90	785	93	878	94,047
	91	784	94	878	93,953
	92	783	95	878	93,858
	93	782	96	878	93,762
	94	781	97	878	93,665
	95	781	97	878	93,568
	96	780	98	878	93,470
8th Year	Total	$9,410	$1,126	$10,536	

I Number of Monthly Payments		II Interest Paid	III Principal Paid	IV Total Payment	V Total Principal Due (Balance)
	97	$ 779	$ 99	$ 878	$93,371
	98	778	100	878	93,271
	99	777	101	878	93,170
	100	776	102	878	93,068
	101	776	102	878	92,966
	102	775	103	878	92,863
	103	774	104	878	92,759
	104	773	105	878	92,654
	105	772	106	878	92,548
	106	771	107	878	92,441
	107	770	108	878	92,333
	108	769	109	878	92,224
9th Year	Total	$9,290	$1,246	$10,536	
	109	$ 769	$ 109	$ 878	$92,115
	110	768	110	878	92,005
	111	767	111	878	91,894
	112	766	112	878	91,782
	113	765	113	878	91,669
	114	764	114	878	91,555
	115	763	115	878	91,440
	116	762	116	878	91,324
	117	761	117	878	91,207
	118	760	118	878	91,089
	119	759	119	878	90,970
	120	758	120	878	90,850
10th Year	Total	$9,162	$1,374	$10,536	
	121	$ 757	$ 121	$ 878	$90,729
	122	756	122	878	90,607
	123	755	123	878	90,484
	124	754	124	878	90,360
	125	753	125	878	90,235
	126	752	126	878	90,109
	127	751	127	878	89,982
	128	750	128	878	89,854
	129	749	129	878	89,725
	130	748	130	878	89,595
	131	747	131	878	89,464
	132	746	132	878	89,332
11th Year	Total	$9,018	$1,518	$10,536	
	133	$ 744	$ 134	$ 878	$89,198
	134	743	135	878	89,063
	135	742	136	878	88,927
	136	741	137	878	88,790
	137	740	138	878	88,652
	138	739	139	878	88,513
	139	738	140	878	88,373
	140	736	142	878	88,231
	141	735	143	878	88,088
	142	734	144	878	87,944
	143	733	145	878	87,799
	144	732	146	878	87,653
12th Year	Total	$8,857	$1,679	$10,536	

Table E–1 (continued)

I Number of Monthly Payments		II Interest Paid	III Principal Paid	IV Total Payment	V Total Principal Due (Balance)
	145	$ 730	$ 148	$ 878	$87,505
	146	729	149	878	87,356
	147	728	150	878	87,206
	148	727	151	878	87,055
	149	725	153	878	86,902
	150	724	154	878	86,748
	151	723	155	878	86,593
	152	722	156	878	86,437
	153	720	158	878	86,279
	154	719	159	878	86,120
	155	718	160	878	85,960
	156	716	162	878	85,798
13th Year	Total	$8,681	$1,855	$10,536	
	157	$ 715	$ 163	$ 878	$85,635
	158	714	164	878	85,471
	159	712	166	878	85,305
	160	711	167	878	85,138
	161	709	169	878	84,969
	162	708	170	878	84,799
	163	707	171	878	84,628
	164	705	173	878	84,455
	165	704	174	878	84,281
	166	702	176	878	84,105
	167	701	177	878	83,928
	168	699	179	878	83,749
14th Year	Total	$8,487	$2,049	$10,536	
	169	$ 698	$ 180	$ 878	$83,569
	170	696	182	878	83,387
	171	695	183	878	83,204
	172	693	185	878	83,019
	173	692	186	878	82,833
	174	690	188	878	82,645
	175	689	189	878	82,456
	176	687	191	878	82,265
	177	686	192	878	82,073
	178	684	194	878	81,879
	179	682	196	878	81,683
	180	681	197	878	81,486
15th Year	Total	$8,273	$2,263	$10,536	
	181	$ 679	$ 199	$ 878	$81,287
	182	677	201	878	81,086
	183	676	202	878	80,884
	184	674	204	878	80,680
	185	672	206	878	80,474
	186	671	207	878	80,267
	187	669	209	878	80,058
	188	667	211	878	79,847
	189	665	213	878	79,634
	190	664	214	878	79,420
	191	662	216	878	79,204
	192	660	218	878	78,986
16th Year	Total	$8,036	$2,500	$10,536	

Table E-1 (continued)

I Number of Monthly Payments		II Interest Paid	III Principal Paid	IV Total Payment	V Total Principal Due (Balance)
	193	$ 658	$ 220	$ 878	$78,766
	194	656	222	878	78,544
	195	655	223	878	78,321
	196	653	225	878	78,096
	197	651	227	878	77,869
	198	649	229	878	77,640
	199	647	231	878	77,409
	200	645	233	878	77,176
	201	643	235	878	76,941
	202	641	237	878	76,704
	203	639	239	878	76,465
	204	637	241	878	76,224
17th Year	Total	$7,774	$2,762	$10,536	
	205	$ 635	$ 243	$ 878	75,981
	206	633	245	878	75,736
	207	631	247	878	75,489
	208	629	249	878	75,240
	209	627	251	878	74,989
	210	625	253	878	74,736
	211	623	255	878	74,481
	212	621	257	878	74,224
	213	619	259	878	73,965
	214	616	262	878	73,703
	215	614	264	878	73,439
	216	612	266	878	73,173
18th Year	Total	$7,485	$3,051	$10,536	
	217	$ 610	$ 268	$ 878	$72,905
	218	608	270	878	72,635
	219	605	273	878	72,362
	220	603	275	878	72,087
	221	601	277	878	71,810
	222	598	280	878	71,530
	223	596	282	878	71,248
	224	594	284	878	70,964
	225	591	287	878	70,677
	226	589	289	878	70,388
	227	587	291	878	70,097
	228	584	294	878	69,803
19th Year	Total	$7,166	$3,370	$10,536	
	229	$ 582	$ 296	$ 878	$69,507
	230	579	299	878	69,208
	231	577	301	878	68,907
	232	574	304	878	68,603
	233	572	306	878	68,297
	234	569	309	878	67,988
	235	567	311	878	67,677
	236	564	314	878	67,363
	237	561	317	878	67,046
	238	559	319	878	66,727
	239	556	322	878	66,405
	240	553	325	878	66,080
20th Year	Total	$6,813	$3,723	$10,536	

Table E-1 (continued)

I Number of Monthly Payments		II Interest Paid	III Principal Paid	IV Total Payment	V Total Principal Due (Balance)
	241	$ 551	$ 327	$ 878	$65,753
	242	548	330	878	65,423
	243	545	333	878	65,090
	244	542	336	878	64,754
	245	540	338	878	64,416
	246	537	341	878	64,075
	247	534	344	878	63,731
	248	531	347	878	63,384
	249	528	350	878	63,034
	250	525	353	878	62,681
	251	522	356	878	62,325
	252	519	359	878	61,966
21st Year	Total	$6,422	$4,114	$10,536	
	253	$ 516	$ 362	$ 878	$61,604
	254	513	365	878	61,239
	255	510	368	878	60,871
	256	507	371	878	60,500
	257	504	374	878	60,126
	258	501	377	878	59,749
	259	498	380	878	59,369
	260	495	383	878	58,986
	261	492	386	878	58,600
	262	488	390	878	58,210
	263	485	393	878	57,817
	264	482	396	878	57,421
22nd Year	Total	$5,991	$4,545	$10,536	
	265	$ 479	$ 399	$ 878	$57,022
	266	475	403	878	56,619
	267	472	406	878	56,213
	268	468	410	878	55,803
	269	465	413	878	55,390
	270	462	416	878	54,974
	271	458	420	878	54,554
	272	455	423	878	54,131
	273	451	427	878	53,704
	274	448	430	878	53,274
	275	444	434	878	52,840
	276	440	438	878	52,402
23rd Year	Total	$5,517	$5,019	$10,536	
	277	$ 437	$ 441	$ 878	$51,961
	278	433	445	878	51,516
	279	429	449	878	51,067
	280	426	452	878	50,615
	281	422	456	878	50,159
	282	418	460	878	49,699
	283	414	464	878	49,235
	284	410	468	878	48,767
	285	406	472	878	48,295
	286	402	476	878	47,819
	287	398	480	878	47,339
	288	394	484	878	46,855
24th Year	Total	$4,989	$5,547	$10,536	

Table E-1 (continued)

I Number of Monthly Payments		II Interest Paid	III Principal Paid	IV Total Payment	V Total Principal Due (Balance)
	289	$ 390	$ 488	$ 878	$46,367
	290	386	492	878	45,875
	291	382	496	878	45,379
	292	378	500	878	44,879
	293	374	504	878	44,375
	294	370	508	878	43,867
	295	366	512	878	43,355
	296	361	517	878	42,838
	297	357	521	878	42,317
	298	353	525	878	41,792
	299	348	530	878	41,262
	300	344	534	878	40,728
25th Year	Total	$4,409	$6,127	$10,536	
	301	$ 339	$ 539	$ 878	40,189
	302	335	543	878	39,646
	303	330	548	878	39,098
	304	326	552	878	38,546
	305	321	557	878	37,989
	306	317	561	878	37,428
	307	312	566	878	36,862
	308	307	571	878	36,291
	309	302	576	878	35,715
	310	298	580	878	35,135
	311	293	585	878	34,550
	312	288	590	878	33,960
26th Year	Total	$3,768	$6,768	$10,536	
	313	$ 283	$ 595	$ 878	$33,365
	314	278	600	878	32,765
	315	273	605	878	32,160
	316	268	610	878	31,550
	317	263	615	878	30,935
	318	258	620	878	30,315
	319	253	625	878	29,690
	320	247	631	878	29,059
	321	242	636	878	28,423
	322	237	641	878	27,782
	323	232	646	878	27,136
	324	226	652	878	26,484
27th Year	Total	$3,060	$7,476	$10,536	
	325	$ 221	$ 657	$ 878	$25,827
	326	215	663	878	25,164
	327	210	668	878	24,496
	328	204	674	878	23,822
	329	199	679	878	23,143
	330	193	685	878	22,458
	331	187	691	878	21,767
	332	181	697	878	21,070
	333	176	702	878	20,368
	334	170	708	878	19,660
	335	164	714	878	18,946
	336	158	720	878	18,226
28th Year	Total	$2,278	$8,258	$10,536	

Table E–1   (continued)

I Number of Monthly Payments		II Interest Paid	III Principal Paid	IV Total Payment	V Total Principal Due (Balance)
	337	$ 152	$ 726	$ 878	$17,500
	338	146	732	878	16,768
	339	140	738	878	16,030
	340	134	744	878	15,286
	341	127	751	878	14,535
	342	121	757	878	13,778
	343	115	763	878	13,015
	344	108	770	878	12,245
	345	102	776	878	11,469
	346	96	782	878	10,687
	347	89	789	878	9,898
	348	82	796	878	9,102
29th Year	Total	$1,412	$9,124	$10,536	
	349	$ 76	$ 802	$ 878	$8,300
	350	69	809	878	7,491
	351	62	816	878	6,675
	352	56	822	878	5,853
	353	49	829	878	5,024
	354	42	836	878	4,188
	355	35	843	878	3,345
	356	28	850	878	2,495
	357	21	857	878	1,638
	358	14	864	878	774
	359	6	774	780	0
	360	—	—	—	—
30th Year	Total	$458	$9,102	$9,560	

Table E-1 Summary
Annual Payments on a $100,000 Loan at 10 Percent
Over a Thirty Year Period

I Mortgage Year	II Interest Paid	III Principal Paid	IV Total Payment	V Total Principal Due (Balance)
1	$ 9,974	$ 562	$ 10,536	$99,438
2	9,916	620	10,536	98,818
3	9,851	685	10,536	98,133
4	9,780	756	10,536	97,377
5	9,699	837	10,536	96,540
6	9,612	924	10,536	95,616
7	9,516	1,020	10,536	94,596
8	9,410	1,126	10,536	93,470
9	9,290	1,246	10,536	92,224
10	9,162	1,374	10,536	90,850
11	9,018	1,518	10,536	89,332
12	8,857	1,679	10,536	87,653
13	8,681	1,855	10,536	85,798
14	8,487	2,049	10,536	83,749
15	8,273	2,263	10,536	81,486
16	8,036	2,500	10,536	78,986
17	7,774	2,762	10,536	76,224
18	7,485	3,051	10,536	73,173
19	7,166	3,370	10,536	69,803
20	6,813	3,723	10,536	66,080
21	6,422	4,114	10,536	61,966
22	5,991	4,545	10,536	57,421
23	5,517	5,019	10,536	52,402
24	4,989	5,547	10,536	46,855
25	4,409	6,127	10,536	40,728
26	3,768	6,768	10,536	33,960
27	3,060	7,476	10,536	26,484
28	2,278	8,258	10,536	18,226
29	1,412	9,124	10,536	9,102
30	458	9,102	9,560	0
Total	$215,104	$100,000	$315,104	

Table E–2 Monthly Payments on a $100,000 Loan at 11% Interest Over a Thirty Year Period (Monthly payment per $1,000 = $9.53)

I Number of Monthly Payments		II Interest Paid	III Principal Paid	IV Total Payment	V Total Principal Due (Balance)
	1	$ 917	$ 36	$ 953	$99,964
	2	916	37	953	99,927
	3	916	37	953	99,890
	4	916	37	953	99,853
	5	915	38	953	99,815
	6	915	38	953	99,777
	7	915	38	953	99,739
	8	914	39	953	99,700
	9	914	39	953	99,661
	10	914	39	953	99,622
	11	913	40	953	99,582
	12	913	40	953	99,542
1st Year	Total	$10,978	$458	$11,436	
	13	$ 912	$ 41	$ 953	$99,501
	14	912	41	953	99,460
	15	912	41	953	99,419
	16	911	42	953	99,377
	17	911	42	953	99,335
	18	911	42	953	99,293
	19	910	43	953	99,250
	20	910	43	953	99,207
	21	909	44	953	99,163
	22	909	44	953	99,119
	23	909	44	953	99,075
	24	908	45	953	99,030
2nd Year	Total	$10,924	$512	$11,436	
	25	$ 908	$ 45	$ 953	$98,985
	26	907	46	953	98,939
	27	907	46	953	98,893
	28	907	46	953	98,847
	29	906	47	953	98,800
	30	906	47	953	98,753
	31	905	48	953	98,705
	32	905	48	953	98,657
	33	904	49	953	98,608
	34	904	49	953	98,559
	35	903	50	953	98,509
	36	903	50	953	98,459
3rd Year	Total	$10,865	$571	$11,436	
	37	$ 903	$ 50	$ 953	$98,409
	38	902	51	953	98,358
	39	902	51	953	98,307
	40	901	52	953	98,255
	41	901	52	953	98,203
	42	900	53	953	98,150
	43	900	53	953	98,097
	44	899	54	953	98,043
	45	899	54	953	97,989
	46	898	55	953	97,934
	47	898	55	953	97,879
	48	897	56	953	97,823
4th Year	Total	$10,800	$636	$11,436	

Table E–2   (continued)

I Number of Monthly Payments		II Interest Paid	III Principal Paid	IV Total Payment	V Total Principal Due (Balance)
	49	$ 897	$ 56	953	$97,767
	50	896	57	953	97,710
	51	896	57	953	97,653
	52	895	58	953	97,595
	53	895	58	953	97,537
	54	894	59	953	97,478
	55	894	59	953	97,419
	56	893	60	953	97,359
	57	892	61	953	97,29°
	58	892	61	953	97,237
	59	891	62	953	97,175
	60	891	62	953	97,113
5th Year	Total	$10,726	$710	$11,436	
	61	$ 890	$ 63	953	$97,050
	62	890	63	953	96,987
	63	889	64	953	96,923
	64	888	65	953	96,858
	65	888	65	953	96,793
	66	887	66	953	96,727
	67	887	66	953	96,661
	68	886	67	953	96,594
	69	885	68	953	96,526
	70	885	68	953	96,458
	71	884	69	953	96,389
	72	884	69	953	96,320
6th Year	Total	$10,643	$793	$11,436	
	73	$ 883	$ 70	$ 953	$96,250
	74	882	71	953	96,179
	75	882	71	953	96,108
	76	881	72	953	96,036
	77	880	73	953	95,963
	78	880	73	953	95,890
	79	879	74	953	95,816
	80	878	75	953	95,741
	81	878	75	953	95,666
	82	877	76	953	95,590
	83	876	77	953	95,513
	84	876	77	953	95,436
7th Year	Total	$10,552	$884	$11,436	
	85	$ 875	$ 78	$ 953	$95,358
	86	874	79	953	95,279
	87	873	80	953	95,199
	88	873	80	953	95,119
	89	872	81	953	95,038
	90	871	82	953	94,956
	91	870	83	953	94,873
	92	870	83	953	94,790
	93	869	84	953	94,706
	94	868	85	953	94,621
	95	867	86	953	94,535
	96	867	86	953	94,449
8th Year	Total	$10,449	$987	$11,436	

Table E–2 (continued)

I Number of Monthly Payments		II Interest Paid	III Principal Paid	IV Total Payment	V Total Principal Due (Balance)
	97	$ 866	$ 87	$ 953	$94,362
	98	865	88	953	94,274
	99	864	89	953	94,185
	100	863	90	953	94,095
	101	863	90	953	94,005
	102	862	91	953	93,914
	103	861	92	953	93,822
	104	860	93	953	93,729
	105	859	94	953	93,635
	106	858	95	953	93,540
	107	857	96	953	93,444
	108	857	96	953	93,348
9th Year	Total	$10,335	$1,101	$11,436	
	109	$ 856	$ 97	$ 953	$93,251
	110	855	98	953	93,153
	111	854	99	953	93,054
	112	853	100	953	92,954
	113	852	101	953	92,853
	114	851	102	953	92,751
	115	850	103	953	92,648
	116	849	104	953	92,544
	117	848	105	953	92,439
	118	847	106	953	92,333
	119	846	107	953	92,226
	120	845	108	953	92,118
10th Year	Total	$10,206	$1,230	$11,436	
	121	$ 844	$ 109	$ 953	$92,009
	122	843	110	953	91,899
	123	842	111	953	91,788
	124	841	112	953	91,676
	125	840	113	953	91,563
	126	839	114	953	91,449
	127	838	115	953	91,334
	128	837	116	953	91,218
	129	836	117	953	91,101
	130	835	118	953	90,983
	131	834	119	953	90,864
	132	833	120	953	90,744
11th Year	Total	$10,062	$1,374	$11,436	
	133	$ 832	$ 121	$ 953	$90,623
	134	831	122	953	90,501
	135	830	123	953	90,378
	136	828	125	953	90,253
	137	827	126	953	90,127
	138	826	127	953	90,000
	139	825	128	953	89,872
	140	824	129	953	89,743
	141	823	130	953	89,613
	142	821	132	953	89,481
	143	820	133	953	89,348
	144	819	134	953	89,214
12th Year	Total	$9,906	$1,530	$11,436	

Table E-2 (continued)

I Number of Monthly Payments		II Interest Paid	III Principal Paid	IV Total Payment	V Total Principal Due (Balance)
	145	$ 818	$ 135	953	$89,079
	146	817	136	953	88,943
	147	815	138	953	88,805
	148	814	139	953	88,666
	149	813	140	953	88,526
	150	811	142	953	88,384
	151	810	143	953	88,241
	152	809	144	953	88,097
	153	808	145	953	87,952
	154	806	147	953	87,805
	155	805	148	953	87,657
	156	804	149	953	87,508
13th Year	Total	$9,730	$1,706	$11,436	
	157	$ 802	$ 151	$ 953	$87,357
	158	801	152	953	87,205
	159	799	154	953	87,051
	160	798	155	953	86,896
	161	797	156	953	86,740
	162	795	158	953	86,582
	163	794	159	953	86,423
	164	792	161	953	86,262
	165	791	162	953	86,100
	166	789	164	953	85,936
	167	788	165	953	85,771
	168	786	167	953	85,604
14th Year	Total	$9,532	$1,904	$11,436	
	169	$ 785	168	$ 953	$85,436
	170	783	170	953	85,266
	171	782	171	953	85,095
	172	780	173	953	84,922
	173	778	175	953	84,747
	174	777	176	953	84,571
	175	775	178	953	84,393
	176	774	179	953	84,214
	177	772	181	953	84,033
	178	770	183	953	83,850
	179	769	184	953	83,666
	180	767	186	953	83,480
15th Year	Total	$9,312	$2,124	$11,436	
	181	$ 765	$ 188	$ 953	$83,292
	182	764	189	953	83,103
	183	762	191	953	82,912
	184	760	193	953	82,719
	185	758	195	953	82,524
	186	756	197	953	82,327
	187	755	198	953	82,129
	188	753	200	953	81,929
	189	751	202	953	81,727
	190	749	204	953	81,523
	191	747	206	953	81,317
	192	745	208	953	81,109
16th Year	Total	$9,065	$2,371	$11,436	

Table E–2 (continued)

I Number of Monthly Payments		II Interest Paid	III Principal Paid	IV Total Payment	V Total Principal Due (Balance)
	193	$ 743	$ 210	$ 953	$80,899
	194	742	211	953	80,688
	195	740	213	953	80,475
	196	738	215	953	80,260
	197	736	217	953	80,043
	198	734	219	953	79,824
	199	732	221	953	79,603
	200	730	223	953	79,380
	201	728	225	953	79,155
	202	726	227	953	78,928
	203	724	229	953	78,699
	204	721	232	953	78,467
17th Year	Total	$8,794	$2,642	$11,436	
	205	$ 719	$ 234	$ 953	$78,233
	206	717	236	953	77,997
	207	715	238	953	77,759
	208	713	240	953	77,519
	209	711	242	953	77,277
	210	708	245	953	77,032
	211	706	247	953	76,785
	212	704	249	953	76,536
	213	702	251	953	76,285
	214	699	254	953	76,031
	215	697	256	953	75,775
	216	695	258	953	75,517
18th Year	Total	$8,486	$2,950	$11,436	
	217	$ 692	$ 261	$ 953	$75,256
	218	690	263	953	74,993
	219	687	266	953	74,727
	220	685	268	953	74,459
	221	683	270	953	74,189
	222	680	273	953	73,916
	223	678	275	953	73,641
	224	675	278	953	73,363
	225	672	281	953	73,082
	226	670	283	953	72,799
	227	667	286	953	72,513
	228	665	288	953	72,225
19th Year	Total	$8,144	$3,292	$11,436	
	229	$ 662	$ 291	$ 953	$71,934
	230	659	294	953	71,640
	231	657	296	953	71,344
	232	654	299	953	71,045
	233	651	302	953	70,743
	234	648	305	953	70,438
	235	646	307	953	70,131
	236	643	310	953	69,821
	237	640	313	953	69,508
	238	637	316	953	69,192
	239	634	319	953	68,873
	240	631	322	953	68,551
20th Year	Total	$7,762	$3,674	$11,436	

Table E–2 (continued)

I Number of Monthly Payments		II Interest Paid	III Principal Paid	IV Total Payment	V Total Principal Due (Balance)
	241	$ 628	$ 325	$ 953	$68,226
	242	625	328	953	67,898
	243	622	331	953	67,567
	244	619	334	953	67,233
	245	616	337	953	66,896
	246	613	340	953	66,556
	247	610	343	953	66,213
	248	607	346	953	65,867
	249	604	349	953	65,518
	250	601	352	953	65,166
	251	597	356	953	64,810
	252	594	359	953	64,451
21st Year	Total	$7,336	$4,100	$11,436	
	253	$ 591	$ 362	$ 953	$64,089
	254	587	366	953	63,723
	255	584	369	953	63,354
	256	581	372	953	62,982
	257	577	376	953	62,606
	258	574	379	953	62,227
	259	570	383	953	61,844
	260	567	386	953	61,458
	261	563	390	953	61,068
	262	560	393	953	60,675
	263	556	397	953	60,278
	264	553	400	953	59,878
22nd Year	Total	$6,863	$4,573	$11,436	
	265	$ 549	$ 404	$ 953	$59,474
	266	545	408	953	59,066
	267	541	412	953	58,654
	268	538	415	953	58,239
	269	534	419	953	57,820
	270	530	423	953	57,397
	271	526	427	953	56,970
	272	522	431	953	56,539
	273	518	435	953	56,104
	274	514	439	953	55,665
	275	510	443	953	55,222
	276	506	447	953	54,775
23rd Year	Total	$6,333	$5,103	$11,436	
	277	$ 502	$ 451	$ 953	$54,324
	278	498	455	953	53,869
	279	494	459	953	53,410
	280	490	463	953	52,947
	281	485	468	953	52,479
	282	481	472	953	52,007
	283	477	476	953	51,531
	284	472	481	953	51,050
	285	468	485	953	50,565
	286	464	489	953	50,076
	287	459	494	953	49,582
	288	455	498	953	49,084
24th Year	Total	$5,745	$5,691	$11,436	

Table E–2 (continued)

I Number of Monthly Payments		II Interest Paid	III Principal Paid	IV Total Payment	V Total Principal Due (Balance)
	289	$ 450	$ 503	$ 953	$48,581
	290	445	508	953	48,071
	291	441	512	953	47,561
	292	436	517	953	47,044
	293	431	522	953	46,522
	294	426	527	953	45,995
	295	422	531	953	45,464
	296	417	536	953	44,928
	297	412	541	953	44,387
	298	407	546	953	43,841
	299	402	551	953	43,290
	300	397	556	953	42,734
25th Year	Total	$5,086	$6,350	$11,436	
	301	$ 392	$ 561	$ 953	$42,173
	302	387	566	953	41,607
	303	381	572	953	41,035
	304	376	577	953	40,458
	305	371	582	953	39,876
	306	366	587	953	39,289
	307	360	593	953	38,696
	308	355	598	953	38,098
	309	349	604	953	37,494
	310	344	609	953	36,885
	311	338	615	953	36,270
	312	332	621	953	35,649
26th Year	Total	$4,351	$7,085	$11,436	
	313	$ 327	$ 626	$ 953	$35,023
	314	321	632	953	34,391
	315	315	638	953	33,753
	316	309	644	953	33,109
	317	303	650	953	32,459
	318	298	655	953	31,804
	319	292	661	953	31,143
	320	285	668	953	30,475
	321	279	674	953	29,801
	322	273	680	953	29,121
	323	267	686	953	28,435
	324	261	692	953	27,743
27th Year	Total	$3,530	$7,906	$11,436	
	325	$ 254	$ 699	$ 953	$27,044
	326	248	705	953	26,339
	327	241	712	953	25,627
	328	235	718	953	24,909
	329	228	725	953	24,184
	330	222	731	953	23,453
	331	215	738	953	22,715
	332	208	745	953	21,970
	333	201	752	953	21,218
	334	194	759	953	20,459
	335	188	765	953	19,694
	336	181	772	953	18,922
28th Year	Total	$2,615	$8,821	$11,463	

Table E–2 (continued)

I Number of Monthly Payments		II Interest Paid	III Principal Paid	IV Total Payment	V Total Principal Due (Balance)
	337	$ 173	$ 780	$ 953	$18,142
	338	166	787	953	17,355
	339	159	794	953	16,561
	340	152	801	953	15,760
	341	144	809	953	14,951
	342	137	816	953	14,135
	343	130	823	953	13,312
	344	122	831	953	12,481
	345	114	839	953	11,642
	346	107	846	953	10,796
	347	99	854	953	9,942
	348	9	862	953	9,080
29th Year	Total	$1,594	$9,842	$11,436	
	349	$ 83	$ 870	$ 953	$8,210
	350	75	878	953	7,332
	351	67	886	953	6,446
	352	59	894	953	5,552
	353	51	902	953	4,650
	354	43	910	953	3,740
	355	34	919	953	2,821
	356	26	927	953	1,894
	357	17	936	953	958
	358	9	944	953	14
	359	—	14	14	—
	360	—	—	—	—
30th Year	Total	$464	$9,080	$9,544	

Table E-2 Summary
Annual Payments on a $100,000 Loan at 11 Percent
Over a Thirty Year Period

I Mortgage Year	II Interest Paid	III Principal Paid	IV Total Payment	V Total Principal Due (Balance)
1	$ 10,978	$ 458	$ 11,436	$99,542
2	10,924	512	11,436	99,030
3	10,865	571	11,436	98,459
4	10,800	636	11,436	97,823
5	10,726	710	11,436	97,113
6	10,643	793	11,436	96,320
7	10,552	884	11,436	95,436
8	10,449	987	11,436	94,449
9	10,335	1,101	11,436	93,348
10	10,206	1,230	11,436	92,118
11	10,062	1,374	11,436	90,744
12	9,906	1,530	11,436	89,214
13	9,730	1,706	11,436	87,508
14	9,532	1,904	11,436	85,604
15	9,312	2,124	11,436	83,480
16	9,065	2,371	11,436	81,109
17	8,794	2,642	11,436	78,467
18	8,486	2,950	11,436	75,517
19	8,144	3,292	11,436	72,225
20	7,762	3,674	11,436	68,551
21	7,336	4,100	11,436	64,451
22	6,863	4,573	11,436	59,878
23	6,333	5,103	11,436	54,775
24	5,745	5,691	11,436	49,084
25	5,086	6,350	11,436	42,734
26	4,351	7,085	11,436	35,649
27	3,530	7,906	11,436	27,743
28	2,615	8,821	11,436	18,922
29	1,594	9,842	11,436	9,080
30	464	9,080	9,544	0
Total	$241,188	$100,000	$341,188	

Table E-3 Monthly Payments on a $100,000 Loan at 12% Interest Over a Thirty Year Period (Monthly payment per $1,000 = $10.29)

I Number of Monthly Payments		II Interest Paid	III Principal Paid	IV Total Payment	V Total Principal Due (Balance)
	1	$ 1,000	$ 29	$ 1,029	$99,971
	2	1,000	29	1,029	99,942
	3	999	30	1,029	99,912
	4	999	30	1,029	99,882
	5	999	30	1,029	99,852
	6	999	30	1,029	99,822
	7	998	31	1,029	99,791
	8	998	31	1,029	99,760
	9	998	31	1,029	99,729
	10	997	32	1,029	99,697
	11	997	32	1,029	99,665
	12	997	32	1,029	99,633
1st Year	Total	$11,981	$367	$12,348	
	13	$ 996	$ 33	$ 1,029	$99,600
	14	996	33	1,029	99,567
	15	996	33	1,029	99,534
	16	995	34	1,029	99,500
	17	995	34	1,029	99,466
	18	995	34	1,029	99,432
	19	994	35	1,029	99,397
	20	994	35	1,029	99,362
	21	994	35	1,029	99,327
	22	993	36	1,029	99,291
	23	993	36	1,029	99,255
	24	993	36	1,029	99,219
2nd Year	Total	$11,934	$414	$12,348	
	25	$ 992	$ 37	$ 1,029	$99,182
	26	992	37	1,029	99,145
	27	991	38	1,029	99,107
	28	991	38	1,029	99,069
	29	991	38	1,029	99,031
	30	990	39	1,029	98,992
	31	990	39	1,029	98,953
	32	990	39	1,029	98,914
	33	989	40	1,029	98,874
	34	989	40	1,029	98,834
	35	988	41	1,029	98,793
	36	988	41	1,029	98,752
3rd Year	Total	$11,881	$467	$12,348	
	37	$ 988	$ 41	$ 1,029	$98,711
	38	987	42	1,029	98,669
	39	987	42	1,029	98,627
	40	986	43	1,029	98,584
	41	986	43	1,029	98,541
	42	985	44	1,029	98,497
	43	985	44	1,029	98,453
	44	985	44	1,029	98,409
	45	984	45	1,029	98,364
	46	984	45	1,029	98,319
	47	983	46	1,029	98,273
	48	983	46	1,029	98,227
4th Year	Total	$11,823	$525	$12,348	

Table E–3 (continued)

I Number of Monthly Payments		II Interest Paid	III Principal Paid	IV Total Payment	V Total Principal Due (Balance)
	49	$ 982	$ 47	$ 1,029	$98,180
	50	982	47	1,029	98,133
	51	981	48	1,029	98,085
	52	981	48	1,029	98,037
	53	980	49	1,029	97,988
	54	980	49	1,029	97,939
	55	979	50	1,029	97,889
	56	979	50	1,029	97,839
	57	978	51	1,029	97,788
	58	978	51	1,029	97,737
	59	977	52	1,029	97,685
	60	977	52	1,029	97,633
5th Year	Total	$11,754	$594	$12,348	
	61	$ 976	$ 53	$ 1,029	$97,580
	62	976	53	1,029	97,527
	63	975	54	1,029	97,473
	64	975	54	1,029	97,419
	65	974	55	1,029	97,364
	66	974	55	1,029	97,309
	67	973	56	1,029	97,253
	68	973	56	1,029	97,197
	69	972	57	1,029	97,140
	70	971	58	1,029	97,082
	71	971	58	1,029	97,024
	72	970	59	1,029	96,965
6th Year	Total	$11,680	$668	$12,348	
	73	$ 970	$ 59	$ 1,029	$96,906
	74	969	60	1,029	96,846
	75	968	61	1,029	96,785
	76	968	61	1,029	96,724
	77	967	62	1,029	96,662
	78	967	62	1,029	96,600
	79	966	63	1,029	96,537
	80	965	64	1,029	96,473
	81	965	64	1,029	96,409
	82	964	65	1,029	96,344
	83	963	66	1,029	96,278
	84	963	66	1,029	96,212
7th Year	Total	$11,595	$753	$12,348	
	85	$ 962	$ 67	$ 1,029	$96,145
	86	961	68	1,029	96,077
	87	961	68	1,029	96,009
	88	960	69	1,029	95,940
	89	959	70	1,029	95,870
	90	959	70	1,029	95,800
	91	958	71	1,029	95,729
	92	957	72	1,029	95,657
	93	957	72	1,029	95,585
	94	956	73	1,029	95,512
	95	955	74	1,029	95,438
	96	954	75	1,029	95,363
8th Year	Total	$11,499	$849	$12,348	

I Number of Monthly Payments		II Interest Paid	III Principal Paid	IV Total Payment	V Total Principal Due (Balance)
	97	$ 954	$ 75	$ 1,029	$95,288
	98	953	76	1,029	95,212
	99	952	77	1,029	95,135
	100	951	78	1,029	95,057
	101	951	78	1,029	94,979
	102	950	79	1,029	94,900
	103	949	80	1,029	94,820
	104	948	81	1,029	94,739
	105	947	82	1,029	94,657
	106	947	82	1,029	94,575
	107	946	83	1,029	94,492
	108	945	84	1,029	94,408
9th Year	Total	$11,393	$955	$12,348	
	109	$ 944	$ 85	$ 1,029	$94,323
	110	943	86	1,029	94,237
	111	942	87	1,029	94,150
	112	942	87	1,029	94,063
	113	941	88	1,029	93,975
	114	940	89	1,029	93,886
	115	939	90	1,029	93,796
	116	938	91	1,029	93,705
	117	937	92	1,029	93,613
	118	936	93	1,029	93,520
	119	935	94	1,029	93,426
	120	934	95	1,029	93,331
10th Year	Total	$11,271	$1,077	$12,348	
	121	$ 933	$ 96	$ 1,029	$93,235
	122	932	97	1,029	93,138
	123	931	98	1,029	93,040
	124	930	99	1,029	92,941
	125	929	100	1,029	92,841
	126	928	101	1,029	92,740
	127	927	102	1,029	92,638
	128	926	103	1,029	92,535
	129	925	104	1,029	92,431
	130	924	105	1,029	92,326
	131	923	106	1,029	92,220
	132	922	107	1,029	92,113
11th Year	Total	$11,130	$1,218	$12,348	
	133	$ 921	$ 108	$ 1,029	$92,005
	134	920	109	1,029	91,896
	135	919	110	1,029	91,786
	136	918	111	1,029	91,675
	137	917	112	1,029	91,563
	138	916	113	1,029	91,450
	139	915	114	1,029	91,336
	140	913	116	1,029	91,220
	141	912	117	1,029	91,103
	142	911	118	1,029	90,985
	143	910	119	1,029	90,866
	144	909	120	1,029	90,746
12th Year	Total	$10,981	$1,367	$12,348	

Table E–3 (continued)

I Number of Monthly Payments		II Interest Paid	III Principal Paid	IV Total Payment	V Total Principal Due (Balance)
	145	$ 907	$ 122	$ 1,029	$90,624
	146	906	123	1,029	90,501
	147	905	124	1,029	90,377
	148	904	125	1,029	90,252
	149	903	126	1,029	90,126
	150	901	128	1,029	89,998
	151	900	129	1,029	89,869
	152	899	130	1,029	89,739
	153	897	132	1,029	89,607
	154	896	133	1,029	89,474
	155	895	134	1,029	89,340
	156	893	136	1,029	89,204
13th Year	Total	$10,806	$1,542	$12,348	
	157	$ 892	$ 137	$ 1,029	$89,067
	158	891	138	1,029	88,929
	159	889	140	1,029	88,789
	160	888	141	1,029	88,648
	161	886	143	1,029	88,505
	162	885	144	1,029	88,361
	163	884	145	1,029	88,216
	164	882	147	1,029	88,069
	165	881	148	1,029	87,921
	166	879	150	1,029	87,771
	167	878	151	1,029	87,620
	168	876	153	1,029	87,467
14th Year	Total	$10,611	$1,737	$12,348	
	169	$ 875	$ 154	$ 1,029	$87,313
	170	873	156	1,029	87,157
	171	872	157	1,029	87,000
	172	870	159	1,029	86,841
	173	868	161	1,029	86,680
	174	867	162	1,029	86,518
	175	865	164	1,029	86,354
	176	864	165	1,029	86,189
	177	862	167	1,029	86,022
	178	860	169	1,029	85,853
	179	859	170	1,029	85,683
	180	857	172	1,029	85,511
15th Year	Total	$10,392	$1,956	$12,348	
	181	$ 855	$ 174	$ 1,029	$85,337
	182	853	176	1,029	85,161
	183	852	177	1,029	84,984
	184	850	179	1,029	84,805
	185	848	181	1,029	84,624
	186	846	183	1,029	84,441
	187	844	185	1,029	84,256
	188	843	186	1,029	84,070
	189	841	188	1,029	83,882
	190	839	190	1,029	83,692
	191	837	192	1,029	83,500
	192	835	194	1,029	83,306
16th Year	Total	$10,143	$2,205	$12,348	

Table E–3 (continued)

I Number of Monthly Payments		II Interest Paid	III Principal Paid	IV Total Payment	V Total Principal Due (Balance)
	193	$ 833	$ 196	$ 1,029	$83,110
	194	831	198	1,029	82,912
	195	829	200	1,029	82,712
	196	827	202	1,029	82,510
	197	825	204	1,029	82,306
	198	823	206	1,029	82,100
	199	821	208	1,029	81,892
	200	819	210	1,029	81,682
	201	817	212	1,029	81,470
	202	815	214	1,029	81,256
	203	813	216	1,029	81,040
	204	810	219	1,029	80,821
17th Year	Total	$9,863	$2,485	$12,348	
	205	$ 808	$ 221	$ 1,029	$80,600
	206	806	223	1,029	80,377
	207	804	225	1,029	80,152
	208	802	227	1,029	79,925
	209	799	230	1,029	79,695
	210	797	232	1,029	79,463
	211	795	234	1,029	79,229
	212	792	237	1,029	78,992
	213	790	239	1,029	78,753
	214	788	241	1,029	78,512
	215	785	244	1,029	78,268
	216	783	246	1,029	78,022
18th Year	Total	$9,549	$2,799	$12,348	
	217	$ 780	$ 249	$ 1,029	$77,773
	218	778	251	1,029	77,522
	219	775	254	1,029	77,268
	220	773	256	1,029	77,012
	221	770	259	1,029	76,753
	222	768	261	1,029	76,492
	223	765	264	1,029	76,228
	224	762	267	1,029	75,961
	225	760	269	1,029	75,692
	226	757	272	1,029	75,420
	227	754	275	1,029	75,145
	228	751	278	1,029	74,867
19th Year	Total	$9,193	$3,155	$12,348	
	229	$ 749	$ 280	$ 1,029	$74,587
	230	746	283	1,029	74,304
	231	743	286	1,029	74,018
	232	740	289	1,029	73,729
	233	737	292	1,029	73,437
	234	734	295	1,029	73,142
	235	731	298	1,029	72,844
	236	728	301	1,029	72,543
	237	725	304	1,029	72,239
	238	722	307	1,029	71,932
	239	719	310	1,029	71,622
	240	716	313	1,029	71,309
20th Year	Total	$8,790	$3,558	$12,348	

Table E–3 (continued)

I Number of Monthly Payments		II Interest Paid	III Principal Paid	IV Total Payment	V Total Principal Due (Balance)
	241	$ 713	$ 316	$ 1,029	$70,993
	242	710	319	1,029	70,674
	243	707	322	1,029	70,352
	244	704	325	1,029	70,027
	245	700	329	1,029	69,698
	246	697	332	1,029	69,366
	247	694	335	1,029	69,031
	248	690	339	1,029	68,692
	249	687	342	1,029	68,350
	250	684	345	1,029	68,005
	251	680	349	1,029	67,656
	252	677	352	1,029	67,304
21st Year	Total	$8,343	$4,005	$12,348	
	253	$ 673	$ 356	$ 1,029	$66,948
	254	669	360	1,029	66,588
	255	666	363	1,029	66,225
	256	662	367	1,029	65,858
	257	659	370	1,029	65,488
	258	655	374	1,029	65,114
	259	651	378	1,029	64,736
	260	647	382	1,029	64,354
	261	644	385	1,029	63,969
	262	640	389	1,029	63,580
	263	636	393	1,029	63,187
	264	632	397	1,029	62,790
22nd Year	Total	$7,834	$4,514	$12,348	
	265	$ 628	$ 401	$ 1,029	$62,389
	266	624	405	1,029	61,984
	267	620	409	1,029	61,575
	268	616	413	1,029	61,162
	269	612	417	1,029	60,745
	270	607	422	1,029	60,323
	271	603	426	1,029	59,897
	272	599	430	1,029	59,467
	273	595	434	1,029	59,033
	274	590	439	1,029	58,594
	275	586	443	1,029	58,151
	276	582	447	1,029	57,704
23rd Year	Total	$7,262	$5,086	$12,348	
	277	$ 577	$ 452	$ 1,029	$57,252
	278	573	456	1,029	56,796
	279	568	461	1,029	56,335
	280	563	466	1,029	55,869
	281	559	470	1,029	55,399
	282	554	475	1,029	54,924
	283	549	480	1,029	54,444
	284	544	485	1,029	53,959
	285	540	489	1,029	53,470
	286	535	494	1,029	52,976
	287	530	499	1,029	52,477
	288	525	504	1,029	51,973
24th Year	Total	$6,617	$5,731	$12,348	

Table E–3 (continued)

I Number of Monthly Payments		II Interest Paid	III Principal Paid	IV Total Payment	V Total Principal Due (Balance)
	289	$ 520	$ 509	$ 1,029	$51,464
	290	515	514	1,029	50,950
	291	510	519	1,029	50,431
	292	504	525	1,029	49,906
	293	499	530	1,029	49,376
	294	494	535	1,029	48,841
	295	488	541	1,029	48,300
	296	483	546	1,029	47,754
	297	478	551	1,029	47,203
	298	472	557	1,029	46,646
	299	466	563	1,029	46,083
	300	461	568	1,029	45,515
25th Year	Total	$5,890	$6,458	$12,348	
	301	$ 455	$ 574	$ 1,029	$44,941
	302	449	580	1,029	44,361
	303	444	585	1,029	43,776
	304	438	591	1,029	43,185
	305	432	597	1,029	42,588
	306	426	603	1,029	41,985
	307	420	609	1,029	41,376
	308	414	615	1,029	40,761
	309	408	621	1,029	40,140
	310	401	628	1,029	39,512
	311	395	634	1,029	38,878
	312	389	640	1,029	38,238
26th Year	Total	$5,071	$7,277	$12,348	
	313	$ 382	$ 647	$ 1,029	$37,591
	314	376	653	1,029	36,938
	315	369	660	1,029	36,278
	316	363	666	1,029	35,612
	317	356	673	1,029	34,939
	318	349	680	1,029	34,259
	319	343	686	1,029	33,573
	320	336	693	1,029	32,880
	321	329	700	1,029	32,180
	322	322	707	1,029	31,473
	323	315	714	1,029	30,759
	324	308	721	1,029	30,038
27th Year	Total	$4,148	$8,200	$12,348	
	325	$ 300	$ 729	$ 1,029	$29,309
	326	293	736	1,029	28,573
	327	286	743	1,029	27,830
	328	278	751	1,029	27,079
	329	271	758	1,029	26,321
	330	263	766	1,029	25,555
	331	256	773	1,029	24,782
	332	248	781	1,029	24,001
	333	240	789	1,029	23,212
	334	232	797	1,029	22,415
	335	224	805	1,029	21,610
	336	216	813	1,029	20,797
28th Year	Total	$3,107	$9,241	$12,348	

Table E–3 (continued)

I Number of Monthly Payments		II Interest Paid	III Principal Paid	IV Total Payment	V Total Principal Due (Balance)
	337	$ 208	$ 821	$ 1,029	$19,976
	338	200	829	1,029	19,147
	339	191	838	1,029	18,309
	340	183	846	1,029	17,463
	341	175	854	1,029	16,609
	342	166	863	1,029	15,746
	343	157	872	1,029	14,874
	344	149	880	1,029	13,994
	345	140	889	1,029	13,105
	346	131	898	1,029	12,207
	347	122	907	1,029	11,300
	348	113	916	1,029	10,384
29th Year	Total	$1,935	$10,413	$12,348	
	349	$104	$ 925	$ 1,029	$9,459
	350	95	934	1,029	8,525
	351	85	944	1,029	7,581
	352	76	953	1,029	6,628
	353	66	963	1,029	5,665
	354	57	972	1,029	4,693
	355	47	982	1,029	3,711
	356	37	992	1,029	2,719
	357	27	1,002	1,029	1,717
	358	17	1,012	1,029	705
	359*	7	705	* 712	0
	360*	—	—	* —	—
30th Year	Total	$618	$10,384	$11,002	

*The total monthly payment is short due to rounding.

214

Table E-3 Summary
Annual Payments on a $100,000 Loan at 12 Percent
Over a Thirty Year Period

I Number of Yearly Payments	II Interest Paid Yearly	III Principal Paid Yearly	IV Total Yearly Payment (II & III)
1	$ 11,981	$ 367	$12,348
2	11,934	414	12,348
3	11,881	467	12,348
4	11,823	525	12,348
5	11,754	594	12,348
6	11,680	668	12,348
7	11,595	753	12,348
8	11,499	849	12,348
9	11,393	955	12,348
10	11,271	1,077	12,348
11	11,130	1,218	12,348
12	10,981	1,367	12,348
13	10,806	1,542	12,348
14	10,611	1,737	12,348
15	10,392	1,956	12,348
16	10,143	2,205	12,348
17	9,863	2,485	12,348
18	9,549	2,799	12,348
19	9,193	3,155	12,348
20	8,790	3,558	12,348
21	8,343	4,005	12,348
22	7,834	4,514	12,348
23	7,262	5,086	12,348
24	6,617	5,731	12,348
25	5,890	6,458	12,348
26	5,071	7,277	12,348
27	4,148	8,200	12,348
28	3,107	9,241	12,348
29	1,935	10,413	12,348
30	618	10,384	11,002
Total	$269,094	$100,000	$369,094

Appendix F
Amortization Table

The following table can be used in buying a home to determine the amount of money one would pay to amortize a loan at varying rates of interest for different periods of time. (This table can also be used for other credit purchases that are amortized, such as cars and major appliances.) For example, if you wish to obtain a $75,000 loan at 12 percent for 30 years, you can figure the mortgage payment (interest and principal) on this amount by looking down the year column to 30 and then reading across to the 12 percent column. The figure 1.24 indicates the dollar amount to be paid annually on each $10 for thirty years. Thus by multiplying 1.24 by $7,500 (75,000 ÷ 10) you arrive at a figure of $9,300. And multiplying $9,300 by 30 years gives you the approximate total future payments due—$279,000. This is a sizable sum to pay for a $75,000 loan. And at 16 percent for 30 years it amounts to about $362,250 (1.61 × 7,500 × 30). It is important to check with at least four lending institutions in order to get the best rate. Don't forget to find out about all other costs—points, insurance, taxes, and closing costs.

Table F-1 Amortization Table for Loans of 1 to 30 Years at Interest Rates of 8 to 20 Percent[1]

Year	8%	8½%	9%	9½%	10%	10½%	11%	11½%	12%	12½%	13%	13½%	14%
1	10.80	10.85	10.90	10.95	11.00	11.05	11.10	11.15	11.20	11.25	11.30	11.35	11.40
2	5.43	5.46	5.48	5.51	5.54	5.57	5.59	5.62	5.65	5.68	5.71	5.73	5.76
3	3.76	3.79	3.82	3.84	3.87	3.90	3.93	3.96	3.99	4.02	4.04	4.07	4.10
4	2.93	2.96	2.99	3.02	3.04	3.07	3.10	3.13	3.16	3.19	3.22	3.25	3.28
5	2.43	2.46	2.49	2.52	2.55	2.58	2.61	2.64	2.67	2.70	2.73	2.76	2.79
6	2.10	2.13	2.16	2.19	2.22	2.25	2.29	2.32	2.35	2.38	2.41	2.44	2.47
7	1.87	1.90	1.93	1.96	1.99	2.02	2.06	2.09	2.12	2.15	2.18	2.22	2.25
8	1.70	1.73	1.76	1.79	1.82	1.85	1.87	1.92	1.95	1.98	2.02	2.05	2.09
9	1.56	1.59	1.63	1.66	1.69	1.72	1.76	1.79	1.82	1.86	1.89	1.93	1.96
10	1.46	1.49	1.52	1.55	1.59	1.62	1.65	1.69	1.72	1.76	1.79	1.83	1.86
11	1.37	1.40	1.44	1.47	1.50	1.54	1.57	1.61	1.64	1.68	1.71	1.75	1.79
12	1.30	1.33	1.37	1.40	1.44	1.47	1.51	1.54	1.58	1.61	1.65	1.69	1.73
13	1.24	1.27	1.31	1.34	1.38	1.41	1.45	1.49	1.52	1.56	1.60	1.64	1.68
14	1.19	1.22	1.26	1.30	1.33	1.37	1.40	1.44	1.48	1.52	1.56	1.59	1.63
15	1.15	1.18	1.22	1.25	1.29	1.33	1.36	1.40	1.44	1.48	1.52	1.56	1.60
16	1.10	1.15	1.18	1.22	1.26	1.29	1.33	1.37	1.41	1.45	1.49	1.53	1.57
17	1.08	1.11	1.15	1.19	1.23	1.26	1.30	1.34	1.38	1.42	1.46	1.50	1.55
18	1.05	1.09	1.12	1.16	1.20	1.24	1.28	1.32	1.36	1.40	1.44	1.48	1.53
19	1.03	1.06	1.10	1.14	1.18	1.22	1.26	1.30	1.34	1.38	1.42	1.47	1.51
20	1.00	1.04	1.08	1.12	1.16	1.20	1.24	1.28	1.32	1.36	1.41	1.45	1.49
21	.99	1.02	1.06	1.10	1.14	1.18	1.22	1.27	1.31	1.35	1.39	1.44	1.48
22	.97	1.01	1.05	1.09	1.13	1.17	1.21	1.25	1.29	1.34	1.38	1.43	1.47
23	.95	.99	1.03	1.07	1.11	1.16	1.20	1.24	1.28	1.33	1.37	1.42	1.46
24	.94	.98	1.02	1.06	1.10	1.14	1.19	1.23	1.27	1.32	1.36	1.41	1.45
25	.93	.97	1.01	1.05	1.09	1.13	1.18	1.22	1.26	1.31	1.35	1.40	1.45
26	.92	.96	1.00	1.04	1.08	1.13	1.17	1.21	1.26	1.30	1.35	1.39	1.44
27	.91	.95	.99	1.03	1.07	1.12	1.16	1.21	1.25	1.30	1.34	1.39	1.43
28	.90	.94	.98	1.02	1.07	1.11	1.15	1.20	1.24	1.29	1.34	1.38	1.43
29	.89	.93	.97	1.02	1.06	1.10	1.15	1.19	1.24	1.29	1.33	1.38	1.43
30	.88	.92	.97	1.01	1.05	1.10	1.14	1.19	1.24	1.28	1.33	1.38	1.42

Table F-1 (continued)

Year	14½%	15%	15½%	16%	16½%	17%	17½%	18%	18½%	19%	19½%	20%
1	11.45	11.50	11.55	11.60	11.65	11.70	11.75	11.80	11.85	11.90	11.95	12.00
2	5.79	5.82	5.85	5.88	5.91	5.93	5.96	5.99	6.02	6.05	6.08	6.11
3	4.13	4.16	4.19	4.22	4.25	4.28	4.31	4.34	4.37	4.40	4.43	4.46
4	3.31	3.34	3.37	3.40	3.43	3.46	3.49	3.53	3.56	3.59	3.62	3.65
5	2.82	2.86	2.89	2.92	2.95	2.98	3.02	3.05	3.08	3.11	3.15	3.18
6	2.51	2.54	2.57	2.60	2.64	2.67	2.70	2.74	2.77	2.81	2.84	2.88
7	2.28	2.32	2.35	2.38	2.42	2.45	2.49	2.52	2.56	2.59	2.63	2.67
8	2.12	2.15	2.19	2.22	2.26	2.30	2.33	2.37	2.40	2.44	2.48	2.52
9	2.00	2.03	2.07	2.10	2.14	2.18	2.21	2.25	2.29	2.33	2.37	2.40
10	1.90	1.94	1.97	2.01	2.05	2.09	2.12	2.16	2.20	2.24	2.28	2.32
11	1.82	1.86	1.90	1.94	1.98	2.02	2.05	2.09	2.13	2.17	2.21	2.26
12	1.76	1.80	1.84	1.88	1.92	1.96	2.00	2.04	2.08	2.12	2.16	2.20
13	1.71	1.75	1.79	1.83	1.87	1.91	1.96	2.00	2.04	2.08	2.16	2.17
14	1.67	1.71	1.75	1.79	1.84	1.88	1.92	1.96	2.00	2.05	2.11	2.13
15	1.64	1.68	1.72	1.76	1.81	1.87	1.89	1.93	1.98	2.02	2.06	2.11
16	1.61	1.65	1.70	1.74	1.78	1.82	1.87	1.91	1.95	2.00	2.04	2.09
17	1.59	1.63	1.67	1.72	1.76	1.80	1.85	1.89	1.94	1.98	2.03	2.07
18	1.57	1.61	1.65	1.70	1.74	1.79	1.83	1.88	1.92	1.97	2.01	2.06
19	1.55	1.59	1.64	1.78	1.73	1.77	1.82	1.86	1.91	1.96	2.00	2.05
20	1.54	1.58	1.63	1.67	1.72	1.76	1.81	1.85	1.90	1.95	1.99	2.04
21	1.52	1.57	1.61	1.66	1.71	1.75	1.80	1.84	1.89	1.94	1.99	2.03
22	1.51	1.56	1.61	1.65	1.70	1.74	1.79	1.84	1.88	1.93	1.98	2.03
23	1.51	1.55	1.60	1.64	1.69	1.74	1.78	1.83	1.88	1.93	1.97	2.02
24	1.50	1.54	1.59	1.64	1.68	1.73	1.78	1.83	1.87	1.92	1.97	2.02
25	1.49	1.54	1.58	1.63	1.68	1.73	1.77	1.82	1.87	1.92	1.97	2.02
26	1.49	1.53	1.58	1.63	1.67	1.72	1.77	1.82	1.87	1.92	1.96	2.02
27	1.48	1.53	1.58	1.62	1.67	1.72	1.77	1.82	1.86	1.91	1.96	2.01
28	1.48	1.52	1.57	1.62	1.67	1.72	1.76	1.81	1.86	1.91	1.96	2.01
29	1.47	1.52	1.57	1.62	1.67	1.71	1.76	1.81	1.86	1.91	1.96	2.01
30	1.47	1.52	1.57	1.61	1.66	1.71	1.76	1.81	1.86	1.91	1.96	2.01

[1]This table gives the annual rate per ten dollars. If you wish to determine the monthly rate, divide the annual rate by 12 (if quarterly, divide by 4; if semiannually, divide by 2).

Glossary

abstract (of title): A summary of the public records relating to the *title* to a particular piece of land. An attorney or title insurance company reviews an abstract of title to determine whether there are any title defects which must be cleared before a buyer can purchase clear, marketable, and insurable title. See *title*.

acceleration clause: Condition in a mortgage that may require the balance of the loan to become due immediately if regular mortgage payments are not made or for breach of other conditions of the mortgage.

agreement of sale: Known by various names, such as *contract of purchase, purchase agreement,* or *sales agreement,* according to location or jurisdiction. A contract in which a seller agrees to sell and a buyer agrees to buy, under certain specific terms and conditions spelled out in writing and signed by both parties.

algae: Microscopic plant life that thrives and multiplies very rapidly, especially in warm, unchlorinated water. Algae cause slimy patches and stains to develop on the bottom and sides of the pool. There are many stains of algae, but the most common are the green, reddish brown, or black.

Definitions of housing terms are adapted from the U.S. Department of Housing and Urban Development booklet *Home Buyer's Vocabulary*. The terms listed do not cover all possible meanings or nuances that a term may acquire in legal use. State laws and custom in use in various states may modify or completely change the meaning of certain terms defined. Source for the pool terms is *Pool Life,* Olin Corporation, Stamford, Conn., 1973, p. 3.

amortization: A payment plan that enables the borrower to reduce his debt gradually through monthly payments of principal.

appraisal: An expert judgment or estimate of the quality or value of real estate as of a given date.

assets: What an individual or organization owns plus what is owed. Assets may be tangible, like a house, or intangible, like good will.

assumption of mortgage: An obligation undertaken by the purchaser of property to be personally liable for payment of an existing *mortgage*. In an assumption, the purchaser is substituted for the original mortgagor in the mortgage instrument and the original mortgagor is released from further liability under the mortgage. Since the mortgagor is to be released from further liability in the assumption, the mortgagee's consent is usually required.

The original mortgagor should always obtain a written release from further liability if he desires to be released fully under the assumption. Failure to obtain such a release renders the original mortgagor liable if the person assuming the mortgage fails to make the monthly payments.

An "assumption of mortgage" is often confused with "purchasing subject to a mortgage." When one purchases subject to a mortgage, the purchaser agrees to make the monthly mortgage payments on an existing mortgage, but the original mortgagor remains personally liable if the purchaser fails to make the monthly payments. Since the original mortgagor remains liable in the event of default, the mortgagee's consent is not required to a sale subject to a mortgage.

Both "assumption of mortgage" and "purchasing subject to a mortgage" are used to finance the sale of property. They may also be used when a mortgagor is in financial difficulty and desires to sell the property to avoid foreclosure.

available chlorine: A measure of active chlorine present in your pool water to combat germs and algae.

balanced water: Pool water that is chemically balanced; that is to say, water that has a pH reading of between 7.2 and 7.5. Water that is neither too alkaline nor too acid.

balance sheet: A financial report on an individual or organization, listing their assets, liabilities, and net worth for one particular period at a time.

binder or **offer to purchase:** A preliminary agreement, secured by the payment of *earnest money,* between a buyer and seller as an offer to purchase real estate. A binder secures the right to purchase real estate upon agreed terms for a limited period of time. If the buyer changes his mind or is unable to purchase, the earnest money is forfeited unless the binder expressly provides that it is to be refunded.

bond: A formal evidence of a debt, in which the borrower agrees to pay the lender a specified amount, with interest at a fixed rate payable on specified dates.

broker; See *real estate broker.*

budget: A schedule for estimating expenses for a given period. It can be used by management as both a planning and control document.

building line or **setback:** Distances from the ends and/or sides of the lot beyond which construction may not extend. The building line may be established by a filed plat of subdivision, by restrictive covenants in deeds and leases, by building codes, or by zoning ordinances.

capital structure or **capitalization:** The amount and type of securities authorized and issued by an organization.

cash items: Cash, bank deposits, U.S. government issues, and other securities that are considered the same as cash.

caveat emptor: "Let the buyer beware."

certificate of title: A certificate issued by a title company or a written opinion rendered by an attorney that the seller has good marketable and insurable *title* to the property he is offering for sale. A certificate of title offers no protection against any hidden defects in the title that an examination of the records could not reveal. The issuer of a certificate of title is liable only for damages due to negligence. The protection offered a homeowner under a certificate of title is not as great as that offered in a title insurance policy. See *title; title insurance.*

closing costs: The numerous expenses that buyers and sellers normally incur to complete a transaction in the transfer of ownership of real estate. These costs are in addition to price of the property and are paid only once, at the closing day. This is a typical list:

Buyer's expenses	Seller's expenses
documentary stamps on notes	cost of abstract
recording deed and mortgage	documentary stamps on deed
escrow fees	real estate commission
attorney's fee	recording mortgage
title insurance	survey charge
appraisal and inspection	escrow fees
survey charge	attorney's fees

The agreement of sale negotiated previously between the buyer and the seller may state in writing who will pay each of the above costs.

closing day: The day on which the formalities of a real estate sale are concluded. The *certificate of title, abstract,* and *deed* pass from the seller to the buyer, the buyer signs the mortgage, and closing costs are paid. The final closing merely confirms the original agreement reached in the agreement of sale.

cloud: (on title) An outstanding claim or encumbrance that adversely affects the marketability of title.

collateral: An obligation or security attached to another to secure its performance.

commission: Money paid to a real estate agent or broker by the seller as compensation for finding a buyer and completing the sale. Usually it is a percentage of the sale price—6 to 7 percent on houses, 10 percent on land.

common stock: Securities with a right to dividends subordinate to all other stock of the organization.

condemnation: The taking of private property for public use by a government unit against the will of the owner but with payment of just compensation under the government's power of eminent domain. Condemnation may also be a determination by a governmental agency that a particular building is unsafe or unfit for use.

condominium: Individual ownership of a dwelling unit and an individual interest in the common areas and facilities which serve the multiunit project.

contract of purchase: See *agreement of sale*.

contractor: In the construction industry, a contractor is one who contracts to erect buildings or portions of them. There are also contractors for each phase of construction: heating, electrical, plumbing, air conditioning, road building, bridge and dam erection, and others.

conventional mortgage: A mortgage loan not insured by HUD or guaranteed by the Veterans' Administration. It is subject to conditions established by the lending institution and state statutes. The mortgage rates may vary with different institutions and between states. (States have various interest limits.)

conveyance: An instrument by which title to property is conveyed.

cooperative housing: An apartment building or a group of dwellings owned by residents (generally a corporation) and operated for their benefit by their elected board of directors. In a cooperative the corporation or association owns title to the real estate. A resident purchases stock in the corporation, which entitles him to occupy a unit in the building or property owned by the cooperative. Although the resident does not own his unit, he has an absolute right to occupy his unit for as long as he owns the stock.

current assets: Cash, cash items, inventories, notes and accounts receivable due within one year.

current liabilities: Accounts and notes payable, accrued taxes, interest, declared dividends, and other claims that are payable within one year.

decision-making process: The decision-making process may draw upon the following management components in order to arrive at a sound solution: objective, resources, areas, and functions. In arriving at management decisions, these questions should be kept in mind: (1) What is your objective? (2) Do you have the necessary facts to make a sound decision? (3) What are your alternatives? and (4) Have you chosen the most profitable alternative?

deed: A formal written instrument by which *title* to real property is transferred from one owner to another. The deed should contain an accurate description of the property being conveyed, should be signed and witnessed according to the laws of the state where the property is located, and should be delivered to the purchaser at closing day. There are two parties to a deed: the grantor and the grantee. See also *deed of trust; general warranty deed; quitclaim deed;* and *special warranty deed.*

deed of trust: Like a mortgage, a security instrument whereby real property is given as security for a debt. In a deed of trust, however, there are three parties to the instrument: the borrower, the trustee, and the lender (or beneficiary). In such a transaction the borrower transfers the legal *title* for the property to the trustee, who holds the property in trust as security for the payment of the debt to the lender or beneficiary. If the borrower pays the debt as agreed, the deed of trust becomes void. If, however, he defaults in the payment of the debt, the trustee may sell the property at a public sale, under the terms of the deed of trust. In most jurisdictions where the deed of trust is in force, the borrower is subject to having his property sold without benefit of legal proceedings. A few states have begun in recent years to treat the deed of trust like a mortgage.

default: Failure to make mortgage payments as agreed to in a commitment based on the terms and at the designated time set forth in the *mortgage* or *deed of trust.* It is the mortgagor's responsibility to remember the due date and send the payment prior to the due date, not after. If payment is not received thirty days after the due date, the mortgage is in default. In the event of default, the mortgage may give the lender the right to accelerate payments, take possession and receive rents, and start *foreclosure.* Defaults may also come about by the failure to observe other conditions in the mortgage or deed of trust.

depreciation: Decline in value of a house due to wear and tear, adverse changes in the neighborhood, or any other reason.

documentary stamps: A state tax, in the forms of stamps, required on *deeds* and *mortgages* when real estate title passes from one owner to another. The amount of stamps required varies with each state.

down payment: The amount of money to be paid by the purchaser to the seller upon the signing of the *agreement of sale.* The agreement of sale will refer to the down payment amount and will acknowledge receipt of the down payment. The down payment is usually a percentage of the total purchase price and varies according to market conditions, availability and type of financing, and the confidence the purchaser and seller have in each other's intent to close the sale. It may not be refundable if the purchaser fails to buy the property without good cause. If the purchaser wants the down payment to be refundable, he should insert a clause in the agreement of sale specifying the conditions under which the deposit will be refunded, if the agreement does not already contain such clause. If the seller cannot deliver good *title,* the agreement of sale usually requires the seller to return the down payment and to pay interest and expenses incurred by the purchaser.

earnest money: The deposit money given to the seller or his agent by the potential buyer to show that he is serious about buying the house. If the sale goes through, the earnest money is applied against the *down payment*. If the sale does not go through, the earnest money will be forfeited or lost unless the binder or offer to purchase expressly provides that it is refundable.

easement rights: A *right-of-way* granted to a person or company authorizing access to or over the owner's land. An electric company obtaining a right-of-way across private property is a common example.

encroachment: An obstruction, building, or part of a building that intrudes beyond a legal boundary onto neighboring private or public land, or a building extending beyond the building line.

encumbrance: A legal right or interest in land that affects a good or clear *title* and diminishes the land's value. It can take numerous forms, such as zoning ordinances, easement rights, claims, mortgages, liens, charges, a pending legal action, unpaid taxes, or restrictive covenants. An encumbrance does not legally prevent transfer of the property to another. A title search is all that is usually done to reveal the existence of such encumbrances, and it is up to the buyer to determine whether he wants to purchase with the encumbrance, or what can be done to remove it.

equity: The value of a homeowner's unencumbered interest in real estate. Equity is computed by subtracting from the property's fair market value the total of the unpaid mortgage balance and any outstanding liens or other debts against the property. A homeowner's equity increases as he pays off his mortgage or as the property appreciates in value. When the mortgage and all other debts against the property are paid in full, the homeowner has 100 percent equity in his property.

escrow: Funds paid by one party to another (the *escrow agent*) to hold until the occurrence of a specified event, after which the funds are released to a designated individual. In FHA mortgage transactions, an escrow account usually refers to the funds a mortgagor pays the lender at the time of the periodic mortgage payments. The money is held in a trust fund, provided by the lender for the buyer. Such funds should be adequate to cover yearly anticipated expenditures for mortgage insurance premiums, taxes, insurance premiums, and special assessments.

first mortgage: A mortgage having precedence over all others.

first mortgage bond: A bond secured by a first mortgage on property of the issuing corporation.

floater: A device used on the surface of your pool water for dispensing dry chlorine in tablet form.

floor joists: Floor framing lumber that extends from the outer foundation walls to interior beams.

footings: The concrete base of a foundation wall.

foreclosure: A legal term applied to any of the various methods of enforcing payment of the debt secured by a mortgage, or deed of trust, by taking and selling the mortgaged property, and depriving the mortgagor of possession.

foreign matter: Materials such as dust, twigs, grass clippings, and algae spores, carried into the pool by wind, rain, and bathers. They may carry bacteria and algae, which would increase consumption of dry chlorine.

foundation wall: A masonry wall supporting the house.

general warranty deed: A deed that conveys not only all the grantor's interest in and title to the property of the grantee, but also warrants that if the title is defective or has a "cloud" on it (such as mortgage claims, tax liens, title claims, judgments, or mechanic's liens against it) the grantee may hold the grantor liable.

grantee: That party in the deed who is the buyer or recipient.

grantor: That party in the deed who is the seller or giver.

hazard insurance: Protects against damages caused to property by fire, windstorms, and other common hazards.

HUD: U.S. Department of Housing and Urban Development. Housing Production and Mortgage Credit/Federal Housing Administration within HUD insures home mortgage loans made by lenders and sets minimum standards for such homes.

interest: A charge paid for borrowing money. See *mortgage note.*

liabilities: What an individual or organization owes.

lien: A claim by one person on the property of another as security for money owed. Such claims may include obligations not met or satisfied, judgments, unpaid taxes, materials, or labor. See also *special lien.*

line: An organizational structure in which the superior-subordinate relationship is delineated.

marketable title: A title that is free and clear of objectionable liens, clouds, or other title defects. A title that enables an owner to sell his property freely to others and that others will accept without objection.

millwork: Doors, trim, shelving, window sills, and other finishing work.

mortgage: A giving of property as security for payment of a debt; a *lien* or claim against real property given by the buyer to the lender as security for money borrowed. Under government-insured or loan-guarantee provisions, the payments may include *escrow* amounts covering taxes, *hazard insurance,* water charges, and *special assessments.* Mortgages generally run from 10 to 30 years, during which the loan is to be paid off.

mortgage commitment: A written notice from the bank or other lending institution saying it will advance mortgage funds in a specified amount to enable a buyer to purchase a house.

mortgagee: The lender in a mortgage agreement.

mortgage insurance premium: The payment made by a borrower to the lender for transmittal to HUD to help defray the cost of the FHA mortgage insurance program and to provide a reserve fund to protect lenders against loss in insured mortgage transactions. In FHA-insured mortgages, this represents an annual rate of ½ percent paid by the mortgagor on a monthly basis.

mortgage note: A written agreement to repay a loan. The agreement is secured by a *mortgage,* serves as proof of an indebtedness, and states the manner in which it shall be paid. The note states the actual amount of the debt that the mortgage secures and renders the mortgagor personally responsible for repayment.

mortgagor: The borrower in a mortgage agreement.

net working capital: Current assets minus current liabilities.

net worth: The true financial worth of a person or organization. It can be determined by subtracting liabilities from assets.

open-end mortgage: A mortgage with a provision that permits borrowing additional money in the future without refinancing the loan or paying additional financing charges. Open-end provisions often limit such borrowing to no more than would raise the balance to the original loan figure.

offer to purchase: See *binder.*

organizational chart: A schematic drawing portraying the formal relationships among the various activities of an organization.

particular lien: See *special lien.*

PERT (Program Evaluation and Review Technique): It serves as a manager's tool for defining and coordinating what must be done to successfully accomplish the objectives of a project within an established time frame.

activity: The actual performance of a task. It is the time-consuming portion of the **PERT** network and requires the resources of men, money, and material.

critical path: The sequence of events that indicates the minimum time required to complete a project.

event: The start or completion of a task.

T_E: earliest completion time. This is the longest time-consuming path.

pH: A numerical rating to indicate acid or alkaline condition of water. pH 7 is neutral. A rating over 7 is alkaline, under 7 is acid.

plat: A map or chart of a lot, subdivision, or community drawn by a surveyor showing boundary lines, buildings, improvements on the land, and easements.

points: Sometimes called "discount points." A point is one percent of the amount of the mortgage loan. For example, if a loan is for $25,000, one point is $250. Points are charged by a lender to raise the yield on his loan at a time when money is tight, interest rates are high, and there is a legal limit to the interest rate that can be charged on a mortgage. Buyers are prohibited from paying points on HUD or Veterans Administration guaranteed loans (sellers can pay, however). On a conventional mortgage points may be paid by either buyer or seller or split between them.

PPM: An abbreviation of "parts per million." It is applied to pool water ratings as the quantity of residual chlorine per million parts of water.

prepayment: Payment of *mortgage* loan, or part of it, before due date. Mortgage agreements often restrict the right of prepayment either by limiting the amount that can be prepaid in any one year or charging a penalty for prepayment. The Federal Housing Administration does not permit such restrictions in FHA insured mortgages.

principal: The basic element of the loan, as distinguished from *interest* and *mortgage insurance premium*. In other words, principal is the amount upon which interest is paid.

purchase agreement: See *agreement of sale*.

quitclaim deed: A deed that transfers whatever interest the maker of the deed may have in the particular parcel of land. A quitclaim deed is often given to clear the title when the grantor's interest in a property is questionable. By accepting such a deed the buyer assumes all the risks. Such a deed makes no warranties as to the title but simply transfers to the buyer whatever interest the grantor has. See *deed; title*.

real estate broker: A middleman or agent who buys and sells real estate for a company, firm, or individual on a commission basis. The broker does not have title to the property but generally represents the owner.

refinancing: The process of paying off one loan with the proceeds from another loan.

restrictive covenants: Private restrictions limiting the use of real property. Restrictive covenants are created by deed and may ''run with the land,'' binding all subsequent purchasers of the land, or may be ''personal'' and binding only between the original seller and buyer. The determination whether a covenant runs with the land or is personal is governed by the language of the covenant, the intent of the parties, and the law in the state where the land is situated. Restrictive covenants that run with the land are *encumbrances* and may affect the value and marketability of title. These covenants may limit the density of buildings per acre, regulate size, style, or price range of buildings to be erected, or prevent particular businesses from operating or minority groups from owning or occupying homes in a given area. (This latter discriminatory covenant is unconstitutional and has been declared unenforceable by the U.S. Supreme Court.)

sales agreement: See *agreement of sale*.

second mortgage: An additional mortgage placed on property already encumbered by a first mortgage.

setback: See *building line*.

sheathing: The first covering of boards or waterproofing material on the outside wall of a frame house.

skimmer: A metal or plastic screen to remove debris from the pool water. Can be either permanently built into the wall of an in-ground pool or can be a simple device attached to the intake line of the filter of an above-ground pool. Some pool owners use a manual skimmer, which is a netlike device attached to the end of a pole.

special lien: A lien that binds a specified piece of property, unlike a general lien, which is levied against all one's assets. It creates a right to retain something of value belonging to another person as compensation for labor, material, or money expended in that person's behalf. In some localities it is called ''particular'' lien or ''specific'' lien. See *lien*.

special warranty deed: A deed in which the grantor conveys title to the grantee and agrees to protect the grantee against title defects or claims asserted by the grantor and those persons whose right to assert a claim against the title arose during the period the grantor held title to the property. In a special warranty deed the grantor guarantees to the grantee that he has done nothing during the time he held title to the property that has or may in the future impair the grantee's title. See also *deed; title.*

speculation: A home built for the purpose of selling it to anyone willing to pay the price. This is in contrast to a custom-built house that has been contracted for prior to construction.

stabilizer (conditioner): A special chemical agent (cyanuric acid), which when applied to pool water in recommended amounts, slows the dissipation rate of the chlorine residual. (Especially useful in warmer climates.)

state stamps: See *documentary stamps.*

statement of income: A financial report of an individual or organization listing their income, expenses, and profit or loss for a given period, normally one year.

studs: Horizontal lumber nailed to vertical lumber which comprises the wall frame. They are usually 16 inches apart.

subfloor: Wood sheeting nailed to floor joists.

superchlorination: Generally referred to as "shock treatment," adding two or three times the normal amount of chlorine to the water in your pool.

survey: A map or plat made by a licensed surveyor showing the results of measuring the land with its elevations, improvements, boundaries, and its relationship to surrounding tracts of land. A survey is often required by the lender to assure him that a building is actually sited on the land according to its legal description.

suspended matter: Particles that do not settle in the bottom and give a cloudy or milky appearance to the water.

tax: As applied to real estate, an enforced charge imposed on persons, property, or income, to be used to support the state. The governing body in turn utilizes the funds in the best interest of the general public.

title: As generally used, the rights of ownership and possession of particular property. In real estate usage, title may refer to the instruments or documents by which a right of ownership is established (title documents), or it may refer to the ownership interest one has in the real estate.

title insurance: Protects lenders or homeowners against loss of their interest in property due to legal defects in title. Title insurance may be issued to either the mortgagor, as an "owner's title policy," or to the mortgagee as a "mortgagee's title policy." Insurance benefits will be paid only to the "named insured" in the title policy, so it is important that an owner purchase an "owner's title policy" if he desires the protection of title insurance.

title search or examination: A check of the title records, generally at the local courthouse, to make sure the buyer is purchasing a house from the legal owner and there are no *liens,* overdue *special assessments,* or other claims or outstanding *restrictive covenants* filed in the record that would adversely affect the marketability or value of title.

trustee: A party who is given legal responsibility to hold property in the best interest of or "for the benefit of" another. The trustee is one placed in a position of responsibility for another, a responsibility enforceable in a court of law. See *deed of trust*.

zoning ordinances: The acts of an authorized local government establishing building codes and setting forth regulations for property land usage.

Recommended Reading

CHAPTER ONE
A MANAGERIAL APPROACH TO BUILDING
YOUR HOME

BOOKS

Anderson, LeRoy Oscar, and Zornig, Harold F. *Build Your Own Low Cost Home*. New York: Dover Books, 1972.

Connolly, William G. *The New York Times Guide to Buying or Building a Home*. New York: New York Times Books, 1978.

Dale, Ernest. *Management: Theory and Practice*. 4th ed. Chapter 1, Management and Its Environment. New York: McGraw-Hill, 1978.

Drucker, Peter F. *An Introductory View of Management*. New York: Harper & Row, 1977.

Eisinger, Larry. *How to Build and Contract Your Own Home,* rev. ed. Greenwich, Conn.: Fawcett Publications, 1971.

Higson, James D. *The Higson Home-Builder's Guide*. Los Angeles: Nash Pub., 1972.

Hotton, Peter. *So You Want to Build a House*. Boston: Little, Brown, 1977.

Koontz, Harold; O'Donnell, Cyril; and Heinz, Weihrich. *Management*. Chapter 1, The Basis of a Theory of Management. New York: McGraw-Hill, 1980.

Neal, Charles. *Do-It-Yourself Housebuilding: Step-by-Step*. New York: Macmillan, 1973.

Stoner, James A., F. *Management*. Chapter 1, Introduction to Modern Management. Englewood Cliffs, N.J.: Prentice-Hall, 1978.

ARTICLES

"A Lot of Conservation." *Money*, October 1979, p. 61.

"Attic Fans." *Consumer Reports*, May 1978, pp. 290–93.

Button, Sally. "The Case for Switching to Gas Heat." *Money*, September 1979, pp. 96–99.

"Can Insulation Lower Your Air-Conditioning Costs?" *Consumer Reports*, August 1978, pp. 447–49.

Eisenberg, Richard. "A Winter's Tale of Two Houses." *Money*, October 1979, pp. 62–65.

"Energy Savers For Your House . . . And Some You Can Live Without." *Money*, October 1979, pp. 66–69.

"Home Energy Audits." *Consumer Reports*, October 1979, pp. 612–14.

"How Much Insulation Do You Actually Need?" *Changing Times*, January 1979, pp. 31–35.

"Lower Utility Bills?" *Consumer Reports*, May 1979, pp. 300–301.

Main, Jeremy. "Houses That Practically Heat Themselves." *Money*, October 1979, pp. 56–60.

"The Push for Energy-Efficient Appliances." *Consumer Reports*, January 1979, pp. 28–29.

"Saving Water When You Flush the Toilet." *Consumer Reports*, May 1978, pp. 296–99.

"Saving Water When You Shower." *Consumer Reports*, May 1978, pp. 300–302.

"Secrets Your Electric or Gas Meter Can Tell." *Changing Times*, August 1979.

Seixas, Suzanne. "Cold Facts about Home Insulation Costs." *Money*, November 1977, p. 113.

"Solar Heating Your House—Would It Pay?" *Changing Times*, April 1978, pp. 6–9.

"Storm Windows and Weather Stripping." *Consumer Reports*, October 1978, pp. 583–87.

"Three Energy-Saving Possibilities: Exterior Caulking Compounds, Energy-Saving Thermostats, Flue-Heat Recovery Devices." *Consumer Reports*, September 1978, pp. 535–42.

"Water: Time to Start Saving." *Consumer Reports*, May 1978, pp. 290–93.

"Ways to Heat Your Home for Less." *Changing Times*, October 1978, pp. 6–14.

CHAPTER TWO
THE IMPACT OF INFLATION AND THE
ENERGY SHORTAGE ON BUILDING YOUR
HOME

BOOKS

Connolly, William G. *The New York Times Guide to Buying or Building a Home*. New York: New York Times Books, 1978.

Daniels, G. *Solar Homes and Sun Heating*. New York: Harper & Row, 1976.

Energy-Saving Home Improvements. New York: Drake, 1977.

The Energy-Wise Home Buyer. Consumer Information Center, Pueblo, Colo., 81009, item no. 1090, current edition.

Fireplaces and Chimneys. Consumer Information Center, Pueblo, Colo., 81009, item no. 046G, current edition.

Firewood for Your Fireplace. Consumer Information Center, Pueblo, Colo., 81009, item no. 047G, current edition.

Gropp, Louis. *Solar Houses*. New York: Pantheon Books, 1978.

Home Heating. Consumer Information Center, Pueblo, Colo., 81009, item no. 048G, current edition.

Hotton, Peter. *So You Want to Build a House*. Boston: Little, Brown, 1977.

How to Improve the Efficiency of Your Oil-Fired Furnace. Consumer Information Center, Pueblo, Colo., 81009, item no. 605G, current edition.

In the Bank or Up the Chimney? Superintendent of Documents, U.S. Government Printing Office, Washington, D.C., 20402, current edition.

Lucas, Ted. *How to Use Solar Energy in Your Home and Business*. Pasadena, Calif.: Ward Ritchie Press, 1977.

Spetgang, I., and Wells, M. *Your Home's Solar Potential*. Barrington, N.J.: Edmund Scientific Co., 1976.

Tips for Energy Savers. Consumer Information Center, Pueblo, Colo., 81009, item no. 610G, current edition.

ARTICLES

"Build Your House with a Few Good Books." *Changing Times*, September 1979, pp. 29–31.

"Building Small, Expanding Later." *Better Homes and Gardens*, April 1975, p. 70.

"Planning Your Own—And Building It Too." *Better Homes and Gardens*, March 1975, p. 42.

Reed, S. "Building Your Own Retirement Home." *The Retired Officer*, March 1976, p. 30.

"Your Home-Building Contractor Could Be You." *Changing Times*, July 1978, pp. 36–38.

CHAPTER THREE
PLANNING YOUR DREAM HOUSE

BOOKS

Dale, Ernest. *Readings in Management: Landmarks and New Frontiers.* 2d ed. Chapter 16, Planning and Forecasting. New York: McGraw-Hill, 1980.

Donelly, James H., Jr.; Gibson, James L.; and Ivancevich, John M. *Fundamentals of Management.* Chapter 4, The Planning Function. Austin, Tex.: Business Publications, Inc., 1978.

Haynes, W. Warren; Massie, Joseph L.; and Wallace, Marc J., Jr. *Management: Analysis, Concepts, and Cases,* 3d ed. Englewood Cliffs, N.J.: Prentice-Hall, 1975.

Miner, John B. *The Management Process,* 2d ed. Chapter 3, Policy Planning: Establishing the Role Prescriptions. New York: Macmillan, 1978.

Stoner, James A. F. *Management.* Chapter 2, Planning and Decision Making. Englewood Cliffs, N.J.: Prentice-Hall, 1978.

U.S., Department of Agriculture. *House Construction* (How to Reduce Costs), Bulletin No. 168. Washington, D.C., current edition.

U.S., Department of Housing and Urban Development. *Solar Energy and Your Home.* Washington, D.C., current edition.

U.S., Federal Housing Administration. *Minimum Property Standards for One and Two Living Units,* current edition.

ARTICLES

"Buying a Homesite? Beware of the Promised Lands." *Consumer Reports,* May 1978, p. 283.

"Buying a House? Analyze the Floor Plan First." *Changing Times,* January 1977, p. 29.

"A Chance to Save on Settlement Costs." *Changing Times,* November 1975, p. 15.

Comarow, Avery. "Home Fire Alarms: Cheaper Can Be Better." *Money,* February 1975, p. 79.

Edgerton, Terry. "Making Your Dream House Come True." *Money,* September 1978, pp. 46–54.

Harris, M. "The Big House Blues." *Money,* May 1978, p. 71.

———. "How to Find an Affordable House." *Money,* August 1977, p. 46.

"House Built with More Muscle than Money." *Mechanics Illustrated,* March 1975, p. 54.

CHAPTER FOUR
MONEY—THE ESSENTIAL INGREDIENT

BOOKS

Hodge, Billy J., and Johnson, Herbert J. *Management and Organizational Behavior: A Multidimensional Approach.* Chapter 17, Measuring Mission Accomplishment Through Financial Analysis. New York: Wiley, 1970.

Stillman, Richard J. *Guide to Personal Finance: A Lifetime Program of Money Management*. Chapter 3, Housing. Englewood Cliffs, N.J.: Prentice-Hall, 1979.

Stoner, James A. F. *Management*. Chapter 24, Budgetary Methods of Control. Englewood Cliffs, N.J.: Prentice-Hall, 1978.

U.S., Veterans Administration. *Pointers for the Veteran Homeowner*. VA Pamphlet 26–5. Washington, D.C., current edition.

U.S., Veterans Administration. Questions and Answers on Guaranteed and Direct Loans for Veterans. VA Pamphlet 26–4. Washington, D.C., current edition.

ARTICLES

"Are Those New Low Payment Mortgages Worthwhile?" *Consumer Reports*, January 1979, pp. 17–21.

Bernstein, E. "Mortgages with Changing Monthly Payments." *Money*, September 1975, p. 65.

Boroson, Warren. "Mortgages Cut to Fit Your Finances." *Money*, October 1977, p. 75.

"Can You Afford To Buy A House These Days?" *Changing Times*, March 1979, pp. 15–17.

Edgerton, Jerry. "The Case for Mortgages—Even at 14%." *Money*, January 1980, pp. 90–92.

"Finding The Best Deal On A Mortgage." *Changing Times*, September 1979, pp. 3–6.

"Got Enough Insurance on Your Home?" *Changing Times*, January 1980, pp. 44–47.

"How to Deal with Closing Costs." *Consumer Reports*, August 1975, p. 482.

Hughes, Charles L. "Why Budgets Go Wrong." *Personnel*, May–June 1965, pp. 19–26.

Main, J. "Here Comes the Minihouse." *Money*, February 1976, p. 50.

Miller, R. W. "How to Plan and Control With PERT." *Harvard Business Review*, March–April 1962, pp. 93–104.

"Need Money? What About Tapping the Equity in Your Home?" *Changing Times*, August 1979, pp. 43–44.

"New Ideas For Home Loans." *Changing Times*, May 1978, pp. 19–22.

"The Overselling of Insulation." *Consumer Reports*, February 1978, p. 67.

Schneider, Frank L. "Return to the City Beginning Here? Some Feel It May Be." *New Orleans Times-Picayune*, February 18, 1973, p. 17.

"Small Luxuries for the Smallest Room in the House." *Money*, October 1978, pp. 90–94.

"Tax Angles to Know When You Buy and Sell a Home." *Changing Times*, December 1979, pp. 33–35.

Tomb, J. O. "A New Way to Manage: Integrated Planning and Control." *California Management Review*, Fall 1962, pp. 57–62.

CHAPTER FIVE
BUILDING YOUR HOME

BOOKS

Huse, Edgar F. *The Modern Manager*. Chapter 7, Organizational Goals and Objectives. St. Paul, Minn.: West Publishing Company, 1979.

Stoner, James A. F. *Management*. Part 3, Organizing for Stability and Change. Englewood Cliffs, N.J.: Prentice-Hall, 1978.

CHAPTER SIX
CHECKING ON WHAT YOU HAVE DONE

BOOKS

Newman, William H., and Warren, E. Kirby. *The Process of Management*. 4th ed. Chapter 5, Controlling. Englewood Cliffs, N.J.: Prentice-Hall, 1977.

Scanlan, Burt K. *Principles of Management and Organizational Behavior*. Chapter 22, Managerial Control. New York: Wiley, 1973.

Stoner, James A. F. *Management*. Chapter 5, Controlling. Englewood Cliffs, N.J.: Prentice-Hall, 1978.

ARTICLES

Sherwin, Douglas S. "The Meaning of Control." *Dun's Review and Modern Industry,* January 1956, pp. 45, 46, 83.

Tannenbaum, Jeffrey A. "Homeowners Outraged by New House Defects and Delays in Repairs." *Wall Street Journal,* April 3, 1973, p. 1.

CHAPTER SEVEN
DO YOU WANT A SWIMMING POOL?

BOOKS

Butler, George D. *Outdoor Swimming Pools: Considerations in Planning, Basic Design Features, Pool Construction Factors*. New York: National Recreation Association, 1955.

Ideal Home Magazine. *Patios and Pools*. London, New York: Hamlyn, 1969.

Jacobs, Bert, and Jacobs, Isabel. *Home Pool Safety*. Chicago, Ill.: Nelson-Hall, Inc., 1978.

Joseph, James. *Poolside Living*. Garden City, N.Y.: Doubleday, 1963.

Kinney, Henry, ed. *Swimming Pool Data and Reference Annual*. 47th ed. Fort Lauderdale, Fla.: Hoffman Pubns., Inc., 1979.

Pedersen, H. W. *Pool Owners Handbook*. Miami Shores, Florida: 1969.

Springer, John L.; Hochman, Louis; and Gladstone, Bernard. *All About Swimming Pools*. Greenwich, Conn.: Fawcett, 1960.

Sunset Magazine. *Swimming Pools*. 4th ed. Menlo Park, Calif.: Lane Books, 1970.

Wills, Norman D. *Build Your Own Swimming Pool: A Guide to Pool Care and Construction*. London: Gifford, 1969.

ARTICLES

Callier, G. W. "Swimming Pools Are His Business." *Ebony*, November 1978, pp. 88–90.

"Gas-Lit Torches around Their Pool." *Sunset*, July 1971, p. 100.

"How to Keep Your Pool Crystal Clear." *Popular Mechanics*, June 1971, pp. 154–157.

LaGregga, F. "What It Really Costs to Maintain a Swimming Pool." *Mechanix Illustrated*, August 1971, p. 63.

"More Than a Swimming Pool." *Southern Living*, June 1978, pp. 94–95.

Murphy, B. "Newest: Pool Domes." *Mechanix Illustrated*, June 1978, pp. 71–72.

"Pool Enclosures: From Domes to Greenhouses." *Business Week*, August 28, 1971, p. 67.

"Pool Is an Entrance Feature." *Southern Living*, July 1978, p. 164.

Pool Life Magazine. Olin Corp., Stamford, Conn., seasonal.

Wicks, H. "Turn Your Above-Ground Pool into a Back-Yard Resort." *Popular Mechanics*, March 1978, pp. 137–39.

CHAPTER EIGHT
PROTECTING YOUR PROPERTY

BOOKS

Arnold, Peter. *Burglar-Proof Your Home and Car*. Los Angeles: Nash Pub., 1971.

Arnold, Robert Taylor. *The Burglars Are Coming*. Santa Ana, Calif.: Arnold Pub., 1972.

Brann, Donald R. *How To Install Protective Alarm Devices*. Briarcliff Manor, N.Y.: Directions Simplified, 1972.

Cunningham, John Edward. *Security Electronics*. Indianapolis: H. W. Sams, 1970.

Eagle, Alyn Bush. *Family and Home Protection Against Crime*. College Park, Md.: Executive House Services, 1968.

Healy, Richard J. *Design for Security*. New York: Wiley, 1968.

Hilts, Len. *Home Security*. Birmingham, Ala.: Oxmoor House, 1975.

Home Repair and Improvement Series. *Home Security*. Morristown, N.J.: Silver Burdett Co., 1979.

Home Security. Home Repair and Improvement Series. Alexandria, Va.: Time-Life Books, 1979.

Kaufmann, Ulrich George. *How to Avoid Burglary, Housebreaking, and Other Crimes.* New York: Crown, 1967.

Nelson, Ralph. *Home Security Manual.* Dayton, Ohio: Rucker Press, Inc., 1977.

Rhodes, R. L., ed. *Homeowner's Security Handbook.* Philadelphia: American Society for Testing and Materials, 1976.

Sootin, Hy. *Burglar Alarm Security.* Miami: Sootin's, 1970.

Treves, Ralph. *Do-It-Yourself Home Protection: A Common-Sense Guide.* New York: Popular Science Pub. Co., 1972.

ARTICLES

"American Home: On Foiling Burglars, Fleeing Fires." *Redbook,* September 1978, p. 72.

"Burglar Alarms You Install Yourself." *Changing Times,* July 1979, pp. 19–20.

Chasen, Nancy. "How Not to Get Hosed by Your Fire Insurance." *Money,* December 1979, pp. 85–91.

Comarow, Avery. "Home Fire Alarms: Cheaper Can Be Better." *Money,* February 1975, p. 79.

Day, R. "How to Protect Your Home With Lights." *Mechanix Illustrated.* March 1971, p. 120.

"Door Locks: Do They Make A House A Fortress?" *Consumer Reports,* March 1979, pp. 132–39.

Dunham, P. "Memo from a Burglar." *Family Handyman,* May 1978, p. 8.

"Escape Ladders." *Consumer Reports,* October 1979, pp. 604–6.

"Fire Extinguishers." *Consumer Reports,* October 1979, pp. 607–11.

"Giving Robbers the Cold Shoulder." *Today's Health,* February 1971, p. 41.

"Here's a Plan Thieves Don't Like: Operation Identification." *Better Homes and Gardens,* March 1971, p. 126.

Hill, R., and Hawkins, W. J. "Do-It-Yourself Guide to Making Your Home Secure." *Popular Science,* August 1972, pp. 94–97.

"Home Safety: An Anti-Burglary Plan That Works," *Better Homes and Gardens,* February 1975, p. 60.

"Home Security: Burglars and Fire Alarms." *Workbench,* March 1978, p. 10.

Johnson, R. D. "How to Protect Your Home against Burglars." *U.S. News,* July 17, 1978, pp. 51–52.

Ingersoll, J. H. "Security For Your Home: More Urgent Than Ever." *House Beautiful,* November 1971, p. 62.

Lee, A. "Ways to Protect Your Home." *Better Homes and Gardens,* June 1972, p. 16.

McCray, M. "Firing Up Interest in Smoke Detectors," *Money,* May 1977, p. 104.

"Protect Your Home Against Burglars." *Good Housekeeping,* September 1972, p. 187.

Rush, A. F. "This Man Can Be Stopped!" *McCalls,* March 1972, pp. 86–87.

"Some Minimum Security Precautions." *Consumer Report,* February 1971, p. 103.

Torok, L. "How You Help the Burglar." *Popular Mechanics,* September 1971, pp. 86–87.

Train, J. "Home Security Hints." *Forbes,* July 24, 1978, pp. 100–101.

"Update: Smoke Detectors." *Consumer Reports,* May 1977, p. 283.

"Window Locks." *Consumer Reports,* March 1979, pp. 140–41.

CHAPTER NINE
HOW TO KEEP YOUR COOL WHILE
MOVING

BOOKS

Alfred, Mary. *Move to a New House.* Nashville, Tenn.: Broadman Press, 1979.

Giammattei, Helen, and Slaughter, Katherine. *Help Your Family Make A Better Move.* rev. ed. New York: Doubleday, 1970.

Hullinger, Robert, and Grosch, Robert. *Move Yourself and Save.* St. Louis, Mo.: Clayton Publishing House, 1979.

Randall, Margaret. *The Home Encyclopedia of Moving Your Family.* New York: Berkley Publishing, 1959.

Rosefsky, Robert S. *The Ins and Outs of Moving.* Chicago: Follett Publishing, 1972.

Sullivan, George. *Do-It-Yourself Moving.* New York: Macmillan, 1973.

Warmington, Carl. *The Family Guide to Successful Moving.* New York: Association Press, 1968.

ARTICLES

Daly, M. "Up-to-Date Tips about Moving." *Better Homes and Gardens,* July 1972, pp. 20–21.

DeMarco, J. "How to Move Yourself." *Mechanix Illustrated,* February 1971, pp. 74–75.

"Easing the Trauma of Moving." *Business Week,* March 13, 1971, p. 101.

Flanagan, W. "Moving Experience." *Esquire,* June 6, 1978, pp. 87–88.

Gant, L. "Money-Saving Moves." *Essence,* November 1978, p. 104.

Hand, J. "How to Get an Honest Move." *Mechanix Illustrated,* June 1971, pp. 67–68.

"Household Moving." *Consumer Reports,* December 1978, pp. 362–64.

Huff, P. "Solving Your Problem: A Step-by-Step Guide to Packing Like a Pro." *Mademoiselle,* May 1978, p. 108.

Irwin, T. "It's Legal: Question of Lost or Damaged Items." *House Beautiful,* September 1972, p. 20.

Murray, N. B. "Moving Day . . . How to Ease the Trials and Tribulations." *Retirement Living,* August 1978, pp. 24–27.

"Pitfalls and Ripoffs in Long-Distance Moves." *Changing Times,* June 1979, pp. 43–44.

Rush, A. F. "Taking the Terror Out of Moving." *McCalls,* March 1971, pp. 35–37.

"Sure You Can Do Your Moving Yourself." *Changing Times,* September 1971, pp. 35–37.

Weinstein, G. W. "Moving Made Easy." *Parents Magazine,* February 1971, pp. 70–71.

"When Moving Men Show Their Worst Side." *Business Week,* August 21, 1971, p. 86.

CHAPTER TEN
LANDSCAPING

BOOKS

Ajay, Betty. *Betty Ajay's Guide to Home Landscaping.* New York: McGraw-Hill, 1970.

Brooks, John. *Room Outside: A Plan for the Garden.* New York: Viking Press, 1970.

Bruning, Walter F. *Home Garden Magazine's Minimum Maintenance Gardening Handbook.* New York: Harper & Row, 1970.

Downing, M. E. *Landscape Construction.* New York: Halsted Press, 1977.

Family Guide Book Serials. *Landscaping Your Home.* Birmingham, Ala.: Oxmoor House, 1974.

Flemer, William, III. *Nature's Guide to Successful Gardening and Landscaping.* New York: Crowell, 1972.

Givens, Harold. *Landscape It Yourself: A Handbook for Home Gardeners.* New York: Harcourt Brace Jovanovich, Inc., 1977.

Ingels, Jack E. *Landscaping Principles and Practices.* New York: Van Nostrand Reinhold Co., 1978.

Kramer, Jack. *Gardening and Home Landscaping Guide.* New York: Arco, 1970.

Landscape Architecture Magazine. *Home Landscape, 1980.* New York: McGraw-Hill Book Co., 1980.

Macleod, Dawn. *Design Your Own Garden.* London: Duckworth, 1969.

Phillips, Cecil Ernest Lucas. *The Design of Small Gardens.* London: Heinemann, 1969.

Robinette, Gary O. *Landscape Architecture Site-Construction Details.* Reston, Va.: Environmental Design Press, 1977.

———. *Landscape Planning for Energy Conservation.* Reston, Va.: Environmental Design Press, 1977.

Smith, Ronald. *Landscape Contracting.* Reston, Va.: Environmental Design Press, 1979.

ARTICLES

Bumgarner, G. M. "Back-to-Nature Landscapes Can Be Both Wild and Civilized." *Flower and Garden* (Northern ed.), November 1978, p. 46.

"Garden Was Already There." *Southern Living,* May 1978, p. 196.

"Gardening with Pebbles and Rocks," *Popular Mechanics,* March 1978, pp. 144–46.

"Keep House Plants Happy." *Changing Times,* September 1978, pp. 39–40.

"Less Paving, More Planting Define Entrance." *Southern Living,* October 1978, p. 150.

Mason, H. "Relaxing Solutions for Landscaping Problems." *Better Homes and Gardens,* March 1971, pp. 46–55.

"Planting for Privacy." *Sunset,* December 1971, pp. 198–99.

"Planting Ideas for Side Yards." *Sunset,* July 1971, p. 161.

"Rocks and Plants: Good Companions." *Sunset,* April 1972, pp. 261–62.

Smith, A. U. "Cool It With Trees." *Horticulture,* August 1971, pp. 18–21.

Tuby, Carrie. "A Down-to-Earth Guide to Yard Gear." *Money,* June 1979, pp. 92–96.

"Walk-About Garden . . . Steppingstones, Pathways, and a Meandering Stony Creek Bed (Usually Dry)." *Sunset,* November 1978, p. 266.

CHAPTER ELEVEN
MAINTENANCE, REPAIRS, AND
IMPROVEMENTS

BOOKS

Adams, Jeanette T. *Home Appliances: Selection, Use and Repair.* New York: Arco Publishing, Inc., 1980.

Alth, Max. *Homeowner's Quick-Repair and Emergency Guide.* Popular Science Skill Book. New York: Harper & Row, Inc., 1978.

Audel, T. *Audel's Do-It-Yourself Encyclopedia.* Indianapolis: How-To Associates, 1968.

Branson, Gary. *Home Maintenance and Repair:* Walls, Ceilings, and Floors. Indianapolis, Ind.: Theodore Audel, 1977.

Brightman, Robert. *Home Owner Handbook of Carpentry and Woodworking.* New York: Crown Pubs., Inc., 1974.

Brumbough, James. *Home Roofing Repairs.* Indianapolis, Ind.: Theodore Audel, 1975.

Cassiday, Bruce. *The New Practical Home Repair for Women: Your Questions Answered.* New York: Taplinger Pub. Co., 1972.

Cobb, Hubbard. *How to Paint Anything.* New York: Macmillan, 1972.

———. *Money Saving Home Maintenance.* New York: Collier Books, 1970.

Curry, Barbara A. *Okay, I'll Do It Myself: or A Handy-Woman's Primer That Takes the Mystique Out of Home Repairs.* New York: Random House, 1971.

Day, Richard. *Home Owner Handbook of Plumbing and Heating*. New York: Crown Pubs., Inc., 1974.

Demski, Dick. *Home Repair Book*. Edited by Margot L. Wolf and Donald D. Wolf. New York: Consolidated Books, 1979.

Evans, Melvin. *Easy Home Repairs*. New York: Western Pub. Co., 1972.

Family Handyman Magazine. *The Family Handyman*, rev. ed. New York: Scribner, 1970.

Hentzberg, Robert. *Home Owner Handbook of Electrical Repairs*. New York: Crown Pubs., Inc., 1974.

Jones, Peter. *Homeowner's Guide to Plumbing, Heating·and Air-Conditioning*. Reston, Va.: Reston Publishing Co., Inc., 1980.

McConnell, Charles N. *Home Plumbing Handbook*. Indianapolis, Ind.: Theodore Audel, 1978.

Nunn, Richard. *Home Paint Book*. Birmingham, Ala.: Oxmoor House, 1976.

Pettit, Tome. *Home Maintenance and Outdoor Repairs*. New York: International Pubns. Service, 1977.

Philbin, Tom. *Home Fix-It Secrets of the Pros*. New York: Dutton, 1980.

Sara, Dorothy. *Home Fix-It Encyclopedia; Complete Manual of Home Repairs and Maintenance*. New York: Westport Corp., 1971.

Schuler, Stanley. *The Homeowner's Minimum-Maintenance Manual*. New York: M. Evans, 1971.

Sharpe, Roger. *Home Insulation Handbook*. Austin, Tex.: S & S Press, 1979.

Sunset Books and Magazines. *Basic Home Repairs Illustrated*. Menlo Park, Calif.: Lane Books, 1971.

Watkins, Arthur Martin. *The Homeowner's Survival Kit: How to Beat the High Cost of Owning and Operating Your Home*. New York: Hawthorn Books, 1971.

Weiss, William. *Home Maintenance: A Guide to Taking Better Care of Your House*. New York: Charles Scribner's Sons, 1978.

Williamson, Dereck. *The Complete Book of Pitfalls: A Victim's Guide to Repairs, Maintenance, and Repairing the Maintenance*. New York: McCall, 1971.

ARTICLES

"Don't Electrocute Yourself!" *Changing Times*, December 1978, pp. 17–19.

Easy Home Repairs. *Mechanix Illustrated*, August 1971, pp. 80–82.

Frankel, C. "Ladies Home Journal Spring Guide to Home Improvement and Decorating." *Ladies Home Journal*, April 1978, p. 165.

"Give Your Home a Safety Checkup." *Changing Times*, August 1977, p. 45.

"Good Tools Make Better Paint Jobs." *Changing Times*, October 1979, pp. 31–34.

Henry, Ed. "A Broad Brush Guide to House Painting." *Money*, June 1978, pp. 84–91.

"Home Ideas Guide." *Popular Mechanics*, April 1978, p. 131.

"Home-Improvement Contracts: How to Protect Yourself." *Consumer Reports*, Feburary 1978, p. 74.

"Home Maintenance." *Consumers' Research Magazine*, October 1978, pp. 103–9.

"Home Maintenance Ideas." *Better Homes and Gardens*, May 1972, p. 22.

"How to Do Your Own Home Improvements." *Mechanix Illustrated*, April 1978, pp. 97–102.

"How to Get Your Money's Worth on Home Improvements. *Good Housekeeping*, November 1970, pp. 168–69.

"How to Save on Home Maintenance Costs." *Good Housekeeping*, January 1970, p. 140.

"Is That Home Improvement A Good Investment?" *Changing Times*, May 1979, pp. 7–10.

"Is Your Home Ready for Winter?" *McCalls*, November 1972, p. 24.

"Master Plan for a Maintenance-Free Summer." *Better Homes and Gardens*, April 1972, p. 22.

McWhirter, W. A. "Horrors of Home Repair: Unskilled and Inaccessible Craftsmen." *Life*, June 1970, pp. 58–60.

O'Brien, R. "Twelve Money-Saving Tips on Maintaining Your Home." *Reader's Digest*, June 1970, pp. 189–90.

Raffel, D. "Home Improvement Ideas for the House Fixer: Spring Checkup." *House and Garden*, April 1978, p. 94.

"Three Good Home Repair Tips." *Popular Science*, October 1970, p. 127.

"Twenty Great Home Fix-Up Ideas." *Mechanix Illustrated*, February 1970, pp. 83–93.

Index